PRAKṚTI

The Integral Vision

VOLUME 4

The Nature of Matter

PRAKṚTI
The Integral Vision

General Editor

KAPILA VATSYAYAN

VOLUME 4
The Nature of Matter

Edited by
Jayant V. Narlikar

Indira Gandhi National Centre for the Arts
New Delhi

D. K. Printworld (P) Ltd.
New Delhi

Cataloging in Publication Data — DK

Prakṛti : the integral vision / general editor,
Kapila Vatsyayan.
Includes bibliographical references.
Includes index.

1. Nature. 2. Cosmology. I. Vatsyayan, Kapila, 1928-

ISBN 81-246-0036-8 (set)
ISBN 81-246-0040-6 (vol. 4)

First Published in India in 1995

Publishers
Indira Gandhi National Centre for the Arts
Central Vista Mess, Janpath, New Delhi - 110001

D.K. Printworld (P) Ltd.
Regd. office : H-12, Bali Nagar, New Delhi-110015

Printed at : D. K. Fine Art Press (P) Ltd., New Delhi

Foreword

In 1986 when the first of the Multidisciplinary and Cross-cultural Seminars was held under the aegis of the Indira Gandhi National Centre for the Arts, there was a trepidation. In my Introduction to the Volume on ***Concepts of Space : Ancient & Modern*** I have shared with the readers the sense of challenge as also of gratification. Then, it was not easy, nor has it been easy in the subsequent years to bring together people from different parts of the world of diverse disciplines and levels of society to speak through a multiplicity of languages to reflect and converse, and have a meaningful dialogue on the fundamental concerns of humanity in the past or present, in science or religion, philosophy and the arts, in civilizations as far apart as Egyptian, Chinese, Greek and Indian, permeating expressions through the written or the oral word, generating a language of myth and symbol which communicates across cultures.

The gathering, the dialogue and the discussion on a single concept of **Space** (*Akasa*) made it evident that the more fundamental and universal the concept, the greater the probability and possibility of diverse interpretations at multiple levels. The single concept of **Space** had taken us through the journey of the concepts of cavity, cave, aperture, fountainhead, body, air, sky, vacuity, cipher, point and much else. The scientist and the technologist explored the concept through their method of empirical investigation, the philosopher and the metaphysician, artists and the sociologist through perennial questioning and speculation. The two approaches and methods we learnt were complementary and not in conflict. The arts, architecture, sculpture, painting, music and dance enclose, embody and evoke space. Poetry creates vast edifices of space as spatial situations, and evoke the experience of outer and inner space.

The concern with **Space** (*Akasa*) could not be dissociated from the concern — the concept of **Time (*Kala*).** Two years later, a similar gathering with many familiar faces (who communicated with one another with greater ease) gathered to deliberate upon the many dimensions of **Time (*Kala*)**. Once again, the discussions at that Seminar revolved round the micro and the macro levels of the single concept, from molecular time to the cosmic time, from the time of biologists to the time of astronomer, from the time of the seer and meditator to the time of the architect, sculptor, musician, dancer and the poet. Besides the familiar faces, there were others who had joined the family of the IGNCA. The enlarged family gave this Seminar a depth and richness, unique and unparalleled. The experiences His Holiness The Dalai Lama articulated in words lucid and resonant, were juxtaposed with the precision and meditation of a scientist – the late Professor D.S. Kothari. The depth of the experience of **Time** in religious traditions, Islamic, Christian, Hindu, Buddhist, Jain and Hebrew, and the embodiment of inner and outer **Time** in poetic language was shared through rapt silence through the voice of the Poet Kathleen Raine.

Logically and naturally, from these two fundamental and universal concepts the next step in our quest for exploration of a single universal theme through diverse paths recalling the Rgvedic Verse, **Truth is one; man knows it by different names**, was to explore the concept of the primal elements (five or four) in different civilizations which have governed and determined the evolution of civilization and culture. Perhaps, the first conscious awareness of Man was the fact that his life depended on water, Earth, air, fire and, above all, space. Understandably, in all civilizations, at the most sophisticated level as also at the simplest level, the recognition that the primal elements were primary and indispensable for Man, is universal. Myths of the origin of the universe, creation, cosmology and cosmogony, have been developed on the concept of the elements which are four or five. There is a vast body of primary sources and equally extensive and complex a history of critical discourse on the nature of primal elements and their indispensability, not only for Man but for all life on Earth.

The subject was too vast and too monumental to be taken up in a single Seminar. Organizationally, therefore, this time it was decided to hold five successive but interlocked Seminars, one leading to the others, so that they could all culminate in a final international cross-cultural multidisciplinary Seminar. Since cultures, disciplines, and levels of society are not completely autonomous and insulated, there was a planned and understandable overlapping between one Seminar or Workshop and another.

The five Seminars were divided more for facility than the autonomous nature of each area or field. The discussions, therefore, at one Seminar were taken up and did interpenetrate into the next.

Logically, the first of these Seminars focused attention on the articulations of cohesive communities in the world who have lived in harmony with nature and who have communicated with the five elements in a continuous unceasing dialogue. To them the nature of the five elements — water, earth, air, fire and space — is not a matter of intellection or breaking down into separation and divisions of totality or a whole; instead, it is a question of life here and now. This is manifested in ritual practices which sacrilize nature so that man can live as an integral part of the universe, the rhythmic movement of the changing seasons, and the symmetrical punctuation and cycle of seed sprouting, growing, flowering, fruiting, decaying and renewing. In modern discourse this is understood as the need for man to live in harmony with the environment for an evolution of socio-cultural systems and methodologies for ensuring the maintenance of ecological balances. The lives and lifestyles of these cohesive groups have begun to acquire renewed validity on account of what man has done to pollute, contaminate, desacrilize and desecrate the very fundamentals that sustain him and make it possible for him to live on earth. The first Volume is based on the papers submitted at this Seminar.

The second Seminar moved the emphasis to the textual traditions. There is a vast body of literature in Greek, Chinese and Indian sources where philosophic discourses have been held on the nature of the universe, the nature of matter, the elements and the possibility of transmutation of the gross to the subtle. In India all branches of the philosophic streams have discussed the nature of the *Bhutas* and the *Mahabhutas*. The discussion ranges from the earliest articulation on the subject in the *Rgveda* to the philosophic schools of Vaisesikas, Vedantins, Saiva and the *Agamas*. The old system of *Ayurveda* in India, as much of medicine in Greece in a very different way, is based on the concept of the *Mahabhutas* in the constitution of the body itself. The very conception of the five elements constitutes the body. Texts for Indian astronomy, chemistry, metallurgy are replete with discussions on the elements. This discussion cannot be dissociated from a speculation, and discourse of, the nature of the universe, cosmology, cosmogony. The second Seminar delved deep into each of these aspects specially in the Indian tradition — Vedic, Brahmanical, Upanisadic and Tantric. In addition, there was a consideration of the concept of the *Mahabhutas* in Buddhism and Jainism. This Seminar unfolded the very complex and subtle aspects of the discourse on the nature of the matter, the fivefold organic matter and the five external objects. It also brought forth the many convergences as also divergences of viewpoint between and amongst these different streams of Indian thought as exemplified in the textual tradition. The Seminar was hosted by the Department of Sanskrit, University of Poona, Pune. The second Volume of this series is based on the papers and the discussions held at this Seminar.

Logically, the third Seminar had to and did explore the discussions as also the manifestations of the five elements in the Indian arts, along with their Agamic background. As is wellrecognized, while the *Upanisads* provide the basis for speculative thinking, the *Brahmanas* give the methodology of ritual practice (*Yajna* and *Prayoga*). Parallel is the development in early and later medieval India where the texts on *Vastu* and *Silpa* provide the frame-work of the abstract principles of creating concrete structures through different media and in different forms. The *Agama* is the twin which provide the methodology of enlivening, giving life and breath to the concrete structures and forms of art. If monumental architecture, sculpture, painting, music or dance, poetry or theatre, is created on the comprehension of space and time, they are even more built on the system of correspondences first for embodying and then evoking the five elements. The fascinating and unceasing cycle of the movement from the inner experience to the creation of form, which would incorporate the five elements and the employment of a methodology of ritual, is outlined in the Agamic texts only to achieve the end experience of the transformation of the gross to the subtle. This was the subject of this Seminar. From different vantage points of the architect, sculptor, painter, musician and dancer, the field was re-opened to examine the structure of the Indian arts at its primal level.

Naturally, theories of aesthetics which have emerged from such a viewpoint had to be discussed and many questions asked. The third Volume incorporates the span of the papers presented and the discussions held at this Seminar.

If the arts deal with the process of transmutation and mutation of the subtle to the gross, and the evocation of the subtle from the gross, in other words, the process of the abstract and the concrete suggesting, stimulating and evoking the abstract, then the astrophysicist deals with the nature of primal matter itself. No discourse on the elements could have been completed by excluding the discussion on modern physics of elementary particles and the most recent developments in microbiology. The fourth Seminar took up the question of the nature and function of matter itself and discussed the theories of the creation of the universe and emergent cosmologies in the modern physics. This was juxtaposed with the consideration on the nature of matter and consciousness. It was obvious that the new developments in science were, perhaps, not all that far remote from the earlier insights in the context of consciousness. The debate between the nineteenth Century mechanistic science and the modern physics was re-opened. This was juxtaposed with speculations and the philosophic discourses in the Indian philosophic schools. If the second Seminar dealt with the textual traditions and the philosophic schools of *Samkhya*, *Mimamsa* and the *Vaisesikas*, this Seminar looked at these traditions as structuralistic traditions from a scientific point of view. The dialogue created between the method of science and the method of speculation was invigorating. The fourth Volume comprises papers and discussions at this Seminar.

The fifth and the last Seminar was a coming together of cultures as also disciplines. Coordinators of the earlier Seminars presented brief Reports on each of the Seminars which provided the background and the landscape. The international community, comprising scientists, biologists, philosophers, anthropologists, ecologists and artists shared not only the myth and cosmology of their particular societies but also there was a most meaningful dialogue between those who lived in the awareness of the primordial myths of the elements and those who had employed the tools of science to explore the nature of the phenomenon of matter.

The putting together of the deliberations of the five major Seminars, as a single or a multiple-volume, is a daunting task. Through the combined efforts of the Coordinators of each of these Seminars and, particularly, the Chief Coordinator – Professor B.N. Saraswati and his associates – it has been possible to prepare the five Volumes based on the deliberations of these Seminars as also a companion exhibition which was called **"PRAKṚTI: The Integral Vision"**.

It is my hope that these Volumes will provide material for further discussion and dialogue. The perennial nature of the theme and its urgent and contemporary validity will, I hope, make these Volumes significant. As I have said earlier in my Introduction, Man stands today at a moment where he is threatened by the pollution, inner and outer, of his own making. The primal elements and the urgent need for purification through austerity and discipline are not the matters of intellectual discourse alone. Their maintenance and sustenance, and the purity of these that are primary and primal, are the objectives of our life, lest death overtakes us.

9th June, 1994 **Kapila Vatsyayan**

Preface

The essays collected here are based on papers delivered at the *Bhutas* seminar held in Inter-University Centre for Astronomy and Astrophysics (IUCAA), Pune, from August 24 to 27, 1992. The seminar was jointly sponsored by IUCAA and Indira Gandhi National Centre for the Arts, New Delhi.

The ancient wisdom contained in the *Vedas*, *Upanisadas*, other *sastras* and the *Ayurveda* discusses the concept of matter in various forms. The word *bhutas* used here is to be taken as symbolising these concepts. The ideas include the nature of matter on the micro-scale as well as on the large scale, the nature of living matter, the origin of life itself, holistic medicine, *Yogasutras,* etc.

Modern science has brought in new perspectives. What is the ultimate micro-structure of matter? In the sequence of atoms-nuclei-quarks – is there an end-point? How, where and when in the universe did the various chemical elements form? Where is the frontier between physics and biology? What is the link between the 'living' and 'non-living' matter? What are the current ideas on the origin and evolution of life? How do they influence modern medical systems?

To what extent is there a commonality between the ancient and the modern streams of thought? The methods of seeking answers are different, but are questions basically the same? Can a dialogue between two systems with such manifest differences be successful?

This seminar was attempting such a dialogue. It sought to bring together intellectuals (who may not otherwise participate in a joint discussion) with the hope that the cross-fertilization of ideas would be productive.

The subject of the seminar covered both the Indian traditional ideas on matter and the modern scientific concepts. The scope was thus fairly wide covering such ideas as:

(i) Origin of matter

(ii) Nature of matter, its hierarchical structure

(iii) Transmutation from one form to another

(iv) Living and inert matter: commonalities and differences

(v) Evolution of living matter

(vi) Any other relevant aspect of matter not covered explicitly in (i)-(v).

On the scientific side there was participation by physicists, biologists, astronomers, chemists, geophysicists, etc., while on the traditional side scholars from humanities, holistic medicine, ancient Indian literature, *Ayurveda*, etc. participated.

The participants cooperated by not being very technical since the workshop was interdisciplinary in nature. They highlighted the basic concepts and march of ideas rather than specific details. The long discussion sessions were enjoyable for their liveliness and spontaneity.

There was a general agreement that the seminar was a success and such interdisciplinary dialogues should continue. There were certain action-points suggested:

1. The database of ancient manuscripts should be made as complete as possible to enable scholars to use it for research purposes. The IGNCA may help sponsor this important activity.
2. An objective assessment is needed about the state of knowledge in past in the various fields listed under the subject-matter of the seminar.
3. Each of the topics listed above deserved extensive interdisciplinary discussions in their own right. As such further seminars could be initiated by the IGNCA and other interested institutions.

I am happy that the views of participants here will give the readers some glimpses of the depth and range of the subject-matter covered. I wish to thank all the contributors to this volume for their cooperation in submitting their articles promptly. Finally, I am grateful to Dr. Kapila Vatsyayan and her colleagues at the IGNCA for making it possible to hold the seminar at IUCAA.

Jayant V. Narlikar

Contents

1

Bhutas

Some Reflections on Modern Scientific Concepts and Traditional Indian Thoughts

Jayant V. Narlikar

Against the background of some elementary knowledge about the many different streams of ancient thoughts, I have ventured to ask some questions vis-a-vis scientific ideas of modern times where I do know a little, perhaps just enough to gauge the extent of my ignorance. About our ancient traditions I do not even know the extent of my ignorance! So I had better begin with the modern scientific end. What does science say about the nature of matter on different physical scales?

Scales of Structure

A few years ago Professor Phillip Morrison had made a beautiful but short film entitled 'Powers of Ten'. It started with a scene very common in the Western world, that of a couple picnicking in a city park. Then the camera zooms out showing the larger scale of the park, then zooms farther to show the city, then the state and so on. Each scene is followed by another with ten times larger scale. How far does this go on?

Taking 1 metre as the scale we measure our local distances in (— the picnicking couple occupied an area of a few square metres), the tenfold increases in length go on till about 10^{26} metres — that is, about a hundred million million million million metres! A few significant steps enroute to this gigantic scale are given in Table I below.

The largest scale in Table I is that of the large scale structure of the universe **as we perceive it today**. Our present cosmological theories tend to suggest that this is absolutely the largest scale we shall ever encounter. But the film does not end there! The second part of the film shows us how things look at small scale. By zooming in the camera takes us to scales smaller than 1 metre from the picnickers to their palms

Table I : Large Structures

Linear Scale (metres)	*Structure*
1	Human being
10^{7}	The Earth
10^{9}	The Sun
10^{21}	The Galaxy
10^{23}	Clusters of galaxies
10^{26}	The observable universe

and then inside the palms to human cells, molecules, atoms etc. Table II shows some important structures on these small scales. The limiting (smallest conceivable) scale in Table II is that of quantum gravity – representing a thousand-million-million-million-million-million-million-millionth part of a metre!

Table II : Small Structures

Linear Scale (metres)	*Structure*
1	Man
10^{-5}	Cell
10^{-10}	Atom
10^{-15}	Nucleus
10^{-29}	Scales probed by present accelerators
10^{-45}	Quantum gravity

Below this small scale scientists can no longer trust the macroscopically familiar notions of space and time. Our laboratory experiments using the biggest manmade accelerators of particles, take us down to length scales 10^{16} (ten thousand million million) times this limit. To probe structures at still smaller scales demands accelerators far more complex and costly than can be built today. So tha human technology is lagging behind what human mind can conceive, by this large factor.

The main conclusion from the film is to tell us how matter exhibits structure on vastly different scales. Why does it exhibit structure? Is there any end to it? There are questions and puzzles. One puzzle relates to the large scale structure : is it fractal in nature? As an example of fracals, consider the map of a country's coastline. It shows zig-zag patterns. It we use finer scale to examine a samller section in greater detail, we will still see the zig-zag pattern. The pattern keeps repeating at finer and finer levels, Likewise, analysis of large scale structure in the universe reveals a grouping at different length scales. Thus stars cluster in galaxies, galaxies in groups, groups in clusters and clusters in superclusters. There are claims that this tendency is of modern cosmology.

An allied puzzle facing cosmologists today is to understand why matter happens to be distributed in such a hierarchical and inhomogeneous way while radiation is so smooth. Here I refer to the radiation in microwaves pending the universe. This radiation is supposed to be the relic of the primordial creation event, the big bang which also produced matter. Why, if both matter and radiation were of primordial origin, did matter distribute itself in this clustered way while radiation remained extremely homogeneous?

A different kind of conceptual difficulty comes at the microscopic (subatomic) level. This arises from the quantum uncertainty principle. Its consequence is as follows. As we think of structures on smaller and smaller length scales, the masses of these structures keep on increasing in inverse proportion! Thus the smaller the system the larger the mass and energy it has. To reconcile this idea with our microscopic notion that mass of the whole is greater than mass of parts is indeed difficult. For example, three quarks make up a proton. Yet the mass of each quark is far more than that of the proton. Of course, the notion can be rationalized but this rationalization becomes more and more difficult as we probe deeper in our search for the 'ultimate' building block of matter.

Attempts at Unification

Scientists do not know the answers to puzzles like these which may call for radical rethinking. Indeed, howsoever objective they may call themselves, the practitioners of science tend to be reluctant to face new evidence that forces them to revise their ideas. Thus many of the puzzles are simply wished away. But science has a self correcting tendency that ultimately helps identify the correct path.

Sheldon Glashow, the Nobel Prize winning physicist likes to illustrate the cosmic puzzle with the figure of a snake swallowing its tail. The concept is of Indian origin, of Shesha Naga who is also portrayed in the tail-swallowing pose. Glashow's snake has its tail pointing towards structure at the smallest scale (quantum gravity). As we progress towards the head we pass through structures on the larger and larger scales, with the head corresponding to the cosmological scale of 10^{26} metres. Thus we transverse 71 orders of magnitude from tail to head. Yet the bringing of the two ends symbolizes the link without which the picture remains incomplete. The snake is fully understood only if the two ends meet. In other words, the largest scale structures cannot be understood without reference to smallest scale ones **and** *vice versa*.

Considerable brainstorming is going on between cosmologists and particle theorists about this link. Many believe that the clue may come from the unification of all known physical forces in a single picture. There are four basic interactions that need to be united this way : the electromagnetic, the strong, the weak and the gravitational interactions. Whether this holy grail of unification will ever be attained reamins to be seen. Some physicists think that the end will be attained very soon.

I hold a pessimistic view that we will never discover the ultimate truth, although we may make progress in the right direction. Thus I disagree with those optimists who are confident that the 'end' of physics is at hand. And so, I do not think that attempts to demonstrate similarities between ancient traditional beliefs and the statements of modern science about nature are worthwhile. For the former are now frozen while the latter are evolving. To argue that the ancients knew about facts of nature that the scientists know today does not take account of the above situation.

Ancient Traditions

To what level had the ancient understanding about nature progressed? Did our ancestors of the Puranik times have high technology? Examples of weapons used — the various *saktis* and *astras* of the Mahabharata War — are cited to demonstrate theat they did have advanced weaponry. However, advance technology has other effects on social structure. Questions arise. Why was a war with remote control missiles fought with chariots, elephants and infantry in a battlefield? And in descriptions of normal life of those days, why don't we find references to such amenities as tap water and household electricity?

A proper claim for advanced technology in the past must be backed by a technical description involving quantitative statements. If there were aircrafts, do we have specifications of a working model? I searched through the *Brihad-vimana-sastra* without finding such details. It is of course possible to argue that such descriptions existed but were lost. But then a sceptic justifiably remains unconvinced. In this connection, I think Pushpa Bhargava and Chandana Chakrabarty have done, within their admittedly limited framework, a commendable exercise in sifting through the statements in life sciences and medicine. If they have drawn negative conclusions in some respects, specific counter-examples need to be produced to shoot them down.

I hope their conclusions would generate fresh activity on this front and I am sure that they themselves would welcome any new evidence they might have missed.

I now make comments on another topic that had generated considerable argument during the seminar.

The question I wish to ask first is, how did the traditional knowledge that we see today in holistic form evolve with time? Science as we know it today has evolved through several processes, sometimes continuously while on ocassions through sudden jumps. Either way, the science of today is vastly different from that in Newton's time, which in turn was vastly different from that in Aristotle's time. Can we likewise see a thread of evolution running through the gems of our traditional knowledge?

This question leads to another. How far was our knowledge based on direct observations and experimentation? If these processes (common in modern science) did operate, did they lead to the modification or even abandonment of any existing line of reasoning? In this connection I may mention that at the time of Galileo, European scholars were in the habit of settling issues by philosophical debates rather than experimental demonstration. Galileo began the then new method of showing a particular claim to be wrong by explicit experimental proof. It was this new approach that heralded the new scientific era in Europe.

This brings me to the last but not the least of my questions about our scholastic history.

Why did our ancient scholastic tradition apparently come to a halt a few centuries ago, to be revived only with the advent of the British Raj? Why the astronomical tradition from Aryabhata to Bhaskara II did not continue beyond the twelfth century? For, during those seven centuries (500-1200 A.D.) India certainly compared favourably with Europe in astronomical know-how.

The question can be debated at length. I find one particular instance indicative of the state of affairs. I refer to the debate between Mandan Mishra and Shankaracharya. The story goes that when Shankara was searching for Mandan Mishra's house he came across some women washing clothes. When he asked for directions to the house he was told :

> *jagaddhruvam syajjagadadhruvam syatkirangana yatra giram giranti,*
> *dwarasthanidantarasannirudha janihi tanmandanamishrasadmah.*
>
> "Is the world permanent or non-permenent? Where you find the female parrots in cages at the front door discussing this question, that you may know to be the house of Mandan Mishra."

I was very impressed when I first saw this *shloka*. Did it not indicate the scholarly atmosphere at the house of Mandan Mishra? And if even the parrots had picked up so much wisdom how wise must Mandan Mishra himself be? And didn't the debate sound so similar to the modern cosmological controversy of 'steady state' *vs* 'big-bang'?

But a careful examination brings out another aspect which is not so complimentary! Parrots pick up words and memorise them without understanding their meaning. They memorise them only when they hear the words recited repeatedly. That implies the practice of rote-learning. Were the students of Mandan Mishra simply memorising the argument as it was passed on to them by their Guru? As Narayan Rana told us in his talk, whatever the teacher told the students was uncritically accepted and memorised by them.

Even in Galileo's time in Europe, Aristotle's ideas were simply propagated through this uncritical process. When Galileo stepped in, he demonstrated by actual experiments why those ideas were wrong – experiments no one had bothered to perform since verbal arguments were considered sufficient.

[There is a similar sequel to the Shankara episode. When Mandan Mishra lost, his wife took up the debate on his behalf. Her questions demanded knowledge of sexual behaviour, which as a bachelor Shankara could not answer. So he asked for time, 'entered' the body of a married man to learn about the details. Whatever be the truth of the matter, here we see an example where experiment was called for to supplement knowledge!]

Thus rote learning and an unquestioning attitude may have been one of the contributory factors to the decline of science in India during 1200-1900 A.D.

I make these comments will all humility. I may also point out that conformity with the traditional dogma has always impeded the march of science. Even today most of the Western science is threatened with this danger. For scientifice research today calls for lots of financial support which is forthcoming only if peer-review is favourable. This guarantees conformism and makes it all the more difficult for new ideas to come in.

Conclusion

I began by discussing the manifestation of *Bhutas* – matter – on different scales. It took me on the one hand to larger and larger scales of interest to astronomers and cosmologists and on the other hand to smaller and smaller scales of interest to the particle physicist. There is the tantalizing possibility of linking the smallest structure with the largest one. How? We do not know yet! Perhaps we never will: for the quest of science is an unending one. And then I turned towards ancient knowledge; for our forefathers too had asked similar questions.

Here I have perhaps digressed too far from the subject of *Bhutas* and raised several questions about the nature and scope of ancient traditions. I would nevertheless be unfair to myself if I did not air these questions. One method of trying to understand these issues is by having interdisciplinary dialogue.

2

Quantum Theory, Elementary Particles
Limits to Divisibility

N. Mukunda

In any effort to compare or bring together ancient insights and current scientific knowledge, there is always the question: what do we hope to achieve or learn from the exercise, if it is to go beyond recounting interesting stories to one another? There is always the problem of communication across disciplines and specialisations. Within science itself this is well-known, but the difficulties are even greater in the present situation. In any case, in matters of detail and recently acquired knowledge of nature through experiment, it is quite unreasonable to look for exact parallels in past thinking. Questions about the nature of matter and the structure of the cosmos have been raised since time immemorial. And in answer there has always been a great deal of speculation based to some extent on experience but also largely on pictorial thinking. We may view this as the first stage in coming to terms with the physical universe. One can generally think of four motivating factors behind speculative thinking: (a) the desire to respond to psychological needs, and even fears, about the unknown; (b) the desire for economy in concepts and independent causes, to unify what appears so diverse at first sight; (c) the wish to inspire and uplift the imagination and create poetic imagery; and (d) to hypothesize about the unknown, in the sense of science, and suggest new experimental tests of one's ideas. Naturally in ancient times there was a tendency for the first three factors to be more prominent; and there was also, apart from astronomy, a general lack of precise and quantitative expression of one's ideas.

Each of these motivations behind speculation is legitimate and has value in its own sphere; problems in comparison arise when different motivations get confused with one another. May be therefore it is wise not to expect too much in advance in any case when comparing ancient and modern insights, and to be cautious.

Let me focus on ideas on the questions: are there such things as the smallest units of matter, out of which all that we see can be built up? Or is there no end to the divisibility of matter? Ultimately is matter discrete or continuous, lumpy or smooth? Schroedinger, in his book *Nature and the Greeks*, explains one line of argument that led some of the early Greek thinkers to the view that there must be an end to the process of dividing matter into smaller and smaller parts. It is worth emphasizing that among the Greek philosophers, and in the course of several centuries, there was certainly no single uniform view about fundamental questions, but several differing schools and points of view existed. Schroedinger traces the views of Thales, his disciple Anaximander and then his disciple Anaximenes, all of whom lived around the sixth century B.C., on this question. Each of them believed that there was **one** basic substance out of which everything else was made up. Thales is quoted by Aristotle as having declared that "Water is the material cause of all things". For Anaximander it was not water but something else unseen, infinite and everlasting, which assumes many forms that we then see. In Anaximenes' view, however, the primary substance was air, subjected to the processes of rarefaction and condensation. Through the development of these successive views, the relationship between being and becoming was gradually highlighted and clarified. For Heraclitus the basic element was fire, combining the attributes of substance and process. Parmenides too clung to a single fundamental principle but there seems to be some vagueness in his statements. In contrast to all these monists – whether it be a primary substance or process or principle – we see a change, a preference for multiplicity, in the views of others. Thus Empedocles hypothesized four basic elements – earth, water, air and fire – acted upon by love and strife. On the other hand, Anaxagoras believed in an infinite variety of infinitely small seeds, undergoing processes of mixing and separation. And then through Leucippus and Democritus we finally arrive at the Greek concept of the atom – the smallest units of matter, indivisible, indestructible, of finite size and located in empty space. Different atoms were of different sizes and shapes, but all of the same substance; with no qualities, mathematically divisible but physically whole. In recalling the development of this chain of ideas leading ultimately to the atom of Democritus, Schroedinger draws attention to a very interesting aspect. It was, according to him, the Greek encounter with irrational numbers and the continuum, and even their fear of these, that led them to the view that matter must ultimately consist of certain smallest indivisible and unchanging parts. And the various changes in the states of matter arose by these parts coming together or going apart, by condensation and rarefaction, in otherwise empty space. I mention this account by Schroedinger mainly because he highlights here a compelling reason based on experience as the motivation for believing that there must be an end to the divisibility of matter.

Contrasted with such views, as expressed by Democritus, Plato had taken the position that the smallest units of matter were certain elementary geometrical forms, so that they had more of a mathematical than a material significance; while Aristotle reverted more or less to the idea that matter is continuous. It would be interesting and necessary to learn in depth about any related and similar, but independent, lines of thinking in those times, in our tradition.

Skipping many centuries, when we come to Descartes we learn that he was a very imaginative and speculative thinker, and also that he was a confirmed opponent of the atomic hypothesis. For him, we read, matter was definitely infinitely divisible. The atomic idea had to wait for Dalton, and the developments in chemistry, to be revived again in compelling and quantitative terms. By that period, of course, the experimental method and the use of mathematical reasoning had been established as the twin pillars of science. In Faraday's experiments on electrolysis too there were hints that there was an ultimate "molecule of electricity", which later turned out to be the electron. But it is interesting to recall that Maxwell had some doubts about it as he felt it would not fit in with his electromagnetic theory! It is also well-known that even around the end of the last century, Ostwald and Mach were strongly against the atomic hypothesis, because in their opinion it had not been demonstrated that the idea was scientifically useful and that atoms could be 'seen'. Indeed one of the important motivations behind Einstein's 1905 work on the Brownian movement was to bring out the reality of the existence of atoms through observable effects.

One sees in these developments spanning many centuries a cyclical process in thoughts about the ultimate nature of matter — like swings of a pendulum, going from the doctrine of existence of ultimate individual entities to their non-existence. It is quite interesting that this tendency has continued even into this century, albeit in a new framework defined by relativity and quantum theory.

The discovery of the electron in the late 1890s by J.J. Thomson, the 1905 explanation of the Brownian movement bringing out the reality of atoms, and the 1911 discovery of the atomic nucleus by E. Rutherford — all these were important steps towards the modern form of atomic theory. In a sense they culminated in the 1913 Bohr-Rutherford model of the atom, which explained Mendeleev's periodic table of chemical elements. We may imagine that we had come to the end of the road on which Democritus first set out. What yet remained was the mathematical and physical framework of quantum mechanics.

In Dirac's justly famous book on the *Principles of Quantum Mechanics*, he explains why, on general philosophical grounds, when one wishes to account for the ultimate structure of matter, there is a need to depart from the ideas of classical physics. His argument is that classical physics is scale invariant and: "So long as **big** and **small** are merely relative concepts, it is no help to explain the big in terms of the small. It is therefore necessary to modify classical ideas in such a way as to give an absolute meaning to size". Then he goes on to say that quantum mechanics provides a resolution by bringing in the concept of disturbance caused by observation, thereby giving an absolute meaning to size: "If the object under observation is such that the unavoidable limiting disturbance is negligible, then the object is big in the absolute sense and we may apply classical mechanics to it. If, on the other hand, the limiting disturbance is not negligible, then the object is small in the absolute sense and we require a new theory for dealing with it".

Even after the discovery of quantum mechanics in 1925-26, though, Schroedinger attempted to go back to a classical continuous model of matter, based on waves and wave packets. His hope was to somehow avoid quantum discreteness and discontinuities. But the attempt did not succeed.

In a few years, by the early 1930s, the atom of chemistry was resolved into a nucleus made up of protons and neutrons, with electrons orbiting on the outside. It must have seemed for a while that all matter was ultimately built up out of three basic building blocks – protons, neutrons and electrons. But then an entirely unexpected and qualitatively new aspect was introduced into the whole problem – this was the prediction, and soon after the discovery of anti-matter. This came about through the understanding of the unexpected features of Dirac's relativistic equation for the electron. It turns out that there is a partner to the electron, called the positron, which is similar in all respects except that the electric charge is exactly the opposite. Moreover, when an electron and a positron collide, with a certain probability they annihilate one another, leaving behind electromagnetic radiation. Thus matter can vanish in a flash. Conversely under suitable conditions matter in the form of an electron-positron pair can be created from radiation. So all these possibilities, which of course obey strictly the laws of energy and momentum and charge conservation, complicate the question of the ultimate nature of matter, by coupling it to radiation. It has turned out that not just the electron, but every other fundamental particle too has a partner anti-particle – in a few cases the two may even coincide! Thus anti-matter, a consequence of relativity and quantum theory, enters the picture in an unavoidable way.

With the steady advance in experimental methods, through the 1940s, 50s and 60s, and even to this day, many additional particles have been found to exist in nature. Some were discovered in the cosmic rays, others were created in man-made accelerators. But as these discoveries accumulated, beyond a certain point, it became rather embarrassing to have to deal with almost 200 or so fundamental particles. This was even more than the number of elements in Mendeleev's table!

So there came a period – in the late 1950s and through the 1960s – when many physicists believed that we had come to the end of the idea of divisibility of matter, but in an entirely new way. It was no longer useful to seek for **the ultimate** constituents of matter — all the 200 or so known particles were made up of each other and could convert themselves into one another freely, subject only to the basic conservation laws. All of them were to be regarded as equally fundamental, their parts were themselves; equally well, they were equally non-fundamental. Thus if you were to ask what went to make up a proton, the answer might be — a neutron and a pi-meson. What about the neutron? Well, a proton and a pi-meson. But then, what is a pi-meson made of? Ah, it is a proton and an anti-neutron! Essentially, it was felt that the search for substructure had ended, because it was no longer a useful question to ask, or a useful view to take. This point of view was particularly strongly expressed by Heisenberg, as recently as in 1975, in the words: "The difference between elementary and composite particles has thus basically disappeared".

But then over the same period and in a few years the pendulum swung again — the concept of quarks, invented in 1962 or so, steadily gained credibility; and all the 200 odd particles, including protons and neutrons and mesons, could be regarded as built up out of a few quarks. It was like the story of Mendeleev's periodic table all over again. The next swing of the pendulum, again an embarrassment, is that today the number of elementary entities at the level of quarks has slowly risen to some 40 or so, so one wonders 'what next'? In this context, I cannot refrain from mentioning one qualitative difference between attitudes today and a few decades ago. At the time he predicted the existence of the positron, Dirac hesitated a great deal because he felt three basic building blocks of matter were good enough, and adding a fourth was somewhat excessive. No such hesitations constrain the speculations and theories of modern times, however. There is also the idea, actively pursued, that the ultimate entities in nature are **strings**, not particles at all, though of a very refined and unimaginable kind.

Against the background of such developments, it is hard to suppose that one will come to a definite conclusion — nature seems to be always hiding behind one more surprise, one more mystery. It is like peeling the layers of an endless onion! At each stage there are some things we have learnt from experiment and theory, and then some educated guesses and speculations which only future developments can decide. Added to these is the fact that relativity and quantum theory put together make the question of constituents and substructure energy dependent.

There is one other general point I would like to make relating to the use of mathematics in the quest for understanding nature. Its value was clearly enunciated by Galileo in his statement: "The book of nature is written in the language of mathematics". In the physical sciences, certainly, mathematics is an essential and powerful language and mode of thinking, which of course gives an abstract quality to the basic theories of physics. One can get a feeling for this abstractness by appreciating that, firstly, the equations of physics are more fundamental than the individual phenomena which they describe. This of course is to be expected. But secondly, going beyond this, one finds that the symmetries of the equations are more basic than the equations themselves! In Dirac's words, "both relativity and quantum theory seem to show that transformations are of more fundamental importance than equations". So the 'stuff' out of which one imagines nature to be made, and the principles underlying our understanding, get more and more refined.

In Heisenberg's writings, he goes back here to ideas of Plato and of Aristotle: ". . . . modern physics takes a definite stand against the materialism of Democritus, and for Plato and the Pythagoreans . . . . The elementary particles in Plato's 'Timaeus' are finally not substance but mathematical forms". And in the context of quantum mechanics, which he himself invented, Heisenberg says we have gone back to the idea of 'potentia' in Aristotle's philosophy. It is truly staggering that our most basic, most fundamental language for physics today is that of deterministic evolution of potentialities and not of actualities. One treats in a quantitative and deterministic way "a strange kind of physical reality just in the middle between possibility and reality".

However, all these comparisons and discovery of parallels between ancient thinking and modern physics must be understood properly. As Heisenberg carefully clarifies, it is the appeal to controlled experiment that gives to modern science a really solid and serious foundation and meaning. The statements of quantum theory are in a very specific context, and are not largely poetic imagery and speculation, however elevating these may be. For one ancient 'insight' corroborated today, may be there are many others not so corroborated. But there is no surprise in all this. It shows the power that speculative thinking can bring in. At the end of his discussion, Heisenberg concludes by saying: "All the same, some statements of ancient philosophy are rather near to those of modern science. This simply shows how far one can get by combining the ordinary experience of nature that we have without doing experiments with the untiring effort to get some logical order into this experience to understand it from general principles".

Coming back to modern physics, it is the reliance on mathematics that provides guidance and rigour in thinking, and helps avoid internal contradictions and inconsistencies. But here it is a quite startling fact to realise that the true impact of careful and rigorous thinking within mathematics itself is a matter of very recent origin. Namely it is no older than the later half of the last century, through the work of mathematicians like Weierstrass, Dedekind and others. Even in this century we have had the striking results of Hilbert and Godel – the former trying to prove the internal consistency and completeness of an axiomatic framework for mathematics, the latter then showing that these can never be achieved!

It is well, then, to keep these facts in mind when we judge the ideas and speculations of ancient times on the nature of matter and the universe.

3

Evolution of Living Matter

S. R. N. Murthy

A Study of the geological record indicates that the grand march of life on the earth is from almost the beginning of the earth. The micro fossils of bacteria and algae found in rocks of more than three billion years old occurring in Africa, Australia and Canada provide evidence on the earliest evolution of life on the earth. According to Barghoorn, the Precambrian interval began when the earth was formed about 4.5 billion years ago and ended about 600 million years ago, when the Palaeozoic era commenced. The geological record shows that there was a great spurt of life in the Palaeozoic rocks. Though there is no geological record to show the gradual development of life from the unicellular organism to the multicellular ones in the Precambrian, it is presumed with good reason for the rocks of the Precambrian have undergone total metamorphism. From the Palaeozoic to the present history of the earth, the grand march of life is recorded with all its details, of course with punctuation. The trilobites and graptolites of the early Palaeozoic gave rise to fishes in the Devonian followed by reptiles in the Mesozoic, mammals in the Tertiary and the human beings in the Recent; on animal side and firns in the carboniferous giving rise to flowering plants in the Tertiary on the vegetative side.

According to Kummel 'The idea of evolution had been known long before Darwin, but he was the first to demonstrate convincingly the general principle of evolution . . .'. Thus it can be surmised that man on the earth is a product of evolution of life from the unicellular organism to the crown creation.

Further Kummel observed that "Two men – the Chevalier de Lamarck (1744-1829) and Charles Darwin (1809-1882) – removed the study of the evolution of life from a theological and metaphysical frame to its proper place in biological philosophy. Lamarck was the first really scientific student of evolution. His book *Zoological Philosophy* published in 1809, aroused a controversy that is still not completely resolved. Lamarck recognised, in the successive organisms he studied, a progressive complication of organisation, and to him that meant evolution; he saw however, that living organisms could not be classified into a simple continuous series of ever increasing complexity. Environment, he believed, was a factor in, but not a cause of, evolution."

Either the concept of disuse or use of organs influenced by environment according to Lamarck or the concept of natural selection by Darwin in advancing organic evolution though brought a kind of revolution in scientific thinking on the grand march of life did not stand the factual criticism and gave way to the modern discipline of genetics which actually originated with Gregor Johann Mendel. From the beginning of the present century this field is being elaborated and it is now known that the chromosomes in the nuclei of the cells contain genes – the paired hereditary factors of Mendel and the spontaneous change in them give rise to new hereditary forms, which is called mutations. It is noted that the cause of mutation is still uncertain.

From the geological record many kinds of evolutionary changes have been known. According to Kummel "Evolutionary changes in animals can be convergent, divergent or parallel. If unrelated groups come to have a similar appearance, we say that their evolution is convergent. Certain genera of fossil brachiopods and pelecypods, for e.g., had a cone-shaped shell that was cemented to the sea bottom like that of the solitary corals – the explanation being that the brachiopods and the pelecypods became adopted to an environmental niche that was similar to that of the corals. If closely related groups become less similar as they evolve, their evolution is said to be divergent. Evolution that is neither convergent nor divergent is said to be parallel. Parallelism is common to the fossil record."

This explains the influence of environment on animals in the fossil record. Also trends like orthogenetic with oriented trends and radiation type are also known from the fossil records. Thus data from the geological record has given us valuable evidence to understand the evolution of life on the earth. While evolution of the living matter as found in the geological record is a product of modern science of the earth, without entering into such details the ancient Indian texts of philosophy and *Ayurveda* deal with the origin of life in a different manner. In the final both the concepts are mutually complementary but not contradictory. The ancient Indian texts do not trace the evolution of life on the earth with such details as the geological sciences do. The entire facts of the geological record can only be considered as only supplementing the ancient Indian thoughts. The ancient Indian thinkers have made a thorough study of the life that is obtained on the earth in its present stage of its long history. Ray and Gupta state that "Man, according to Caraka, is an epitome of the macrocosm. Following the philosophical doctrines of *Samkhya* and *Vedanta*, Caraka holds that the individual is a replica of the universal; both the external world and the individual man are the manifestations of one and the same eternal spirit (*Brahman*). In other words, spirit and matter are not two separate entities but one integral whole. Both man and the visible world are composed of six elements. *Prthivi* (earth), *ap* (water or liquid), *tejas* (fire), *vayu* (air) and *akasa* (ether) are common to both. The sixth element, the spirit or self in the individual, is equivalent to *Brahman* in the universe." Further they observed that "Conception occurs inside the womb by the union of semen, ovum and the spirit. By the physical act of mating union takes place between the semen (sperm cell) and the female ovum (germ cell); then the spirit, associated with the mind, descends and enters into the zygote formed, and a new embryonic life is created. If the spirit does not descend, no life is created and conception fails to occur." and "It is the mind which yokes the living organism to the spirit and holds the senses together. With the departure of mind, the organism becomes a lifeless matter."

They also deliberate further on the concepts of Caraka on heredity and environment. These factors indicate that in spite of large gaps in their knowledge about the modern scientific data on the evolution of life, the ancient Indians succeeded in understanding the origin and evolution of life in its broad outline. The modern science is trying hard to unravel the origin of life. Experiments on amino-acids etc. have only indicated the frame that would be necessary to hold life but not its cause, i.e., the spirit. The identification of the spirit and its role in the origin of life is the prime contribution of ancient Indian thought, which fact is to be recognised by modern science. Hence, there is need for a close collaboration of modern science and ancient Indian thought to fully understand the evolution of living matter in the universe in general and on the earth in special. The earth being a representative of the universe, and in dynamic equilibrium with the universal bodies, its evolution to catch the spirit to manifest life is a matter of deep reflect from both the occident and the orient.

The Unique Earth

That the earth is a representative of the whole universe and is set in dynamic motion is realised both in the East as well as in the Western thinking, is not a matter for deep deliberation. Both the occident and the orient have influenced each other in arriving at the idea. But advancement in modern earthscience has something more to contribute in giving us details of the earth which made its frame aminable for life to enter. The primary geochemcial differentiation of the earth dividing it into an external shell of crust, middle shell of mentle and inner shell of core is something salutary. This has not happened in any other member of the solar family or if it had happened it is not complete in all respect to have produced a geomagnetic field as has been done by the earth. As a result of the generation of a geomagnetic field by the virtue of which the surface of the earth is having solar light filtered of all harmful types of rays like x-rays, a protective field for life to manifest on the earth was created. In this sense the importance of the generation of the electromagnetic field of the earth is something superb.

Soon after the primary geochemical differentiation of the earth, it may be taken that the sedimentary cycle started functioning on the earth with the origin of oceans in between the land masses. This was a second fact which fecilitated the life to manifest on the earth. Without the appearance of water sheet on the surface of the earth, the mere mineral or chemical frame would have hardly held life within it. Even if such a structure had been encased life, its activity having been limited and perceptions quelled, would hardly been realised that life did exist.

The above two stages can be deciphered from the modern geological point of view in tracing evolution of living matter. So far no life is reported on other members of the solar family. Also it is uncertain that life exists in other galaxies of the universe. As much as that the earth is the only planet to give birth and protect life in its numerous forms make it really fit to be addressed as 'Mother Earth'.

Why only that the earth has undergone primary differentiation of its matter and not others is a matter of deep research. The facts may be related to its early faster motion, its chemistry and other factors. The factors defining the developments of the physico-chemical condition of the earth to encase life is therefore unique and this uniqueness is difficult to be satisfactorily answered. The chemistry of the earth generally represented by that of its mantle which makes up a major portion possesses a chemistry comparable to that of the solar chormosphere and the meteorites. This chemistry of the earth set in such a dynamic motion has slowly acquired shell structure with different composition during the course of its history. All these factors need be taken into consideration when we are discussing the optimum conditions for the chemical material structure to hold life in it.

The Life Force of Field of Life

Matter can exist without life but life to manifest matter is essential. That does not mean that the matter will, on attaining optimum condition should automatically contain life. It may also mean life that. But that may mean that until such conditioning life force will not be able to be held by matter. Or life may be in gross form in the inanimate things and gradually transform into living form when the matter gets conditioned to hold it.

Life is equated with *prana* in Sanskrit. *Prana* is a kind of air or *vayu*. Along with other kinds of air namely *apana*, *samana*, *udana*, *vyana*, *naga*, *kurma*, *krakara*, *devadatta* and *dhananjaya*, it resides in the human body. Life is between the first and the last breath. Thus the life force is the kind of air which enters the body and makes it living. Therefore the body or *shareera* which is *parthiva* or made of earth and also water becomes living on the application of air. Thus the body is of earth, water and air and can exist only under certain condition of heat or temperature accounting for the four *bhutas* of the *Pancamahabhutas*. *Prthivi* confers hardness; *ap* confers fluid constitutents; *tejas* the body heat; *vayu* the vital breath and *akasa* the bodily orifices.

It is also noted that the various kinds of air reside in the following parts of the body:

prana	*hrdaya*
apana	*guda*
samana	*nabhi*
udana	*kantha*
vyana	*sarva-shareera*
naga	*vagdvara*
kurma	*unmilana*
krakara	*chaksu*
deavdatta	*vijrmbhana*
dhananjaya	*sarvavyapi*

and it is also mentioned that the air *dhananjaya* will not leave the body even after death. That means that one kind of air exists in the dead or non-living body also. This indicates that the life force exists in different form from the non-living to the living in more than one form. Even after the body is capable of breathing it may not be epitheted to be 'living' but for the spirit of life enters the body. The spirit of life charges the body with mind and holds senses together.

Therefore the case made by the *pancamahabhutas* alone cannot make it live. The most important thing is the spirit of life. The spirit of life can be separated from the body by yogic practice when the body can only be said as a case of *pancabhutas*. It is motionless and static. No life for that matter. But soon spirit descends into it, it electrifies the mind and senses. The body can be held for long period by yogic practices. This is clear evidence of the relationship that spirit holds with the body which is only *parthiva*.

Analyses through Modern Science

Developments in genetics about the detailed and elaborate researches in the DNA and RNA and the tremendous scope for the field of study has taken us to much advanced areas. However, the study of these complex molecules have not been able to help ascertain the role of spirit in the induction of life. One of the leading research laboratories in the U.S.A. has this as the Director's introduction to a department of embryology, one of the most advanced fields in genetics. It states that "Consider the window to developmental biology presented just by this small department alone. We are asking about how genes are regulated, i.e., "Differential gene action". What is the basis of tissue specificity, of developmental specificity on a time axis? What molecules instruct cells to specialise? How do cells migrate to a precise position during embryogenesis? What is the role of harmones in development? etc. etc." All these researches belong to the *parthiva* field only as has been described earlier. Though a knowledge of the material world is essential, it is not the be all and end all. The importance of spirit underlying life must be realised after the research and the differences between life with spirit and life without spirit must be brought out.

The Wisdom of *Taittiriya Upanisad*

The *Taittiriya Upanisad*, one of the ten most important *Upanisads* of Indian philosophy, has made important observations in the evolution of life. It traces the life evolution to space. Accordingly, space is noted to evolve into air, air into fire, fire into water and water into the earth. Earth generates the vegetative kingdom which gives rise to food. From food is life on the earth, it contends. The life or *purusa* is constituted by *anna-rasa*. Subtle is this *annamaya-kosa* which is the field of food and subtler is *pranamaya-kosa* the field of life. Also the *manomaya-kosa* or the field of mind (*cetana* or spirit) is still subtler and the field of science still subtler — *vijnanamaya-kosa*. The final and the subtlest of all these fields is the *anandamaya-kosa,* i.e., the field of bliss-eternal bliss.

This text very briefly traces the evolution of living matter from space. But then it also advances and traces the steps to realise the underlying truth of the universe, true to a research oriented philosophy. Infusing all the *pancabhutas* in certain proportions, life has evolved through various stages of the geological history and has been becoming more refined and subtle. The coarser frames of early eological ages has given rise to more advanced and refined kind of life as time has advanced. This has been made clear by the geological record.

Conclusion

The geological record shows the various stages of the evolution of living matter from the time of the origin of the earth to the present. This is unique of the earth. Though these individual stages were not known to ancient Indian seers, they have been able realise the truth underlying the evolution from a philosophical point of view and have brought out in very brief outline the essence of the modern scientific results.

References

Barghoorn, E.S. (1971), *The Oldest Fossils.* Scientific American, v. 224, no. 5 pp.30-42.

Kummel, B. (1961), *History of the Earth.* Eurasia Publishing House, New Delhi, p.610.

Ray, P. & Gupta, H.N. (1965), *Caraka Samhita.* National Institute of Sciences of India, New Delhi, p.120.

4

Nature and Function of Matter

E.C.G. Sudarshan

Science is the discipline which organizes our experimental communicable 'public' knowledge. It is rooted in experience ('experiment') and draws on all our linguistic and computational expertise and is thus both a branch of philosophy ('natural philosophy') and of semiotics: compare with a page of a research paper in theoretical physics! Depending upon the aspects of experience that are emphasized the kind of science is also altered. If we are dealing with planetary orbits we may treat the planets as moving mass points in the first approximation but if we are sailing in a lake or driving on a road the local geography is very important. It is therefore not surprising that physical science takes on many points of view and many aspects. But amongst them we may distinguish two dominant themes: the materialistic, chemical, structural tradition inherited from chemistry: and the abstract, mathematical functional tradition inherited from mechanics. In the development of physics these two traditions complement each other and enhance each other.

The Structuralist Tradition

In the first tradition we can ask what is matter made of? Studies in chemistry lead us to believe that all the myriad substances that are found on the earth can be composed from a few chemical **elements** combining with each other according to a set of (empirical) laws, some combine eagerly, some reluctantly: flourine, carbon, oxygen, chlorine, hydrogen all combine readily while gold, platinum, argon, helium, etc. combine only with great reluctance. Some elements like carbon, silicon, hydrogen, nitrogen and oxygen are plentiful on earth while some like gold and platinum are rare. (Some plentiful elements like carbon have special allotropic forms like diamond which are rare!) The multitude of chemical elements and their groupings into families like halogens, alkali atoms, alkaline earths etc. suggests that far from being indivisible they are composite objects and their qualities depend on the components and **their** qualities.

The study of the composition of the atoms became the discipline of atomic physics, which began with spectroscopy. (Each atom emits its own characteristic spectrum which serves as its signature). It was soon found that electrons were constituents of every atom; and that most optical and chemical properties could be understood as aspects of the behaviour of electrons. This great unification had a price: we had to develop the strange discipline of quantum mechanics with noncommuting quantities being used for representing dynamical quantities like position, momentum or energy. At the same time quantum mechanics elevated the mystery of light emission and absorption by atoms. Light is not a constituent of atoms but is associated with its functioning; it is a *vibhuti* rather than an *amsa*.

The atom shorn of its electrons is the (atomic) nucleus: and the various nuclei are themselves composed of neutrons and protons. This is the realm of nuclear physics: to understand the structure, properties and spontaneous reactions of various nuclei. While chemical forces could be traced to the electrical interactions between electrons there is a new force which must exist between the nuclear particles. This new kind of force was eventually understood to be the result of the spontaneous creation and absorption of particles called mesons. In the beginning one hoped for one meson (or one multiplet of similar mesons) but today we seem to need a great many!

Such a multitude of 'elementary' particles suggest that these particles are themselves not elementary but composite. What are they composed of? The present picture is that they are composed of a family of quarks. Quarks have not been found experimentally despite diligent searches. So efforts are being pursued to construct a theory in which the elementary objects would not be observable at all!

The odyssey thus ends in a curious place. The essential ingredients of all tangible concrete matter are ultimately unobservable in principle.

In these searches for the basic constituents, experiment and theory have gone hand in hand: new sophisticated techniques have been developed for experiments with superfast computers as an essential link. But theory also has had to develop new tools: quantum theory itself and the mathematical disciplines of group theory and algebra in infinite dimensional spaces.

The story is not complete without weak interactions and gravitation. Of these gravitation is truly universal; and is therefore treated as a modification of the behaviour of the space-time manifold. Space-time itself became a dynamical entity capable of sustaining vibrations. Once this is accepted Cosmology is within reach. Cosmology becomes a part of standard physical science.

This programme reveals new interconnections between the very large and very small. If the universe is dynamical conditions at earlier epochs may be much different from what it is today. There is then the possibility that in the far past there was a stage in which matter and light were compressed into very high density, from which stage we have an explosive expansion. On the basis of such a picture we can attempt to **compute** nucleo-synthesis rates and the chemical abundance of elements at the present time. Thus what was a 'given' in chemistry becomes a computable quantity in physical cosmology; by the way, apart from the agreement that the observed abundances of various elements it also explains that this composition is valid throughout the universe, except perhaps in the interior of the stars where thermonuclear reactions are still taking place.

A by-product of such a view is the prediction that there should be a cosmic microwave background; several decades after this prediction it was discovered experimentally.

The Functionalist Tradition

The other tradition in physics is that of abstract functional description of matter. We say 'wind blows' and are talking about wind, detect wind velocity and direction yet we also know that wind is but air in motion. Waves are water (or other fluids) in motion. We thus invent new categories because it is convenient to describe what is 'observed'. It is a time honoured tradition: Newton's laws of motion are about 'bodies' or 'particles'. What are these? They are **those that move**. The process of motion is best viewed as the motion of something. Energy is that which is conserved: when energy of motion is converted into heat we talk of the conservation of energy and view energy as a permanent entity which only changes from one form to another much like chemical elements combine with, substitute, or dissociate from a chemical compound. The eternal verities are not directly observed but their manifestations are!

When electromagnetism was properly understood to have wave-like vibrations people were ready to invent a mysterious 'aether': that does the vibrations. When quantum theory has states that exhibit wave-like properties some people worry about what is the medium in which the vibrations take place.

It takes some degree of insight and experience to recognize that the equations of motion themselves suffice to make a model of reality. Newton's equations are the model of physical reality: a 'particle' is that which has position and momentum and hence realizes the motion. Position and momentum are variable but no particle is seen without some position and some momentum. Once one realizes this way of recognizing a particle the way is open to deal with chaotic and 'mixing', motion where the notion of a particle trajectory is not very useful and one has to consider phase space 'flows'.

Electromagnetism is described in classical theory by Maxwell's equations. What is the 'object' described by these equations? What is the realization of these dynamical laws? The present style is to call this the electromagnetic **field** which is nothing but space-time equipped with potentialist. This field, *ksetra*, is the dynamical entity.

Quantum mechanics advances such abstractions one step further. The quantum particle is that which is described by Schroedinger's equation. The physical state is best described by a complex-valued wave function. This object has only some similar features to Newton's 'particles' there is a limitation to the degree of precision with which the position and the momentum can be assigned described by the uncertainty relations of Heisenberg:

$$\Delta q \, \Delta p \leq \tfrac{1}{2} \hbar$$

and of Schroedinger:

$$(\Delta q)^2 \, (\Delta p)^2 - (\Delta(qp))^2 \leq \tfrac{1}{4} \hbar$$

These **uncertainty relations** are the price we pay for using an **inappropriate description:** much like the distortions in a map of the spherical earth on a plane sheet of paper, where whatever we do there are distortions. We can trade one kind of distortion for another. Mercator's projection gives the directions correctly but greatly distorts the higher latitude areas. Polar projections represent the neighbourhood of the pole accurately but vastly distort the other hemisphere. Bartholomew's projection tears up the map in various locales while Buckminister Fuller's projection distributes these tears more uniformly with small triangular regions rendered faithfully. **No one causes these distortions**: Alaska and Kamchatka appeared on opposite ends of the world map that we used in school, but clearly they are close together on the earth!

When we penetrate to the subnuclear level particles occur in **multiplets** which are identified as **representations** of symmetry groups. The neutron and proton furnish a two-dimensional representation of the isospin group of which the pi-mesons (whose exchange between nucleons cause the longer range part of the nuclear force) furnish a three-dimensional representation; and the deuteron (the nucleus of heavy hydrogen) furnishes a one-dimensional representation.

An extension of group theory is to the theory of **gauge groups** which may be thought of as "field of groups", a group at each space-time point. Whenever such a group is postulated there are gauge particles that correspond to them and gauge interactions between the various particles. Modern particle physics makes use of such gauge forces to account for most of the particle reactions.

While these two approaches are different they do not contradict each other; on the contrary they enhance and supplement each other. Nevertheless, when one talks about a physics of matter, we must recognize these two threads of ideas. It becomes even more important when we compare contemporary physics with knowledge in the Indian tradition.

Before concluding this section I must point out that quantum mechanics and particularly quantum particle physics have erased the category difference between **substance** and **process**, between particles and interactions. Interactions are carried by particles which binds particles together which in turn modifies the interactions. Forces and particles are but two manifestations of the dynamical system. Since processes are **noncommutative** and often depend upon their sequence, so do observations of dynamical attributes. The Heisenberg-Schroedinger uncertainties and their generalizations are expressions of this noncommutativity.

Vaisesika and *Sankhya*: Structuralist Traditions

In the Indian tradition we find these two threads. In the *Vaisesika* system of philosophy we find the closest parallel to the chemical physics approach; to describe matter in its elementary and composite forms, the qualities (*gunas*) of the fundamental *kanas* (quanta) and the primary substance (*dravya*) of the universe. There are nine of them: Earth (*prthivi*), water (*jalam*), Air (*vayu*), substratum (*Akasa*), Time (*kalam*), Space (*dik*), Mind (*manas*), radiation (*tejas*), and self (*atma*) are these nine. Note the prophetic inclusion of space and time anticipating modern cosmology and the use of the substratum (*akasa*) as distinct from it. But *Vaisesika* system goes beyond it in including mind and the self as relational entities so that the world is treated as a **perceptual** discipline. The *dravyas* are but the raw material for the world-building: one must include the relationships: Quality (*guna*) was already mentioned; Action (*karma*) which are dynamical relationships including static stable situations; Universal (*samanya*) properties, 'beingness' Individuality (*visesa*), the distinguishing characteristics, necessary intimate relations (*samavaya*); and Negation (*abhava*). The first four *dravyas*: *Prthivi*, *Jalam*, *Tejas*, and *Vayu* are divisible and their elementary indivisible units are the *paramanu* or *kana* (quanta). These four *dravyas* together with *Akasa* constitute the five *Bhutas* (*pancabhuta*).

The ultimate particles of the four *dravyas* are endowed with quality by virtue of which they can coalesce: either primary or secondary (molecules?) of the same elements or of distinct elements. When threads come together we have aggregation (*samyoga*); but when it is woven into a fabric we have the fabric itself as a new creation, non-existent until then; this new relationship is merging (*samavaya*). Spatial extensions of ponderable bodies arose from them being composed of secondary compounds and not due to the extension of the atoms.

What is created can also dissolve. All creations are impermanent and the association of two or more *dravyas* will unravel eventually echoing Nagarjunas aphorism: All that is composed shall decompose!

It is also noteworthy that self (*atma*) is plural and is a *dravya*.

Sankhya system begins with two primary functionalities: Sentience (*purusa*) and Nature (*prakrti*). The Sentience is without specific qualities, discriminating (judgemental), alive (spontaneous), free of entanglements, beyond causality but plural; in contrast Nature both in its manifest (*vyakta*) and unmanifest (*avyakta*) aspects is non-discriminational (non-judgemental), universal, not spontaneous and entangled in transformations. Nature is also endowed with three fundamental qualities (*guna*): integrity (*sattva*), dynamism (*rajas*) and inertia (*tamas*). This Nature undergoes a sequence of modifications and the later stages include ego (*ahamkara*), mind (*manas*), subtle elements (*tanmatra*) and gross elements (*bhuta*). Nature in its state of dissolution (*pralaya*) has all the *gunas* in balance; by the very presence of the sentience (*purusa*) integrity (*sattva*) dominates and intelligence (*mahat*) arises, which in turn yields Ego (*ahamkara*). Mind (*manas*) is then born, and sensory organs, motor organs, subtle elements and gross elements. From vibration (*sabda*) arise the substratum (*akasa*), from vibration and contact (*sparsa*) arise air (*vayu*), from vibration, contact and colour (*rupa*) arise radiation (*tejas*); adding taste (*rasa*) yields fluid (*ap*); finally including smell (*gandha*) yields earth (*prthivi*). *Sankhya* system also has a novel way of dealing with causality; the effect is merely the gross manifestation of that which was subtly present in the material cause.

Finally, according to *Sankhya*, sentience is not to be sought for in matter; nor do Intelligence (*mahat*) or Mind (*manas*) come from matter **alone**. Sentience is reflected in Nature to generate Intelligence and Mind, and even the sense and motor faculties.

Since *Yoga* and *Purva-Mimamsa* are primarily concerned with individual spiritual discipline I shall not comment on them here except to note that *Yoga sutras* clearly points to the possibility of perception being refined to the point that the individual awareness can transcend the limitations of material laws.

Uttara-Mimamsa: The Functionalist Tradition

Uttara-Mimamsa philosophy as contained in the *Upanisads* is clearly akin to the functionalist tradition in physical science (or rather the other way around!). This is a vast area of literature and therefore I have to content myself with a few characteristic examples.

The *Aitareya Upanisad* has a graphic account of creation: how Prajapati created a sentient being out of a blob (*pinda*) and then created the sense principles (*devata*), their sense-organs; and how the sense principles told Prajapati that they were hungry and needed nourishment and in response food was created but to no avail since no sense-organ could consume it; and how finally the downward vital breath (*apana vayu*) was able to assimilate the food and nourish the sense-organs and the sense principles. It sounds like a fanciful legend about creation unless you happen to recognize in it the perception of the world by someone waking up from deep sleep. The downward breath, the *prana* that digests the food in one that liberates the nourishing chemical energy necessary to sustain life. It is the first explicit account of the Second Law of Thermodynamics and its sequel that of dissipative structures. It is only in recent years that Prigogine has brought to our attention the essential role played by dissipation in the creation of new structures in open systems.

The variability of the perceived universe in different states of awareness is the opening subject of the *Mandukya Upanisad*. In the waking state (*jagrat*) the person is outward directed and the sense-organs perceive the "external universe" and feeds this information to the mind and the mind builds up its world-view. But when one is dreaming (*svapna*), even though similar processes take place the person is inward directed. In non-dreaming sleep (*susupti*) all perceptions are negated. What happened to the waking person or the dreamer? When one wakes up from a dream where does the dreamer go? Where did he come from? *Mandukya* goes on to identify the Self as the **integration** of all this, **yet beyond** all this. When one sees stereoscopically, two different visions are merged into one and the object viewed acquires a new dimension: the view is neither picture, nor the two alternately or a collection of them both. Yet the three-dimensional perception subsumes the individual views and they can be obtained by projection. So too, the world is transmuted when different perceptions are integrated.

The two aspects of experience, one as an involved doer and one as awareness unsullied and unentangled implicit in *Mandukya* is made explicit in the *Mundaka Upanisad*. Here there is the metaphor of two birds in amicable ambience perching on two branches of the same tree: one partaking of the sweet and the bitter fruits while the other merely looks on. In *Chandogya Upanisad* there is a discussion on the nature of light: What is the light with which we see when the sun has set, the moon is obscured by clouds and the fire has gone out? It is obviously not a discourse on optics but on perception. In *Katha Upanisad* the young boy Nachiketa asks the Just Lord (*Yama dharma raja*): Where do people go when death has overtaken them? The subsequent discourse is a systematic exposition of the hierarchy of perception and transformations much like in the *Yoga sutra*.

The non-Vedic Jaina and Buddhist systems also treat world-views in characteristic ways. The Buddhist views are closest in methodology with modern science in its phenomenological discussion and the care with which causality is treated. I will not be able even to outline these systems. I shall content myself with pointing out that all these traditional systems do allow for intention (*sankalpa*) which would enable one to transcend: whether it be from the misery of unfulfilled lives, from unsatisfied desires or irremovable attachments. So not everything can be predetermined: there is to be an element of freedom. Without it there is no liberation (*moksa*) or freedom from attachments (*kaivalya*). The purpose of all these systems is happiness: and practice of the discipline is to restore to us our true nature; and our true nature is happiness. *Anandeti abhyasat: anandam brahmah.* In this one essential aspect the Indian philosophic systems, explicitly theistic or otherwise, differ and stand above contemporary science. Contemporary Science looks in terms of utility (technology and standard of life) or, in rare cases, the joy of creativity. But never does it aim to see uninterrupted happiness as the aim of all disciplines, including the discipline of science. Science is not yet seen as a spiritual discipline. In the Indian tradition not only the systems of philosophy but even other disciplines like grammar, politics, music or dance, all of them are for **restoring us to happiness**. There seems to be nothing incompatible with or contrary to scientific principles so to enlarge science.

5

Scientific Philosophy
with reference to Buddhist Thought

Raja Ramanna

Early Buddhist philosophy is very close to scientific philosophy of modern times, and many a distinguished scientist has expressed great admiration for the clear exposition of the Buddha on the Nature of the Universe and the interaction between its various components. The more recent discoveries of science make it necessary to study Buddhist epistemology in order to get a proper view of the Universe and man's position in it.

We start with a classification of the Universe into three parts, a classification which must have had an early origin but is attributed to the great *Bhakti* Philosopher Ramanuja (11th century). This classification is not only scientifically appealing but is as valid today as it was a thousand years ago. Ramanuja divides the Universe into three parts: *Achit*, *Chit* and *Isvara*, and the interaction between the three divisions, brings Science and Philosophy into a proper focus. In this classification the original meanings of the divisions are:

Acit: Things which have no consciousness,
Cit: Things which have consciousness, and
Isvara: God.

We interpret the divisions hopefully without any distortion in the following manner:

Acit: All material things, and whose behaviour is best explained by modern science.
Cit: All things which have life and exhibit biological behaviour and hence possess a consciousness. The exhibited consciousness being higher in quality, depending on the evolutionary status of the concerned object.
Isvara: A power which develops a consciousness with a desire to do good to all life.

The definitions of the above classifications and the interactions between the sets, bring philosophy and science to a common plane. Some of the discoveries in modern science emphasise that a close interaction is necessary if we have to understand the Universe in all its aspects. There seem to be contradictions both mutually and internally in both aspects of knowledge and this paper strives to analyze some of them.

It will be observed that early Buddhist thought, based as it is on rationality and logic, comes closest to an understanding of the Universe in all its aspects without many arbitrary assumptions or coming into conflict with observed data.

Figure 1 shows the division of the Universe according to Ramanuja by Venn Diagrams. S(A) stands for the *Acit* set, S(C) stands for the *Cit* set and S(I) for the *Isvara* set.

We note that in its original definition the reality of S(I) is rejected by the Carvaka materialistic philosophers, Mechanistic Science, early Buddhism, Jainism and in general by the *Sankhya* philosophers.

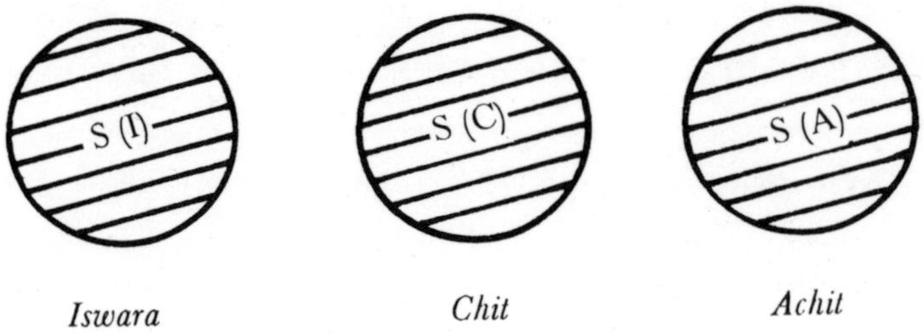

Figure 1 : Universal Classification

S(I) as an Anthropomorphic Absolute Entity isolated from the world and as a father figure, is the description in the Jewish, and hence the Christian religions and Islam. The contact with life and the material world is held through prophets, saints and in the case of Christianity a Messiah (son of God).

A kind of anthropomorphic entity of a polytheistic nature exists in Puranic Hinduism, but the entity is not isolated from ordinary life and is one in which the God or Gods identify themselves with human weakness and errors, much like the Greek divinities. However, Vedantic influence has brought all these divinities together by a monism of the most comprehensive type.

The Vedantic interpretation of S(I) is very abstract and as we shall see later it interacts with the other sets in a very subtle way as interpreted by Sankara (8th century) and Ramanuja. This interaction is denied by Madhva (14th century) and God is completely separate from *Cit* and *Acit* and in this sense his interpretation of *Vedanta* begins to resemble the conclusions of the Mediterranean religions.

Later Buddhism admits of the Divinity of the Buddha which seems like an obvious influence of Hinduism. The phase of Buddhism during which the *Sunyata* theory was developed, is another interesting phase of philosophy which has parallels in scientific thought. We discuss this in some detail.

All the interpretations of the interactions between the sets, depend on the meaning of **Reality.** This word is a deeply intuitive one. Even in science the word has found no clear definition and its meaning has been and is still being debated at great length. One would have expected that Science with its dependence on quantification, the language of mathematics and possibilities of experimental verification, would have no difficulty in defining Reality, but this has not been the case.

To return to the Venn diagrams, *Figure 2* gives the way the Carvaka and Mechanistic Scientists look at the interactions. There is no Reality for S(I), and S(C) is embedded in S(A), i.e., consciousness is created by material forces.

S (C) S (A)

Not real
S (I) is a null set
Evolution : Natural Selection
Survival of Fittest

(Developement of thought
Not Explained)

Figure 2 : Mechanistic and Charvaka (Pre-Buddhist)

In *Figure 3a* and *Figure 3b* are shown the interactions as given in *Vedanta.* S(I) is considered as the only Reality. It is, however, so pure and isolated that only through the forces of *Maya* the material world has become observable/measurable. The Universe has become observable because of our consciousness. In this way S(A) is a subset of S(C). The relationship of the abstract *Isvara* set to that of S(C) and S(A) is one of projection through *maya.* The interesting aspect of the Vedantic theory is that *Brahman* is in all living things. In fact it leads to the famous aphorism 'Thou Art That'. It implies that S(C) and therefore S(A) are a part of S(I). An important aspect of this interpretation is that it points to a unification of the entire Universe. Just as all the laws of Physics will presumably be unified, the *Brahman* takes the role of that Unification. The interpretation of *Brahman* and *Maya* is due to Sankara (8th century) but it is clearly enunciated in the *Vedanta*.

Sankara's theory has, however, been modified by Ramanuja by denying that the *Isvara* set is an abstract one. He believes that the set interacts with human consciousness in a direct way through *Bhakti,* i.e., love and affection. It is in this way the love of fellowmen and mankind in general arises. In *Advaita Vedanta*, S(I) is the only set having Reality, the rest is a projection of that Reality through *Maya*. The Madhva version of *Vedanta* insists that God and the rest are separate (*Dvaita*) and thus S(I) is separate from the other sets. In this way it resembles the Mediterranean religions.

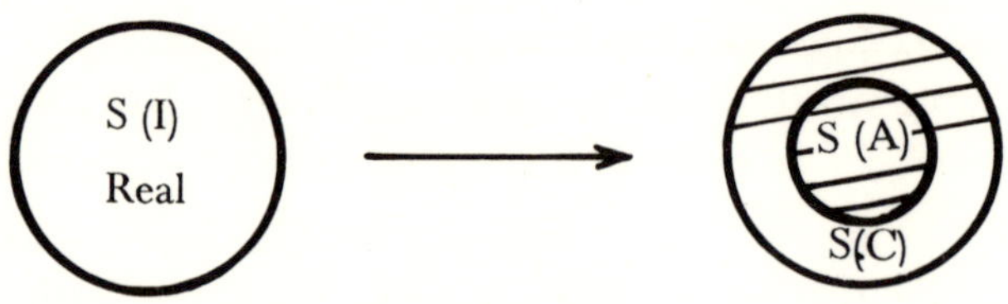

Supreme, Symmetric, Pure, Unchangable

Projection or Illusion
(Due to Unchangability of Supreme *Brahman*)

Evolution: Symmetry to Symmetry (*Chandyogya Upanisad*)
". . . . . though some held that chaos alone was before a second, and order come of it, how can it ever be so. Order indeed was alone in the beginning . . . . ."

Figure 3 (a) : *Advaita* (Shankara, 8th century)

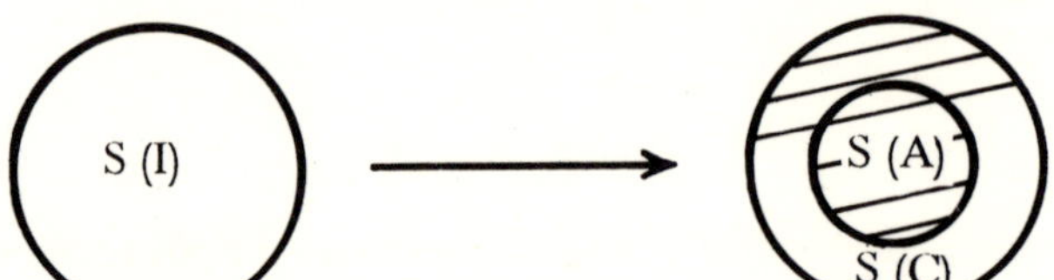

S (A) S (C)

Supreme
Pure
Changable

Real Therodynamic
Consideration to express human feelings possible in this process

Evolution : From Chaos to Symmetry

Figure 3 (b) : *Visista-Advaita* (Ramanuja, 11th century)

In *Figure 4* the view of the Mediterranean religions is shown

S(I) represents a fatherly anthropomorphic entity whose relationship with the rest of the world is through parental concern and fear.

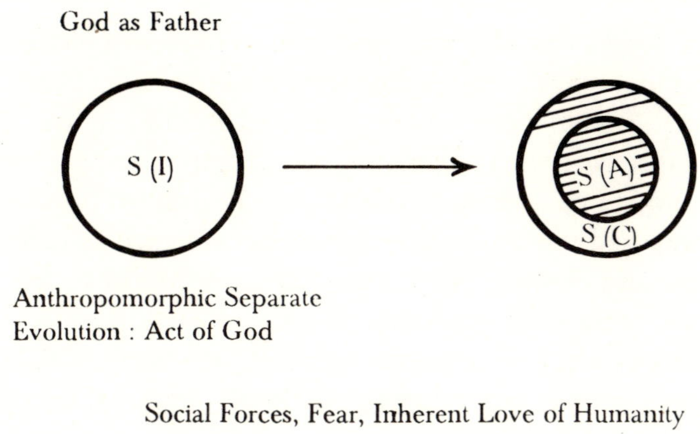

Figure 4 : Mediterranean Religions & Madhav (*Dvaita*)

In *Figure* 5 the Buddhist view is given. To be as accurate as possible we quote from Stcherbatsky's[1] book on *Buddhist Logic*, which effectively summarises the Buddhist standpoint.

> At the time of Buddha, India was seething with philosophic speculation, and thirsty of the ideal of Final Deliverance. Buddhism started with a very minute analysis of the human personality into the elements of which it is composed. The leading idea of this analysis was a moral one. The elements of a personality were, first of all, divided into good and bad, purifying and defiling, propitious to salvation and averse to it. The whole doctrine was called a doctrine of defilement and purification. Salvation was imagined and cherished as a state of absolute quiescence. Therefore life, ordinary life, was considered as a condition of degradation and misery. Thus the purifying elements were those moral features, or forces, that led to quiescence. The defiling ones were those that led to, and encouraged, the turmoil of life. Apart from these two classes of conflicting elements, some general, neutral, fundamental elements were also found at the bottom of every mental life, but nothing in the shape of a common receptacle of them could be detected: hence no Ego, no Soul, no Personality. The so-called personality consists of a congeries of ever-changing

elements, of a flow of them, without any perdurable and stable element at all.

This is the first main feature of early Buddhism, its Soul-denial. The No-Soul theory is another name for Buddhism.

The external world was also analysed in its component elements. It was the dependent part of the personality, its sense-data. There were other systems of philosophy which preceded Buddhism and which envisaged the sense-data as changing manifestations of a compact, substantial and eternal principle, the Matter. Buddhism brushed this principle away and the physical elements became just as changing, impermanent and flowing, as the mental were found to be. This constitutes the second characteristic feature of early Buddhism: no Matter, no Substance, only separate elements, momentary flashes of efficient energy without any substance in them, perpetual becoming, a flow of existential moments.

However, instead of the abandoned principles of a Soul and of a Matter, something must have come to replace them and to explain how the separate elements of the process of becoming are holding together, so as to produce the illusion of a stable material world and of perdurable personalities living in it. They were in fact, substituted by causal laws, laws of physical and moral causation. The flow of the evanescent elements was not a haphazard process. Every element, although appearing for a moment, was a 'dependently originating element'. According to the formula 'this being, that arises' it appeared in conformity with strict causal laws. The idea of moral causation, or retribution, the main interest of the system, was thus receiving a broad philosophic foundation in a general theory of Causality. This is the third characteristic feature of early Buddhism. It is a theory of Causation.

To find the place where Buddhist philosophy can be included in the diagram given in *Figure 5* involves the following modifications. Buddhism does not explicitly assume the existence of a God. Therefore the interpretation of the *Isvara* state is not that of a God, but all the unifying forces based on causal laws which includes the status of *Nirvana*. *Cit* and *Acit* are clearly defined except that the overlap between the *Cit* and *Acit* takes into account the dynamics involved in the state of the universe and evolution in the state of conscious matter.

Sunyata Theory

Later Buddhism, through the work of Nagarjuna (around 2nd century A.D.), Dignaga (5th century), Dharmakirti and Dharmottana (8th century), has many interesting contributions to make towards the philosophy of causality (*Sunyavada*) and logic.

Nagarjuna in a most general way shows in his *Sunyavada* that while one can have ontological monism, it is possible for dual states to exist in epistemology – a conclusion of great implications to science.

In order to be as accurate and at the same time concise, a note from the *Encyclopaedia Britannica*[2] on Nagarjuna and *Sunyavada* is given in the appendix. The note also includes Buddhist views on ego-consciousness and memory, and pure sensation as perception. All these have a bearing on what follows on physical reality.

(A) Early Buddhism

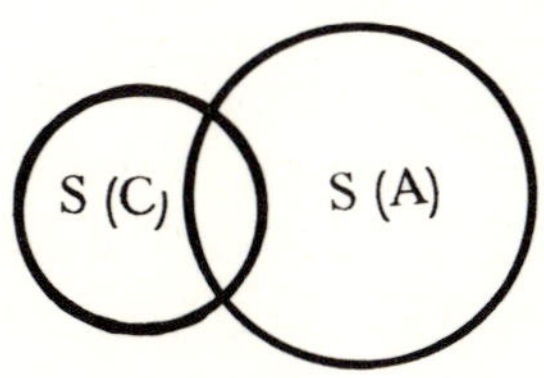

1. No God
2. No Soul
3. Interaction purely by Causal Laws
4. S (C) mainly dealing with Good and Evil and prosper knowledge as part of Causal Laws. Origin big bang or bangs
5. Existence of *Nirvana* (as absorption into nothingness)

(B) Buddhism : Middle Period

S (I) now represents the Buddha as a Divine personality
S (A), S (C) interaction dealing with individual salvation
Nirvana – close to the idea of Vedantic *Brahman*

(C) Buddhism : Final Period

Theory of *Sunyata*

Figure 5 : Buddhist View

One would have expected that in Science there could hardly be any conflicting views on Reality, but as we shall see from what follows this is not the case and problems of philosophy enter the domains of pure science in no uncertain way.

We now consider the problems of Physical Reality.

It is to the credit of physics that all words used have a meaning defined within the framework of mathematics. However, in recent times the foundations of physics and the foundations of mathematics have been rudely shaken by new discoveries which not only make the older definitions ambiguous but lead to inconsistencies which would just not have been allowed in the past.

The two problems which have caused this situation are in the Foundations of Quantum Mechanics and the discovery of the Godel Theorem in mathematics. We consider here only the first of the problems, since it involves the concept of Reality, a concept which as we have seen has been discussed over the ages.

Most scientists are very happy with the successes of new Quantum Mechanics, (Q.M. for short), as opposed to Newtonian mechanics, in explaining a wide and complex range of physical phenomena. This, however, has been possible by not only introducing new laws of physics but even revising basic concepts concerning Reality itself. The scientists are so satisfied with the way Q.M. has worked, that if any blemish in its foundations is pointed out, they would rather call the questioner a person of unsound mind than take the criticism seriously. Even the great Einstein himself was treated in this manner, when he objected to the claim that quantum theory was a complete theory of all matter, and pointed out some inconsistencies which could lead to a paradox of a serious nature. His criticisms, however, require a clear understanding of Reality which has, as we know, metaphysical overtones.

The other great scientist of the period Niels Bohr, believed that the inconsistencies pointed by Einstein were the result of an obsolete method of viewing the methods of Physics. In order to clarify the new approach, Bohr proposed a principle, known as the Complementarity Principle which permits different (even contradictory) aspects of physical phenomena, particularly in the microscopic world to exist. To support this, Bohr suggested that in the description of phenomena, inconsistencies are bound to come up, when Quantum effects dominate, but this has to be pictured in a classical sense. The principle of complementarity envisages situations where a system can exhibit particle-like properties and wave-like properties, though they are opposite descriptions of nature. However, it is expected that both the descriptions never appear simultaneously.

Most scientists have supported the interpretation of Bohr, since it provided an epistemological base to describe many observed phenomena quantitatively, particularly in the atomic and nuclear regime. While most scientists were happy with the new mechanics even if it contained inconsistencies, only Einstein, Schroedinger and a few others, though impressed by the predictive successes of Q.M., were never convinced of the validity of the principle of complementarity. In recent times, more people have come out against the views of Bohr. One of the ways of raising objections is to discuss the problem with the aid of 'imaginary experiments' and interpret it, based on Q.M. which would show up the parodoxes, if any. This was the method used by the above-mentioned scientists. The use of imaginary experiments is a method of creating idealised situations for the sake of discussion to show the consistency of the assumptions that have been made. However, in recent time technologies have greatly advanced, such that these idealised experiments can now be actually performed and their results are used to clinch issues.

In order to show that the Quantum Theory was at best only a working theory but incomplete, and would one day have to be modified, Einstein and two of his collaborators Podolsky and Rosen in 1956, published a paper (usually referred to in literature as EPR), to show that Q.M. has in its structure inconsistencies which if properly interpreted could lead to a serious paradox. The paper generated heat at the time when it was published some forty years ago, but it was not taken as too serious an objection, because much of it centered round the almost metaphysical problem as to what is Reality, and metaphysics is not popular among physicists. Further, the arguments on both sides relied on idealised experiments. They could only be discussed at a philosophical plane and not actually performed and the best bet then was that the results of the experiment would confirm the ideas of Bohr.

Now that new technologies have made difficult experiments possible, the results of the experiments have to be taken into account and they do not seem to support the Theory of Complementarity conclusively.

Through this paper, we state the foundations of physics, first in the way a classical physicist would like to have it. They have now had to be given up, in view of all the information we now have on microscopic phenomena, which has clearly shown that classical theory is untenable. The latest experiments,[3] also seem to suggest all is not well with the definition of Reality as proposed in Q.M. also.

We start by summarising the relevent differences between the classical (Newtonian) approach to physical problems with that of Q.M., if at least to show that the latter is an entirely new theory, with a very different epistemology. Later we indicate why the Complementarity Principle of Bohr was introduced – in an effort to bridge the gap between the classical and the quantum views – taking note of the fact that while microscopic phenomena are governed by Q.M., the observer is however a macroscopic object and thus guided by the earlier concepts.

The main differences between the two theories can be summarised as follows:

Classical Theory

1. The theory is deterministic. Given the initial conditions and the laws of motion, it is in principle, even in the most complicated of cases, possible to predict the behaviour of the system at a subsequent time and place.

Quantum Systems and Theory

1. The theory is basically probabilistic and abstract.
2. It requires the intervention of an observer to determine its state, and this intervention suddenly makes the observation deterministic.
3. Objects under examination can behave in a contradictory manner from the point of view of classical theory, e.g. an object can exhibit itself as either a particle or a wave. Such descriptions are mutually contradictory in the framework of classical physics but it is this duality that gives Q.M. its flexibility to explain phenomena.
4. A measurement interferes with the state of the object under measurement. A measurement of one of the parameters, of the object under study, can make the measurement of an associated parameter uncertain, to the extent that a simultaneous measurement of both parameters is impossible. This is known as the Uncertainty Principle.

Since finally the measurement has to be made by an observer — eventually a macroscopic being, the principles of the two theories come into conflict. Thus we have a situation where Classical Theory which at first sight seems to be rational is unable to explain all observed phenomena. At the same time, we have Quantum theory able to explain nearly all observed phenomena, but with assumptions which are at variance from the observer's point of view.

We now take up the question of what is Reality. According to Classical Physics a system is real if the parameters of the system under consideration for example Position, Momentum etc. have a definite value even before it is actually measured. Further the process of measurement should not, in principle, affect the system.

In Q.M. every observable is somewhat abstractly connected with a mathematical operation. When this operation is carried out, specific rules tell one what its likely values are. The moment the measurement is made the wave aspect of the system collapses and the system assumes a particular value, which it may not have had earlier (*Figure 6*).

It is with a view to interpreting these abstract processes, Bohr proposed his

Principle of Complementarity. Essentially it states the wave-particle duality is something that nature follows. This duality forces on us the fact that the theory can only give the probabilities of the parameter that are being measured. But only a measurement determines the value of the parameter. In this way, we can say that prior to measurement the system had no particular predetermined value and it is the measurement process that created the value of the concerned parameters. All these aspects of Q.M. lead up to a Reality which states that nothing that is not directly observable (measurable) has an existence. All this happens only because of the dual nature of matter which gets more prominent as the object becomes smaller. These effects become negligible as we go into the macroscopic region.

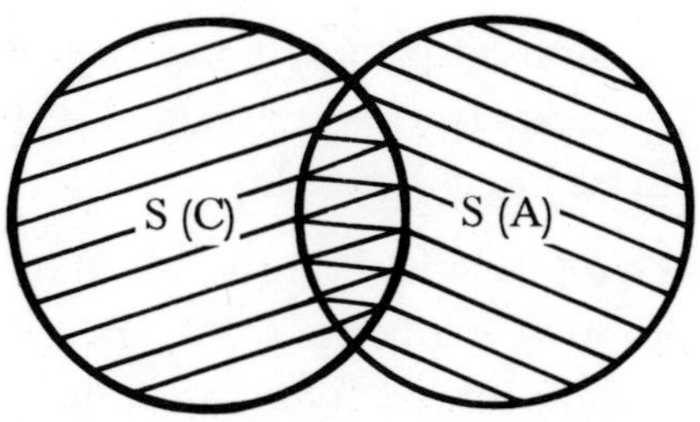

Interaction to allow for:

a. Collapse of wave function
b. Immeasurability (Uncertainity)
c. Holistic Approach

S (C) U S (A)

Evolution : Molecular and Symmetry Process

Figure 6 : Quantum Mechanics

Several distinguished scientists of the period, like Einstein and Schroedinger to name only a few, were unhappy with the principle of Complementarity. They believed Quantum theory can only be an incomplete theory and one day a new theory would arise in which determinism would return and duality would disappear.

Reality in Q.M. is thus at variance with Classical Reality which insists that the system can exist before one noticed it. In Q.M., it acquires its quantitative existence only after measurement which itself is restricted by many constraints, e.g. the Uncertainty Principle. In this way Q.M. Reality depends not only on the system but the measuring instrument and the observer.

In order to show that Q.M. is an incomplete theory, Einstein, Podolsky and Rosen (EPR) proposed the following experiment. If performed, the experiment would show that the assumptions of Quantum Theory would lead to a situation, where interactions can take place between systems, which are so far away that the signal from one to the other will have to travel at a speed faster than the velocity of light, or one has to invoke a "mysterious superfast interaction at a distance". Both these possibilities would be untenable to a physicist. The rejection by the physicist is based on a fundamental principle known as **Causality**, which means that there is a physical cause for everything. A principle of deep significance in a discussion in early Buddhist philosophy. A more restricted Causality called Local Causality is one when something is real only if it changes within a system and can be measured within it or sufficiently near it, so that the principle of the Theory of Relativity, i.e., no signals can travel faster than the velocity of light, is not violated.

To understand the implications of the 'imaginary experiment' and its consequences requires a knowledge of physics. However, a very sketchy description of it is given as it introduces the concept of Local Causality.

Consider a system which emits two photons, i.e., light simultaneously in opposite directions. Such systems are now available. Q.M. states that the position of each of the particles (x), (y) can be determined by some suitable experiment and another experiment can determine the momenta (p), (q) of each of the particles. However (x) and (p) cannot be measured simultaneously, because of the Uncertainty Principle. Similar is the case with (y) and (q). The paradox appears when we take into account that the distances between the particles are always known and the total momenta of the two particles are fixed. If this is so, by measuring (x) of the first particle and later the momentum (p) of the same particle, one can know all about the second particle without having made any measurements directly on the second particle and not disturbing it in any way. In this way we have already violated the principles of Q.M.

If however, the supporter of Q.M. objects to the fact that the parameters (x) and (p) have not been measured at the same time, and what was measured earlier would have lost its validity, the paradox worsens in that the second particle somehow seems to have got to know the sequence of measurements made on the first particle, [since any change in (x) and (p) has to show itself on (y) and (q), because x-y and p and q are fixed]. With Q.M. as it is presently formulated, this effect on the other must take place however far off the distance between the photons, perhaps even thousands of kilometres or more and the interaction must be instantaneous. This can happen only if the information is travelling faster than that of light!

The epistemological problems of Q.M. involve the dual behaviour of matter. In a measurement, the wave function representing the particle has to collapse. How or why this happens has never received a proper explanation. It has been pointed out that one may have to accept the existence of a human consciousness on the completion of a measurement, which is responsible for the collapse of the wave function, and to make the measurement deterministic. These are complex issues but are stated here only to show even physicists wedded to physical reality are forced to invoke the physical existence of consciousness.

The comparison with Buddhist philosophy becomes relevant if we consider ontological monism as the situation before measurement and epistemological dualism as equivalent to wave-particle dualism. These ideas require greater study especially using the original works of Nagarjuna. Physicists who are interested in Reality must take these earlier works into account because of their generality.

As stated earlier the complementarity principle has come under severe scrutiny in recent years. Some new experiments[3] using optical methods seem to indicate that a particle can be observed to be both wave-like and particle-like simultaneously and not one or the other as assumed by complementarity. *Figure 7* gives the experimental set-up based on an earlier experiment done by J.C. Bose, a hundred years ago, to demonstrate the wave nature of micro-waves.

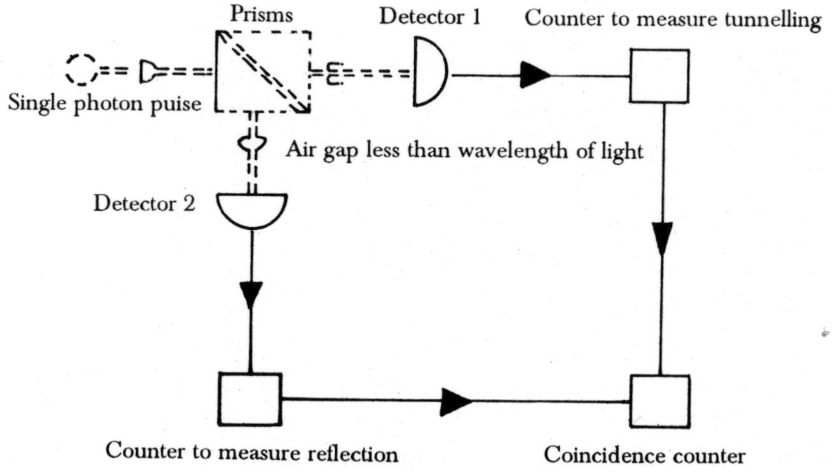

Figure 7

In conclusion, by referring to *Figure 7,* we note that the registrations by the counter 2 to measure the tunnelling rate pertain to a propagation of light pulses which is consistent with a classical wave picture. However, at the same time let us consider the rates measured by the coincidence counter (connected to detectors 1 and 2) when the incident light pulses are in states that are close approximations to single photon states. If the coincidence rates are found to be lower than the minimum bound derived from the classical wave picture (perfect anti-coincidence for 'ideal' single photon states), as reported by Mizobuchi and Otake,[3] the propagation cannot be comprehended using a classical wave-picture, but is amenable to a description in terms of the particle picture. We, therefore, contend that an understanding of this experiment in terms of classical pictures [which Bohr's complementary principle (BCP) necessarily requires] can only be obtained by using both particle and wave-pictures; in other words, the experimental data recorded in the three counters of *Figure 7* contain both wave-like and particle-like information about the propagation of light pulses. It is in this sense that the experiment 'confronts' BCP by showing that there is a situation allowed by the formalism of quantum mechanics where the notion of 'mutual exclusiveness of classical pictures' is not applicable.

The purpose of referring to the experiment is to show the methods of science to decide on the complexities of interpretation. Even then one cannot be sure that the last word has been said about the subject because one is never sure how ontology affects epistemology which is basically a philosophical question.

Philosophy has always had a place in science. The following quotation from Einstein[4] on 'pre-established harmony' shows how science cannot quite depend on epistemology alone:

> The supreme task of the physicist is to arrive at those universal elementary laws from which the cosmos can be built up by pure deduction. There is no logical path to these laws; only intuition, resting on sympathetic understanding of experience, can reach them. In this methodological uncertainty, one might suppose that there were any number of possible systems of theoretical physics all equally well justified; and this opinion is no doubt correct, theoretically. But the development of physics has shown that at any given moment, out of all conceivable constructions, a single one has always proved itself decidedly superior to all the rest. Nobody who has really gone deeply into the matter will deny that in practice the world of phenomena uniquely determines the theoretical system, in spite of the fact that there is no logical bridge between phenomena and their theoretical principles; this is what Leibnitz described so happily as a 'pre-established harmony'. Physicists often accuse epistemologists of not paying sufficient attention to this fact.

Appendix[2]

Ontological Monism and Epistemological Dualism

Developments in *Mahayana*, Nagarjuna and *Sunyavada*. Though the beginnings of *Mahayana* are to be found in the *Mahasangikas* and many of their early sects, Nagarjuna gave it a philosophical basis. Not only is the individual person empty and lacking an eternal self, according to Nagarjuna, but the *dharmas* also are empty. He extended the concept of *sunyata* to cover all concepts and all entities. 'Emptiness' thus means subjection to the law of causality or 'dependent origination' and lack of an immutable essence and an invariant mark (*nihsvabhavata*). It also entails a repudiation of dualities between the conditioned and the unconditioned, between subject and object, relative and absolute, and between *samsara* and *Nirvana*. Thus, Nagarjuna arrived at an ontological monism; but he carried through an epistemological dualism, i.e., a theory of knowledge based on two sets of criteria between two orders of truth: the conventional (*samratti*) and the transcendental (*paramartha*). The one reality is ineffable. Nagarjuna undertook a critical examination of all the major categories with which philosophers had sought to understand reality and showed them all to involve self-contradictions. The world is viewed as a network of relations, but relations are unintelligible. If two terms, A and B, are related by the relation R, then either A and B are different or they are identical. If they are identical, they cannot be related; if they are altogether different then they cannot also be related, for they would have no common ground. The notion of "partial identity and partial difference" is also rejected as unintelligible. The notion of causality is rejected on the basis of similar reasonings. The concepts of change, substance, self, knowledge, and universals do not fare any better. Nagarjuna also directed criticism against the concept of *pramana* or the means of valid knowledge.

Nagarjuna's philosophy is also called *Madhyamika*, because it claims to tread the middle path, which consists not in synthesizing opposed views such as "The real is permanent" and "The real is changing" but in showing the hollowness of both the claims. To say that reality is both permanent and changing is to make another metaphysical assertion, another viewpoint, whose opposite is "Reality is neither permanent nor changing". In relation to the former, the latter is a higher truth, but the latter is still a point of view, a *drsti*, expressed in a metaphysical statement, though Nagarjuna condemned all metaphysical statements as false.

Nagarjuna used reason to condemn reason. Those of his disciples who continued to limit the use of logic to this negative and indirect method, known as *prasanga*, are called the *prasangikas*; of these, Aryadeva, Buddhapalita, and Candrakirti are the most important. Bhavaviveka, however, followed the method of direct reasoning and thus founded what is called the *svatantra* (independent) school of *Madhyamika* philosophy. With him Buddhist logic comes to its own, and during his time the *Yogacaras* split away from the *Sunyavadins*.

Ego Consciousness and Stored Consciousness

Contributions of Vasubandhu and Asanga. Converted by his brother Asanga to the *Yogacara*, Vasubandhu wrote the *Vijnaptimatratasiddhi* ("Establishment of the Thesis of Cognitions Only"), in which he defended the thesis that the supposedly external objects are merely mental conceptions. *Yogacara* idealism is a logical development of *Sautrantika* representationism: the conception of a merely inferred external world is not satisfying. If consciousness is self-intimating (*svaprakasa*) and if consciousness can assume forms (*sakaravijnana*), it seems more logical to hold that the forms ascribed to alleged external objects are really forms of consciousness. One only needs another conception: a beginningless power that would account for this tendency of consciousness to take up forms and to externalize them. This is the power of *kalpana*, or imagination. *Yogacara* added two other modes of consciousness to the traditional six: ego consciousness (*manovijnana*) and storehouse consciousness (*alaya-vijnana*). The *alaya-vijnana* contains stored traces of past experiences, both pure and defiled seeds. Early anticipations of the notions of the subconscious or the unconscious, they are theoretical constructs to account for the order of individual experience. It still remained, however, to account for a common 'world-which' in fact remains the main difficulty of *Yogacara*. The state of *Nirvana* becomes a state in which the *alaya* with its stored 'seeds' would wither away (*alayapravrtti*). Though the individual ideas are in the last resort mere imaginations, in its essential nature consciousness is without distinctions of subject and object. This ineffable consciousness is the 'suchness' (*tathata*) underlying all things. Neither the *alaya* nor the *tathata*, however is to be construed as being substantial.

Vasubandhu and Asanga are also responsible for the growth of Buddhist logic. Vasubandhu defined 'perception' as the knowledge that is caused by the object, but this was rejected by Dignaga, a fifth-century logician, as a definition belonging to his earlier realistic phase. Vasubandhu defined 'inference' as a knowledge of an object through its mark, but Dharmottara, an eighth-century commentator pointed out that this is not a definition of the essence of inference but only of its origin.

Pure Sensation as Perception

Contributions of Dignaga and Dharmakirti. Dignaga's *Pramanasamuccaya* ("Compendium of the Means of True Knowledge") is one of the greatest works on Buddhist logic. Dignaga gave a new definition of 'perception': a knowledge that is free from all conceptual constructions, including name and class concepts. In effect, he regarded only the pure sensation as perception. In his theory of inference, he distinguished between inference for oneself and inference for the other and laid down three criteria of a valid middle term (*hetu*), viz., that it should 'cover' the minor premise (*paksa*), be present in the similar instances (*sapaksa*), and be absent in dissimilar instances (*vipaksa*) In his *Hetucakra* ("The Wheel of Reason"), Dignaga set up a matrix of nine types of middle terms, of which two yield valid conclusions, two contradictory, and the rest uncertain conclusions. Dignaga's tradition is further developed in the seventh century by Dharmakirti, who modified his definition of perception to include the condition 'unerring' and distinguished, in his *Nyayabindu*, between four kinds of perception: that by the five senses, that by the mind, self-consciousness, and perception of the *yogins*. He also introduced a threefold distinction of valid middle terms: the middle must be related to the major either by identity ("This is a tree, because this is an oak") or as cause and effect ("This is fiery, because it is smoky"), or the *hetu* is a non-perception from which the absence of the major could be inferred. Dharmakirti consolidated the central epistemological thesis of the Buddhists that perception and inference have their own exclusive objects. The object of the former is the pure particular (*svalaksana*), and the object of the latter (he regarded judgements as containing elements of inference) is the universal (*samanyalaksana*). In their metaphysical positions, Dignaga and Dharmakirti represent a moderate form of idealism.

Notes & References

1. F. Th. Stcherbatsky, *Buddhist Logic*, Vol. 1, Oriental Books Reprint Corporation. pp, 3-5, 1984.
2. *The New Encyclopaedia Britannica*, Chicago, Vol 21, pp 201-02, 1992.
3. Partha Ghose, Dipankar Home and G. S. Agarwal, *An Experiment to Throw More Light on Light Implications*, Preprint.
4. Albert Einstein, *Ideas and Opinions*, Rupa and Co, Calcutta, pp 226, 277, 1992.

6

Matter is Consciousness

S.C.Malik

> *A human being is a part of this whole, called by us 'Universe', a part limited in time and space. He experiences himself, his thoughts and feelings as something separated from the rest – a kind of optical delusion of consciousness. This delusion is a kind of prison for us, restricting us to our personal desires and to apportion for a few persons nearest to us. Our task must be to free ourselves from this prison by widening our circle of compassion to embrace all living creatures and the whole of nature in its beauty.*
>
> — ALBERT EINSTEIN

Traditional Western thought has consistently modelled those world-views which have generated ontological gaps that runs across the whole domain of existence. For example, human and other organisms, in spite of the fact that they share the same cosmic niche, are considered to be literally worlds apart. This dualism is one of the fundamental, often, tacit tenets of Western metaphysics, epistemology and ethics. Dualist conceptions of human beings themselves are rooted in this deep-seated anthropocentrism. This dominant world-view has assimilated evolutionary theory and historicised this ontological gap. All – religious or secular – teleological perspectives construe the variety of life-forms as the result of a process leading to the advent of humankind. *Homo sapiens* is not seen as a stage in an indefinte flux of change, but as an end, the glorious result of a history of trial and error. Is there any difference between this view and that of creationism? This dichotomy between human and non-humans was extended often to other races, often treated as slaves and even women were not exactly placed in the same category as evolved humans – this was especially the case with many nineteenth century Darwinians. Social differences within Europe itself were classified in this line of thought. (Bouissac:1991). In the context of a discussion on Matter, it is important to note the specific historical-philosophical climate of Europe during the sixteenth-seventeenth centuries, within which the Scientific Revolution took place. It is also worth our while to recall some basic presuppositions, essentially Western, which dominate our times, summarised as follows:

The Universe

1. A mechanical machine,with no intention or purpose; not an organism having consciousness. In being so, it is indifferent to man – hence it needs to be conquered.
2. It is real to the extent it can be externalised, quantified, measured in terms of mass, dimensions of size, colour, taste, etc., characteristics that are ultimately not real.
3. The internal nature of man is subjective and different to the external which alone can be objective and true.
4. Matter precedes intelligence; the latter must be explained in terms of the former which may be dead, though subject to purposeless forces.
5. Time is linear, sequential; and space essentially uniform. Energy is basically the same, not gross or subtle – though it may be more or less in quantity. Time, space and energy are only externally real, and are independent at the level of perceiving consciousness.
6. Importance is given to the causal notion in terms of the evolution of complexity and intelligence.

Man

1. Man is essentially a rational cognizer, a body with a mind localised in it or an "engine with a will" (Descartes and Behaviourism); he is an atomic being, an individual without any transpersonal spirit.
2. There is no essential hierarchy of being or consciousness among men or within man; even if so, it is irrelevant to knowledge and the organisation of society, governments, etc.
3. As he is, Man is an imperfect being, yet the measure of all things.

Knowledge-Truth

1. Knowledge is an end in itself, except for the betterment of the estate of man.
2. There is one truth, if it was Christianity once, it is Science now.

3. Subject and Object can be completely separated, i.e., without a need for earlier studying oneself.
4. Reason is the only faculty by which knowledge may be obtained, even experiments are extensions of this faculty. But sensations and feelings are not true perceptions.
5. True knowledge is obtained by proceeding from the parts to the whole.
6. The importance of detaching oneself from the subject of study, rather than by participation and experiencing the object.
7. Reality is a mental construct; knowledge is abstract and general, not a vision or experience of particulars.
8. True knowledge is quantitative, not qualitative – what can be quantified is independent of place and function.
9. True knowledge leads to predictions of what is known, since it is based on external, repeatable perceptions; only that which is externalised is available to true knowledge.
10. The truth and falsity of propositions is self-evident, irrespective of the person who says it.
11. As knowledge has nothing to do with being-ness or consciousness, it is not esoteric, i.e., it requires no moral preparation to be discovered or to be understood.
12. In principle, in the making of actual observations (not in the interpretation of data), the observer can always be replaced by scientific instruments.
13. The dichotomy of faith-knowledge, is perhaps more a consequence of the Scientific Revolution rather than a presupposition that truth and knowledge reside in dimensions different from those in which religious considerations about God, etc. reside.

The point of the above summary is to indicate how these concepts, world-views and classifications have effected the understanding of the elements, of matter. But these issues do not merely rest at the theoretical level. They have had, and continue to have, pragmatic consequences. For example, the idea of slaves, racial inequalities, ethnic conflicts which one sees all around – even the exploitation of depressed classes – emerge from this higher and lower idea in the rung of the evolutionary ladder; the experiments on animals, and humans, that are treated as objects because they are known to be driven by blind instinct and hence are dispensable. The exploitation of the environment also follows from this world-view, since the non-human world is devoid of an autonomous agency and exhibits only passive resistence. This is due to the use of such metaphorical categories as mind, matter, conscious and unconscious life, blind instinct and clear-minded intentionality, automatism and free will, and objects and subjects. In such a conceptual framework animals are defined negatively as devoid of mind, plants as devoid of mobility, etc. Thus, philosophies and world-views, not always as abstract models, are powerful reinforcers with definite pragmatic consequences through their authoritative legitimisation.

In contemporary terms these systems may seem aberrant. Nevertheless, many of the biases continue covertly. For example, what is considered universal today usually implies a dominant Western world-view — whatever way one may define it — and all other categories have to be subsumed within it in the name of universalism. In this one may include the idea of linear time and progress towards a certain state. But this makes these approaches less flexible, against those cultures which see evolutionary developments in terms of cyclical time wherein catastrophes are part of nature and reality and, further, encompassed within a larger context.

Of course, the notion of the earth as a complex system within which organism interact with each other and with geophysical and chemical processes in a predictable manner is at the root of modern science. It permeates Western and Westernised cultures and prevails across the spectrum, beginning with elementary textbooks. But the interrelatedness is still in terms of a mechanical interpretation, as one to one cause-effect relationship. For instance, earthquakes have geophysical causes since we know that the earth is made of inert matter explainable locally and regionally rather than in any global systemic terms. No notion of an independent variable — say, a god in heaven — would suffice for an explanation of the earthquake (*Ibid.*).

The belief of inert c nponents of the earth has also lead to the passive exploitation of the resources. The belief of the Navaho, who treat the earth as mother and have sacred places, would consider coal mining as digging into mother's body — a heinous crime; or other groups of the non-Western world who apologise to the tree before cutting it. Both are equally compelling truths within the boundaries of their world-views. The holistic view perhaps helps in a sustainable development for a long time, while the exploitation of maximum resources for development and progress is a short time approach even in historical — evolutionary terms. No longer can one describe the earth and life merely in terms of the laws of physics and chemistry; that life just happened on earth by chance. Shifting world-views within the Western tradition is reflected by not only the developments in physics, chemistry and biology but also in the Gaia hypothesis (Lovelock:1979,1988); this particular world-view that is both holistic and multi-centered developed within the scientific tradition of the West — in the framework of evolutionary biology. It is congrunt with many Eastern world-views and, if such convergences are possible, it is also imperative if humankind is to survive, provided that the idea of interrelatedness within the framework of Consciousness is taken seriously.

Based on the above assumptions, the prevailing world-view in terms of humanistic psychology, of modern man contrasts with the traditional world-views, all over the world, i.e., nature unfriendly and confrontational, so the need for control and, therefore, the feeling of alienation and separation. Hence, the necessity to provide orderliness, protection and predictability for its members through structure, property rights, laws, enforcement agencies and a central hierarchy of authority and so on.

The transformational world-view which the new science and ancient insight suggest, is that of a friendly universe, to be accepted, experienced and celebrated; space and time are relative-infinitely small or large units. Nature is an evolving eco-system of which you and me, the human species, are a part. Therefore by enhancing nature we enhance ourselves. Life is a matter of contributing through myself and others to the universe. The purpose of human society is to increase the service of its members to other human beings and to themselves. To do this, I must realise my fullest potential of body, mind, and spirit. To do this requires an environment that supports and encourages self-actualization and self-responsibility. I am unique, but I am also one with the human species.

Many a Western poet and mystic have felt at odds with the cultural implications of modern science and technology. Recent advances in science are ahead of these early assumptions, especially in physics. But in general there has been no serious challenge to these assumptions from many quarters and have a hegemony which remains unchallenged by and large. It has widely spread like a surgical transplant, such as in India, subverting all that is there in the indigenous and inherent to Indian traditions in a deep sense. No doubt one should be conversant with all that the West has to offer. But the quality of Being-Consciousness — a fundamental basis of Indian thought — needs to be taken into account in any discussion of Matter. But let us turn to contemporary developments in science for our purpose.

Physical Whole

The Universe is everything that is and ever has or will be; there can be only one. To speak of many universes is therefore misuse of the term. If there could be many, they must somehow, in some sense, be mutually related; otherwise they could not be distinguished, or counted, or regarded as a many. They must constitute a single complex, within which there may be many distinguishable regions or epochs, but these would not be strictly be Universes, even if between them no communication of information could pass. If they exist they must have some kind of togetherness. So long as they can be at all conceived and postulated, they will all form part of the all-inclusive Universe.

But serious objections can be brought against the notion of an infinite universe, however subdivided. Infinity is a concept that has given cosmologists trouble ever since Newton, and physicists today do all they can to eliminate from their calculations. Contemporary quantum physicists have invented a method of removing it that they call 'renormalisation', and Einstein adopted a similar stratagem. Special Relativity establishes an equivalence between matter and energy, and general relativity identifies fields of force with space curvature. Accordingly, matter introduces curvature into space and bends it round an hypersphere, so Einstein introduced the cosmic constant into his gravitational equation, which eliminates infinity from the resulting model of the universe. The full spatio-temporal extent of the world is now described as finite but unbounded — like the surface of a Euclidean sphere but having three instead of two surfaces.

In thermodynamics, the random activity presumed is that of molecules dashing hither and thither in a volume of gas or liquid. But molecules are highly structured entities, as are also the atoms of which they are composed. Any random movement must presuppose the existence of some such entities (involving their own order) that can be shuffled around. Prior to such order, there is no discoverable chaos. Present-day particle physics discovers no hard, impenetrable granules. The elementary units are quantum entities that as much waves as particles, and have been called 'wavicles'. They are conceived as wave-packets, superposed waves, at once both energy and matter. Again waves have structure and are periodic, and prior to them there is nothing except time, the metrical field, which itself is an ordered manifold. If it were not ordered it could have no geometry. Where then are we to find the primary bodies that move randomly? But indeterminacy exists only at the particle level, or wave-packets, not at the macroscopic level in which they are embedded. One has therefore to conclude that random activity is always parasitic on some sort of order and cannot have ultimate priority. It is precisely in the primordial form of order that the conditions for the development of life and mind implicitly reside.

The idea of the unity and wholeness of the physical universe has received enthusiastic support from particle physicists in the last decade of this century. At the turn of the century, Planck's discovery of the quantum of action and Einstein's formulation first of Special and then of General Relativity immediately had revolutionary effects. Space and time ceased to be viewed as separable parameters, but were fused together as a single metrical field, and its organising structure provided principles of order governing all physical laws and events — particle and wave became complementary concepts. The energy system, taken as a whole, thus assumed priority over determination of the exact position, or the precise momentum, of particles within it, so that these properties along with others became conjugate. Pauli's principle of exclusion, and Heisenberg's indeterminacy laid the foundations as is well-known, as the latter said, "The world thus appears as a complicated tissue of events, in which connections of different kinds alternate or overlap or combine and thereby determine the texture of the whole".

Without going into the history of theoretical developments, more recently, David Bohm has maintained, by way of discovering a credible interpretation of the quantum theory, that the physical substance of the world is a dynamic totality, which he calls 'the holomovement', in which a principle of order is implicated and expresses itself variously in the emergence of phenomena and entities (such as elementary particles), so that, on the analogy of the holograph, the whole is implicit in every part. This is an ontological interpretation of the quantum theory, consistent with experimental findings and conforms to Bell's theorem, satisfies Schroedinger's equation. In short, the theory is then able to account for the experimental facts, but requires us to regard what is measured and the measuring instrument as a single indivisible complex, within which what is measured comes to be. The theory has not been adopted by many physicists, but it illustrates afresh the contemporary trend to interpret physical facts holistically in terms of the field.

If dogmatic idealism fails to recognize the dialectical character of the whole immanent in finite experience, it commits the epistemologist to a subjectivism that is as disastrous as dogmatic realism. The first because it leads inevitably to self-contradiction in solipsism; the second because, by confining consciousness to an effect in the brain of an assumed (but ex-hypothesi unknowable) external cause, it excludes from knowledge the very object that the knowledge seeks and claims to embrace. The one feasible resolution of the contradictions involved is in the self-specification of the universal whole as a dialectical scale of forms, manifest in the physical universe and bringing itself to fruition through the organic world in the self-consciousness of intelligent life.

What, then, is to be taken as the criterion of truth? By what standard do we assess the validity of our knowledge of the world? It is the degree of coherent wholeness of the experience judged, both observation and theory together. When they do not agree, contradiction arises,due to some oversight or omission in one or the other, and corrections are needed, or presuppositions must be changed, in order to restore coherence and systematic wholeness.

Artificial Intelligence and Consciousness

To speak of mentality in terms of sentience and consciousness is now-a-days anathema to many. A long history of materialism, mechanism, and behaviourism – largely a hangover from the Renaissance world-view – has resulted, more recently, in an enthusiasm for artificial intelligence and the opinion that the human brain is some kind of highly complex digital computer or general Turing Machine, to the functioning of which consciousness, if it exists at all, is irrelevant.

To deny the existence of consciousness is self-refuting. It is that of whose existence we are directly assured by its very occurrence, and without which we could be assured of nothing. No theory of artificial intelligence, no opinion about the epiphenomenal character of awareness, could be entertained without it. Moreover, the behaviourist, demanding cognizance only of what can be "publicly observed", disregards the fact that such observation, so far as it is perception – as it must be, is the private experience of the observers, and that they can communicate it only on the assumption that others can become aware of their means of communication. All this, again, presumes the use of the senses and, therefore, the existence and presence of sentient experience. We ourselves are consciousness.

A general Turing Machine, the theoretical archetype of all computers, does no more than operate a mathematical algorithm; that is, a procedure in accordance with set rules – howsoever complex and sophisticated. But no algorithm can be devised except by a human mind – no Turing, no machine. So if we try to pretend that the human brain is no more than a complicated computer, we beg the question. Godel's Theorem proves that in any formal system whatsoever, a legitimate proposition can always be formulated that is unprovable in the system, and so it establishes that there is some mathematical thinking that is not formalizable and therefore cannot be computable. This statement seems to be true, because seeing it as true requires insight, which is not the product of this or any algorithm albeit the brain unconsciously in its operation acts like one for some functions.

That insight involves consciousness must be accepted if we recognize consciousness as the activity of organizing sentient presentation. In the first place, such organization is the establishment and comprehension of relationships within a whole, and the perception of relations precisely is what constitutes insight. In the second place, the relations are established between elements in the sentient field, and nascence is what characterizes all consciousness. Thinking, including mathematics, continues this activity at a high level of abstraction, but is never wholly devoid of sentient content.

But how, we may be asked, have we established the existence of sentience itself? To this the answer is: By the self-certainty of consciousness, the presence of which is undeniable without self-refutation – for one must be conscious to deny it, and could postulate it without having it. And consciousness is nothing other than the awareness of elements in the sentient field. Methods of investigation that ignore the occurrence of sentience and consciousness, or which refuse to make reference to it, may in some circumstances, and for acceptable reasons, be justified, but the pretense that sentience and consciousness do no exist can only be an affectation on the part of those who seek to deny what, by its very nature, is ineluctably manifest to themselves and to all other cognizant beings.

Observation and Perception

Normally sentience has been compared to a camera, in which the entire surround is reflected through a single lens on to a screen within a limited space. But this analogy is limited as it tells of a clear articulated scene, where sentience is an indiscriminate mass of diverse feelings. But this has further disastrous epistemological results, as it eliminates the viewer from the scene, who sees, recognises, and interprets the reflected objects. We are lured into believing that perceiving is the result of the transmission of physical effects from the outside world, through our sense-organs, to create some kind of replica or model in the brain. Even neurophysiologically this is an unsupportable theory, since it is the mind set, or subset which is crucially involved in the act of perceiving the external world — that is why the world differs individually. May be in order to know the true nature of perception, one ought to say what it is not, first, and why.

As stated above, perception is not the end result of a causal chain of physical and physiological processes that converted into a psychical cognition. First, the causal relation between the object and the percept is excluded from this end result. The percipient is certainly never aware of any such causation. Second, it is usually assumed that the sensation caused from without is an indubitable datum. But perception cannot be such immediate acceptance of data, assumed to be indubitable, or hard. All that is undubitable about any experience is that it occurs when it does. The immediate sensum, moreover, is not and cannot be apprehended as such, unless it is distinguished from a background and identified as an object, an accomplishment requiring inchoate comparative judgment — some degree of discursive activity. Third, it is said that causal theory requires as its compliment the 'idea' — it should a copy or representation of the external thing taken to be its object. It means some archetype, to which we have no independent access, in order to make the necessary comparison. But we did know it then we would have no need to apprise us of it.

The sense-datum theories, the building blocks from percepts are constructed are erroneous, as unrevisable bases of all knowledge. Yet when we perceive objects, we seem to apprehend them as a whole, beyond mere sense-datum. Perhaps, language interferes here, since 'seeing' implies what is seen as an external object either perceived veridically, or 'seen as' what we take it to be. May be one can distinguish the two by using the word seeing for the former, and looking for the latter, to remove ambiguity. We need some valid criterion to judge between cases in which we actually see — veridically — and those in which we only think we see. But again this become a problem of the language and the theory of appearing. We need not go into the whole range of such philosophical discussions available in literature. The point is that whatever we perceive, the object of which we become aware is not what we directly sense. Neurophysiologists and psychologist have demonstrated this for even simple perceptions, which are the products of quite complicated incipient thinking.

Sense-datum theories are the progeny of empiricism, which declares all knowledge to be derivative from sense and is then committed to discovering the sensuous data on which it is based. But it ignores the fact that all knowledge is organised experience, which is essential to cognition, without which there can be no perception. This is an analytic-synthetic activity, involving thought, attention, senses and a Gestalt, in accordance with the principles of organization essential to its nature. Perception is thus the activity of structuring the contents of primitive sentience — from the physical and biological levels as traced elsewhere — and at every stage, from the most elementary to the most complex, it is always the comprehension of a whole.

Cognition begins with perception, when the object — singled out from a whole background — by attention; and, by successive stages, objects are identified and distinguished and relations are established between them. The existence of the organism in the world, in its interaction in the world, is registered in sentience. Apprehending mutual relationships, identifying them, and distinguishing them is the thinking activity of the conscious subject thus awakened; each individual act being one of judging, initially implicit but, in the more developed phases, explicit and articulate. Perceiving and thinking can therefore not be separated. Or, concepts without intuition is hollow while intuition without concepts is blind. Massive experimental evidence shows that the perceived object is formed and conditioned by context, spatial and temporal, and by past experience. Thus no physical thing is presented ever as a whole to the senses, yet it is perceived, when at all, as a whole. But the cognitive result, the implicit judgment, implicit inference and interpretation — subject to the principle of ordering — arises in relation to the funded knowledge of the experienced world. The realisation comparatively recently by scientists and philosophers of science that all observation is theory-laden is therefore hardly surprising.

The experienced life-world, its experience and awareness and perception is a unified one in the ordinary sense also, its natural for it to be so; an integral whole, even if its intrinsic coherence varies in degree according to the extent to which the experience has developed and is systemised by the thinking activity of the subject. The unity is organic as consciousness; the experience of structured whole, of subject and object, could only be cognised as related to other presented objects if both or all were held together by the cognizant subject within its own consciousness. It is not as if it is brought from the outside; for the subject is nothing less than the universal principle of wholeness that has been immanent throughout the process of nature, and is intrinsic to the organic unity now come to consciousness through the sentience of the organism, operating throughout nature also. It is the same organising principle that integrates the physical cosmos and unites the biosphere, which unifies conscious experience and ensures the integrity of the experienced world.

In practical terms the belief in the reality of the life-world is immediate and innate, its initial justification is primarily pragmatic. But as stated above, it is the coherence of the experience as a whole that is implicit even in pragmatism. The process of bringing the world to consciousness is, in the first place, the imposition of order and systematic relationships upon the sensory flux. In the life-world – physical and biotic – all are mutually continuous dialectical phases or specific forms in the necessary differentiation of the universal duality. Since the world is a whole it must, of necessity, be complete, both synchronically and diachronically. And as no whole can be complete unless brought to consciousness, the universal principle of structure comes to self-awareness in the consciousness of a cognizant subject, through the natural process that issues in human experience of a perceived world.

In the course of becoming organised, self is distinguished from not-self, and the spontaneous activity of thinking becomes aware of its own agency as subject concomitantly with its apprehension of its object, and that object is nothing other than its own self in process of generation. Throughout mental life, the object of awareness is always the prior phase of the dialectical process. This generates the perceptual world of spatio-temporal bodies and their properties; but, as accepted in the natural attitude or common sense, the life world is still far from being fully coherent; so that perceptual consciousness itself becomes an object to a further stage of conscious reflection. Admittedly, we cannot get outside our own consciousness, but consciousness is itself the activity of ordering the contents of sentience; and that is, as we have asserted, a unified whole of feeling which, in the very course of the process of organisation, is revealed as the focused registration of a world external to the sentient body.

The difference between common perception and scientific observation is not one of kind but only of degree of sophistication. Both are active efforts to discern presented objects by a subject framing hypotheses and trying to confirm them by correlating evidence for and against; in the first case the process is largely subconscious, or prejudicial, and in the second it is deliberate and explicit. But it is the paradigm that dictates in scientific advancement, and attention is selective – what guides it is interest, on the one hand, and previous knowledge, on the other. What is perceived is partly what is expected and partly what is sought; it is simply never what is there. A vast amount of material is therefore overlooked, and often in this lack of perception it is not credited as possible. In this sense scientific observation is continuous with common sense, in that it raises observation to a high degree of systematisation what is already the experience of an ordered world. One may thus say that it is the same totality throughout, in different phases of self-articulation.

Mentality and Sentience

An organism, as organized being, involves a concept because it is a whole constituted by parts that are mutually adapted and are equally adjusted to the overall structure of the whole. Hence, in order to exist at all, such organism must be organized, and it can arise only out of what is already organized being. The very functioning of the parts and processes of the organism involves a concept — a principle of order and relationship. But a concept implies the existence and activity of a cognising mind, while the material existence and operation of the organic being is in space and time, dependent on physical laws and external causes that are antithetical to the purely ideal. This contradiction can be resolved only if, on the one hand, the concept immanent in the material system qua organized is somehow objectified or actualized in its practical functioning, and, on the other hand, the organizing principle in the organic system is brought to self-consciousness.

Sentience is not only the feeling of the integrated physiological whole of the body but is also the feeling of all these focused into a single complex whole. Hegel identified sentience with the soul, and Aristotle maintained that the soul was the form of the body. The soul is not a separate 'thing', attached to, or associated with, the body, acting upon it from the outside, or acted upon by it to generate sensation. It is the form of the body, the new quality evinced at a specific, critical threshold of intensity of integrated physiological activity. Feeling, the self-revelation of this new form, is not just something triggered in particulate flashes by special processes in the nervous system; it is basically bodily feeling, the body as felt — the 'lived body' is sentience.

From primitive forms to ourselves, the registration of the natural world in sentience is copiously exemplified in the felt response to the experience of seasonal changes, the weather, and climatic conditions. All this is related to the flow of energy into and through the organism from external physical sources, and to the felt needs of its body and the supply through its physiological and behavioural activities. It is believed that primitive sentience must be pre-conscious. But it is the material content of all consciousness and becomes its immediate object. How far down the evolutionary scale sentience occurs, and at what level consciousness proper emerges, is of necessity a matter of speculation and can only be inferred from the behaviour of the organic body. It is hard to believe that the behaviour of Paramecium and so on, is not prompted by sensibility to outside influences. How is the response to lack of oxygen possible unless it is somehow sensed? No inorganic reducing substance can migrate to seek an oxygen supply, however we may imagine that it is some way sensitive to the presence of oxygen when that is available. Such imputation of sensitivity in physical bodies to physical forces is only metaphorically justifiable, except if one advocates panpsychism. But the hypothesis is not necessary if one regards holism as a matter of degree — a higher degree of wholeness than simple chemical combinations, for instance, or physical cohesion. The relation between sentience and consciousness, at any rate, is one of degree, if only of clarity and articulation, and that in the evolutionary scale the latter must have emerged out of the former gradually, and probably concomitantly with the development of brain capacity and organization.

In thus bringing itself to awareness, the universal principle of wholeness remains immanent, as subject, in the experience; and without such immanence the experience could not be true. The immanent universal is what Kant called the transcendental synthetic unity of apperception. It is what constitutes the self, as distinguished within the sentient and conscious whole, a transcendental ego, transcendentally aware both of itself and its other, and cognizant of the whole immanent in its own experience of the world.

Attention,Consciousness and Cognition

Attention selects an element within the felt whole, distinguishes it from the felt background, and creates a figure — and — ground structure within the psychical field, making it an object for consciousness, which is this way directed upon it. Consciousness thus varies in clarity and definition with the degree of sharpness and articulation of attention. There is no consciousness without an object which it is intentionally directed. Whereas sentience does not, consciousness does imply the distinction between subject and object. The object is, as it were, projected and held 'before' the subject, which contemplates it as a whole. Consciousness has been compared to a searchlight playing upon successive objects and illuminating the surrounding landscape; it is an activity. While it presents itself as hierarchical structure, it also has the capacity to extricate itself from it all and grasp the whole, the general form; in some way consciousness is also self-transcendent.

Attention, creating the object, by singling it out of the psychical field, is thus initiation of consciousness, the experience described as cognitive when perception is born. Concurrently, the various sense modalities are distinguished. As objects are related to one another and to the body in which sensation are felt, self becomes opposed to not-self, and an outer world is built in which the subject is conceived as one member and the organism that it inhabits is placed to its encompassing environment. It is in the virtue of the self-transcendent character of consciousness that the mind reaches the point at which a fresh tresh transition, a further self-enfoldment, takes place: the stage at which self-reflection is achieved.

It is the crucial point at which the self becomes aware of its own identity and knows itself as 'I', at which it makes itself, along with its ideal content, object to itself as subject. Here the mind enters upon the stage of self-reflection; reflection upon the nature of its objects and its own relation to them. This is the dawn of intellect, the birth of wonder, and the awakening of self-criticism and self-appraisal. Reflection is the distinguishing mark of the human. Without it there can be no morality, no civil society, no science or philosophy, no art or religion, no materialism, no behaviourism, no scepticism, and no theoretical deconstruction; and the first fruit of reflection is the indefeasible revelation to the self of its own existence. Those who remember the traditional idealistic problematic will no doubt wish to challenge this account of the emergence of knowledge, to ask how, if the life-world is thus constructed from the contents of the sentient field, we can ever know whether anything in the outer world corresponds to our subjective construction. The question is however misplaced and misguided. Objective and subjective is a distinction made within the life-world, which the experience embraces as a whole. We can in no way get outside our own consciousness. There is no outside, if only because outer and inner is an opposition constituted within experience.

On Complementarity

In modern scientific terms, the Principle of Complimentarity, based mainly on the work done by Neils Bohr, stresses the ancient viewpoint at least seemingly in essence at least. It states that the seemingly opposites or what one at present calls irreconcilable points of view need not be contradictory. In fact, on deeper analysis are mutually illuminating, i.e., these are part of the same totality, seen from different perspectives (Kothari: 1989). At the social, ethical level, like the uncertainty principle mentioned elsewhere, one is allowed for the possibility of accommodating widely divergent views and human experience. From the scientific viewpoint of the educational curricula, this needs to be emphasized. For example, thinking and thought, how they arise and how one gets an idea which have existed goes on infinitely; and this infinity is enclosed in an instant, moving yet not moving thoughts, like Zeno's paradox of an inexplicable contradiction. This is like matter (brain) and consciousness (mind) that are complementarities. This is what Pauli has stated in his Pauli's Extension Principle, the oneness of quality and quantity, matter and mind. Thus scientific principles are applicable to life too, we just have to look at these at the subatomic levels, of which we are made of too. It is easy to see how scientific knowledge has allowed for the possibility of giving new meaning to words unlike those that exist in ordinary language. Even in mathematics, concepts like Infinity lead to contradictions, or what Godel's theorem tries to prove. Thus the ambiguity of ordinary language can further undergo changes to provide insights of greater understanding between human mind and reality. Not that this is not known in Buddhist, Jain, Upanisadic ethics and philosophy. But all this has to be relevant in our times by our own discoveries and perceptions, and in terms of scientific understanding and technological developments. A new vocabulary, a new language, a reinterpretation in terms of contemporary needs and society is essential. Insights (as ancient these might be) need to experienced again and again and restated, afresh. As said earlier, truths have to be said anew for out own purposes albeit supported perhaps by earlier ideas (or *vice-versa*) which confirm our experiences and insights. Each age, generation has to do it over and over again, afresh. Each one has to stand on its own feet, breathe first hand and feel for itself whatever it is now; and be a lamp to one's self. And, this has to be manifested over and over again in its own unique yet universal way. In this way there is fresh creation, moment to moment, age after age. In an abstract sense, there is nothing new of course, unless it is experienced in that perception-action manner, in a timeless yet creative way. Yet this is not a paradox, i.e., I am the same yet I am different or *vice-versa*; I am moving yet am not also.

In an abstract sense, pain, hunger, feelings, and all that is the same for all of humankind. These experiential states are beyond any socio-cultural boundaries. Nevertheless, the universal nature is forgotten by narrow boundaries of conceptual notions; and also it must be remembered that each experience is unique even if its cultural manifestation is bound. Thus there are unique and universal states at the same time. Several such paradoxes may be mentioned; being and non-being, I am and I am not, etc. These pairs of the binary systems from the phenomenal world in Upanisadic sense has been stated by many, and some examples are given as:

1. Noumenon and Phenomenon —— one is the other.
2. God and Nature —— one is the other.
3. *Sansara* and *Nirvana* —— one is the other.
4. *Brahman* and *Maya* —— one is the other.
5. Self and self —— one is the other.
6. Thought and Time —— one is the other.
7. Self and thought —— one is the other.
8. Knower and Known —— one is the other.
9. Renunciation and Enjoyment —— one is the other.
10. Action and Non-action —— one is the other.
11. Being and Becoming —— one is the other.
12. *Vidya* and *Avidya* —— one is the other.
13. Birth and Non-birth —— one is the other.
14. Work and Knowledge —— one is the other.
15. Spiritual and Phenomenal Nature —— one is the other.

16. Subjective and Objective —— one is the other.
17. Actor and Spectator —— one is the other.
18. Future and Past —— one is the other.
19. A and not-A —— one is the other.

etc. etc. etc.

The problem asked, the questions that arise are in themselves having the answer, since the two levels are not distinct and contradictory except from the purely limited phenomenal viewpoint. How is one to make a jump, a quantum jump which is required of one to the other, since it is a continuous transition, a gradual movement up the ladder. But this is not the way, i.e., from the finite self to the infinite self is not possible, through time-thought. If the latter was possible it would have happened again and again in these 5000 years. But it has become worse with repeated attempts. Of course there are complementarities of higher and lower levels when one conceptualises the issue. But the simplest and best understood complementarities is that of the wave-particle duality in physics. In brief, in ordinary language it means simultaneity, coupling of past and future, in every observation which implies freedom of choice and objectivity, i.e., free will between mutually exclusive alternatives, is in a sense a participation in genesis, i.e., actor and the spectator.

The observer and the observed are not two separate entities as was revealed by the discoveries of quantum mechanics in 1920s. It was assumed until then that such objectivity was possible, as the world of matter consisted of discrete entities and man was a distinct entity, at least in principle. But this picture has changed, of the self and the other which are part of the whole, if one were to project to the human world this subatomic reality. At the subatomic level, the interaction is not predictable, and therefore the unpredictable nature of things is inherent in their very nature, according also to Plank's constant. This is to say not only atoms, their physics and chemistry is what humans are also made up of. We all thus function in a unified system, for anything to happen at one, everything in the universe has to participate for it to happen and unless this is so, nothing will actually happen at the conceptual level. Hence all the suffering we see all around where one sees one's self as a separate entity unrelated to all else. The words perhaps cause the problem. In physics things can no longer be explained simply and be describable so easily. This is not to say that all the work done in physics is not objective and scientific. But it provides an insight into the working of all of nature, of which man is an essential part.

Thus, scientific truths and ethical truths are not contradictory but complementary.[1] There can be no advancement in science without some measure of ethics in society. Equally, on the other hand, in the modern world there is not much room for the practice of ethics without science and technology. In other words, the quest is for seeking a unified field in science and in other areas, of a unity in nature and man.

But it all begins with a personal yearning. Throughout human history, in every endeavour, human beings have searched for connections, for ways to make a harmonious whole out of the parts. Today, the Holy Grail of modern physics is the Grand Unified Theory.

To be asked is the question, is there a unity, in fact, say in the brain or the interpreter sitting in it, since the unity of thought is an illusion? The brain has a multiplicity of functions and voices that speak independently. But despite the fact that the brain is multipartite, it represents itself to the mind as unified. Were conscious selves fully unified, we would feel justified in concluding that for all the disparity of its parts the brain is in truth a fully unified system. But, instead, we find that our sense of the personal unity and command over the brain is something of an illusion.[2]

So, is the idea of unity and its quest a mere assumption, does unity really exist ? In the world of art this assumption may depend only on aesthetics but in science, it would seem some concrete forms have to be taken into account. The assumption of Lovelock, for instance is that there is probably a mechanism that will reduce the carbon dioxide in the atmosphere when it is too low for trees; and particle physicists assume a single force that produces electromagnetic forces, gravitational forces, and nuclear forces. Nature may, or may not accommodate these assumptions. Paradoxically, as science digs deeper into nature, it uncovers alternating layers of unity and variety, simplicity and complexity. Copernicus's sun-centered cosmos was simpler than Ptolemy's earth-centered universe, but twentieth century astronomers found that the sun is merely a resident in the suburbs of the Milky Way galaxy. The atom was once the indivisible unit of matter; then hundreds of subatomic particles such as neutrons and protons were found; then the genealogy of this multitude was simplified by tracing their lineage to three constituent particles called quarks; now the number of quarks has grown to six or more.[3]

Twentieth century has thus exploded a metaphysical bomb, namely, quantum physics. It shows that the scientist is inextricably tangled with the objects she observes, as no longer is she a passive observer as it was believed one could observe the pendulum swing without changing its motion. Chemists believed they could measure the rate at which coal burned in air without altering that rate; naturalists believed they could quietly listen to a sparrow without dictating its song; and scientists assumed they could put a box around their subject and peer into that box. Quantum physics has shown that scientist are always inside the box. The answers scientists get to their questions depend on the way they ask the questions. Thus, the enigma of whether unity exists outside the mind of the scientist and dissolves in a mist of ambiguity and meaninglessness. A baffling experiment in quantum physics, called the double-slit experiment, demonstrates how 'the observer' finds that he is not really an observer but part of the experiment. Without going into details of it the baffling part is: How does each electron know in advance whether there are additional detectors behind the openings? How does each electron know whether to remain whole like a golf ball or to subdivide and spread like a ripple on a pond? Somehow, the properties of the electron depend on the mind asking the questions.[4]

Physics and Biology

Ernst Mayr in his *Towards a New Philosophy of Biology* (1991) asks the question, Is evolutionary biology a science ? If so, what kind of a science is it ? His central theme is that the concepts which underlie evolutionary biology, make it an autonomous science, and not merely a subbranch of physics. Not that he does not believe in the unity of science; in particular he believes that the law of physics and chemistry are the same in living and inanimate matter. The claim for autonomy rests on the existence of concepts — for example, natural selection, genetic programme, species — that are needed if we are to understand biology. These concepts are consistent with physical laws but could not be deduced from them.

In distinguishing between physics and biology, he points to the different role of laws in the two sciences. In physics, laws are intended to be universal. Such laws do exist in some branches of biology. For example, the "central dogma of molecular biology" that information can pass from nucleic acid to protein, but not from protein to nucleic acid, is intended to be such a law, universal as far as life on earth is concerned. As yet, there is no convincing falsifying evidence. The law is important for evolutionary biology, because it provides one explanation for the non-inheritance of acquired characters. In evolution such laws are hard to come by. Even the law that acquired characters are not inherited has exceptions, because not all heredity depends on the sequence of bases in nucleic acids.

The message is that evolution is contingent. It is not the case that, initially, there were a few simple organisms, and that, as time passed, there was a steady increase in diversity and complexity, leading inevitably to the emergence of an intelligent, tool-using, talking animal-ourselves. If there was a replay of it all again, there may not be chance for the same to be repeated since it is a matter of chance which body, phyla, survive; no guarantee or likelihood of the emergence of vertebrates, or mammals. Evolution is not a stately law-governed progression leading inevitably to human intelligence.

Throughout evolution function has preceded the organ through which it is to be exercised; the organ developed in response to a need. So why should the brain be any exception? In other words Intelligence came first, quite able to function in its own realm. Working from such a premise, is it not true that life, intelligence, and consciousness are primal realities? Is it scientific heresy to suggest that biological forms are secondary events, to the primary substratum? It is somewhat ridiculous to maintain the position of a mechanistic, chance creation which insists that thought originates and depends upon the physical brain. For example, with regard to the brain, no special 'box'equivalent to the computer's 'memory'store has been identified; nor is memory to be found in a particular cell, synapse, or chemical molecule. All experience is not stored in the brain (Smith:1975). Today, physics and other allied disciplines are clear that there is a non-mechanical reality more like a great thought rather than like a machine-mind is no longer an accident of matter but the creator and governor in the realm of matter.[5]

On Consciousness

In the modern world most explanations are mechanistic interpretations of the processes of life, such as, that it is in the brain that consciousness appeared as an epiphenomenal process occurring in evolution. But this is like a dreamer explaining a dream while asleep. It is explaining consciousness through the mechanism of the brain, which itself is the product of the mind – Universal Mind or Consciousness. It is like looking for the programmer in a television set, or a radio set, in its tubes or circuits, etc. which when taken out would cause some disturbance of the audio-visual programme; and this would then be attributed to a part of the set as if something was located in that part of the set (brain). But all the while forgetting that apparently there is some logical connection between the part and the dislocation, nevertheless this is only a receiving set, since the broadcast is being transmitted from elsewhere. All the problems, conflicts about the brain, soul, existence and so on are part of the individual mind's own firmament and have no existence apart from Consciousness or Intelligence. Those who try to prove that the mind begins and ends with the brain, can only testify it or not with the mind alone.

It appears falsely so, that the mind is a mere bio-chemical activity. But this has never been proved, shown or analysed. The linguistic and languaging powers located and residing in the brain is not the mind, i.e., the tape or commentary, and the audio-visual apparatus is not the mind or its dynamics. The enterprise of social sciences and sciences is based on this notion of the mind – again a statement of the mind, counteracted in the mind itself by an opposite statement! This is the game a language plays, as mentioned elsewhere as the dual nature of thought (Malik:1989,1993). In any case, consciousness cannot be known through rational language left-brain activity, nor can it make it to the ineffable and indescribable through all its striving. This is not possible by the intellect any way; it can only deal with matters agreed upon by the social set up and thus must realise its limitations. Nevertheless, many of us desire to know or have an experiential state. This is only possible through an intuitive mystical knowing and not by the left-brain language categories. But is this knowing located in the individual brain or the mind? The brain-body mechanism is an instrument, a very sophisticated one at that but, self-referentially, like a computer it cannot know about these intimations which are beyond its limited sphere. The issue at the moment is not the functioning of the brain, at any rate.

The essence is thus missing, an aspect that many today long for; it is a consequence of the agnostic intellect that feels essenceless and dry and hence is having a dream of itself. There is a possibility of these brain activities being connected to biochemical workings. But is it all the by-product of such mechanical activities? If so, who or what is the knower? Surely, it cannot be a transient derivative, arising out of the atoms or molecules of lesser known matter. If so, how can it answer questions regarding creation and existence, or what is real or unreal? All this occurs in whatever this mind or no-mind maybe; the questions and answers in the mind-stuff itself, its debates, the arguments, the verdict and those against it. There are in this sense no others actually, its all **Me**, the Self or Consciousness; being the sceptic, the judge, the opponent, the believer, the non-believer; and all our hopes, ideas, theories, doctrines, concepts,etc. arise in the mind and subside in it only. It is like lines drawn on water, and vanishing as soon as they are drawn. All the stuff going on is the universal stuff itself — the rays of sun is the sun. Is not matter then nothing but the Universal Mind or Consciousness ?

And, what is the mind, without Consciousness, and that too in the shoreless, measureless ocean on whose surface it arises like foam. And from the mind arise various universes that appear very tangible, which they are not except to be seen as metaphors of another dimension, another reality. Both the universe and our personal observing minds would not exist but for an omnipresent Intelligence. But all modern goals run counter to this embellishment of the brain's desire for spiritual needs; it craves merely of food for the body and bodily comforts and material wants. Even the atoms and the subatomic particles are not everlasting, albeit they are part of the universal energy present everywhere; even protons consist of jumping up and down quarks that are omnipresent in and out of the body. Thus, the two clash. The current trends thwart the opening of supersensory channels, and this course of collision is malevolent functioning, not the benevolent plan of nature to move to the Omega point of Chardin (1959).

Consciousness may be seen as transcendental and immanent from the human viewpoint, but this is not so by itself; like air, it is everywhere and where is it not? Is the space inside and outside the building different, except until the time the building is there and the moment it falls off, the space is once again one — it appeared like two, inside and outside, only because of the building being the focus of attention.

This knowledge of Consciousness is known by Consciousness (the mind-stuff); it partakes of itself through various ways in the functioning of the brain-mind's confluence. It itself is the knower, the known and the knowing, of its significance. It is known or seen when the general facilities are open in the brain-body mechanism that is a vehicular instrument — an instrumentality. For example, the occurrence of paranormal telepathic communication, etc. for which there are many examples (the photographer who got lost in the jungles of the Amazon and began to communicate with the Shaman of a tribe non-verbally and he communicating among other things that the tribe is moving away from civilization since the more it contacts it the less its ability to communicate non-verbally!) But much the same fate awaits them, as it has been the case with other non-Western cultures in America, Africa and Australia. Contemporary science, despite evidence to the contrary in even one's personal life, is ignoring it. Perhaps, because it has neither the tools or means to verify it and it is so, since the rational-theoretical models are limited by their own frameworks of scientific instruments, which are extensions of the five senses only and cannot detect the sixth sense areas, an atomic reactor would be the wrong laboratory for it. The laboratory and its verifiability would come from another area or dimension, beyond current scientific vision at the moment, i.e., its assumptions do not take these areas into account at all. This is another kind of dogmatism and fundamentalism. The essence of Knowledge, of Mind and Consciousness, and of the notion of Self, when absent from the entire universe of discourse, can one really get at any other actuality, a dimension of reality and leave aside Truth?

Of course, if such extra-sensory perception was amenable to empirical scientific verification, especially moments of personal-impersonal existential-experiential states that are taken to have some validity, this would become a fearful threat to all that has been invested all these years into the current state of knowledge — theoretical and practical — in the world. Such a state would shake the foundations not only of social sciences and anthropology, but even one's own life at all — individual and collective — levels especially one's relationships. To point out the reality behind our obvious phenomenal world, would be to create a void; one would be in a limbo, a transitional state between the known and the unknown. One is referring simply at the moment to the mystical dimension — not the mysterious — that is known and knowable but not by any so-called concrete means. These are areas which are governed by laws beyond those of space, time and causality, states which one may call meditative ones. These are therefore not beyond anyone's means, or beyond directions of research separate from the 'material' empirical one of science and social science — beyond one's scope as one may imagine. The primary aspect of consciousness is of crucial importance. This is part of a human-being's mental-experiential aesthetic-states which were as much familiar to the pre-industrial man as a way of life, as today's non-industrial communities. These are states expressed in their life-styles, states of mind that manifest the grand creations and expressions seen in all civilizations. All this is beyond the rational-empirical methodology of a positivistic and reductionistic philosophy that has so determined modern life, to its own detriment.

Obviously, Consciousness exists in all states, during wakefulness, dreams and in sleep — since there is a knowing even while dreaming, even in dreamless states when one gets feeling so fresh, not remembering one's name or problems about the body. If this was not so, one would not know that one slept well and it would all switch off if it were only an epiphenomenon of brain's activity. It would seem as if there is a kind of Witnessing to various activities by Consciousness. But we dismiss all this since we have separated the observer from the observed. The external evidence of the study of societies may not indicate all this, since one has eliminated consciousness and mind as the subject of study, how can one show this dimension by gross tools of measurement? It implies that the sense of history will also be different, since the past, present and the future becomes an awareness of the **now**, the *bindu* of Now, the big-bang is happening Now. The Now, Now, Now is all a Presence! How does one know anything, without taking into account Consciousness or Intelligence, one may ask?

Science is irressitibly coming to the conclusion that there is no separation between the observer and the observed; that matter by itself cannot observe itself. It is awareness — Consciousness — that creates this division; how this mysterious division, this separateness takes place — of the drop thinking it is separate from the ocean — forgetting its primary existence; this perhaps is the veil of *maya*, or *mahamaya*. The awareness to see this screen created by the ego which believes it is the supreme entity to do so is to identify with the Being of a human being. It is to know that the One becomes the many and the latter also being the One. But the discovery of this universal has to be discovered uniquely in each experience, paradoxically, at each moment by an personal-impersonal state, over and over again newly every Now, in the Now. That is the game.[6]

As the basal substance of the universe, how can Consciousness cease to be or die? Consciousness, to use an old analogy or even in terms of physics, that there is an infinite ocean of energy in which matter, condenses in many forms without any diminishing of the energy which is prevalent everywhere 'within and without'. This is the boundless ocean, void which is full, which is dotted with globular icebergs of colossal proportions floating in it, of matter. Our senses know only the tip of the iceberg, they cannot feel the imperceptible oceanic waters of Consciousness which includes space, time, etc. albeit it is beyond all of its contents, i.e., the Context of all contexts is a limitless, infinite creative energy of a universal order which is beyond even any conceptions of the brilliance of a thousand suns. Normally one sees merely the ice-formations and that conceptually and intellectually one imagines or believes, or does not, the rest. But in a silent state, beyond words or chatters, in a purified mind-state without the 'me', it is possible to catch a glimpse of that state of eternity, the eternal moment of Now or Presence, of *Samadhi*, of a union or *Yoga* beyond duality or multiplicity. In these states the ice-formations, the tips or gross matter vanishes as one knows its superficialness and ephemeral nature. One knows the boundless energy, the ocean of pure effulgent light. It is now all '**me**', as Sri Krsna says in the *Gita*, either in the pure state, or in its multiple states like seeing light through a prism (the mind-brain complex) which is still the same light—just like the often stated jewel-gold metaphor. Thus is Immanence and Transcendence One, as it always was, is; it is one in all and all in one, witnessed in mystical experience, in the moments of Now, when the 'me' vanishes — states of ecstasy and bliss knowable in everyday mundane life, not as something exclusive. It is the '**me**' experiencing itself in all its activities through its creations of the so-called other which is itself, for what is it that it is not?

Thus, this is the only conceivable theory of creation one can frame being consistent with the latest trends in physics and the mounting evidence posited by the study of extra-sensory perceptions. Call it soul, spirit, or whatever, it is that, and sees its own glory unhampered by the senses perceived by the 'me'. Is this not Saivite, Vedantin, Sakti, Vajrayana Buddhist or Tantra philosophies too? These *turya* and *turyatitta* states are knowable and experienceable by one and all, we are told, as it is the self-reflection and self-perceptive powers of that which **is**. What clouds it all is the dust gathered in the mirror of the mind — the memories of pleasures, pains, regrets, resentments—which distorts that One. It needs cleaning every time, not any different to breathing that must be done every moment afresh; or that dusting of the house has to be done everyday and not once for all, in order for it to reflect truly. This is the awakening of the mind, created by the mind itself, for a new transformation, a vision of the discovery of the **being** for this is who one is, always was — not who one thinks one was, is.

As indicated above, we understand the world in a topsy-turvy manner, i.e., the world seen by the senses is real while that which allows this to happen is unreal or abstract. But the opposite is true, i.e., the world of senses is governed by a mind-set socially conditioned through concepts and images represented symbolically and is therefore abstract in fact. This is the commentary which one takes to be real, whereas the action is at the experiential level that is indescribable beyond words — even like the taste of water. To know this, one has to wake up from the conditioning. Then one knows that it was always available, it is, provided one stops clinging and hanging on to the known.

Contemplating in this manner creates problems since the social system one lives in feels threatened by these manifest expressions and statements, for these go against the old generalisations of mostly the nineteenth century notions, ideas to which most of social sciences and even science in many parts of the world where it is equated to technology and scientism, continue to cling to. Not all of the current states of science perhaps accepts this notion of an ocean of Intelligence, of a universal energy or a unified field. If it is so, it has not penetrated to the larger society of scientists or society at large. It also speaks of an attributeless, nameless and formless energy; all name and form fixed in any way will limit it. How does one know it, then? It is like light or electricity which is known by its effects in a cognisable form as such by our senses. The infinite is present in the finite albeit often in a diluted form, as it is often clouded and limited but reveals itself when awakened and purified, this body-brain instrument which in its subtler aspects is light and sound vibrations speaking in material terms. The universe is a Play of Consciousness, *Krsna-Leela*; it is the clouds that hide the sun which is always there; it was not so that it never was, it is.

Mysticism and Science

The movement from a religious metaphor guiding the ancient past to a scientific metaphor of modern times continues to go further ahead, since the latter is increasingly being recognised as incomplete for telling us about the various contemporary issues, the crisis, such as environmental pollution, ecological imbalances, and so on. The modern movement marked a departure from the old dynamics of life when humankind lived closer to nature, sustained and motivated by an understanding of our higher nature — an understanding that came easily and naturally to them; as against the confidence of the modern era to achieve better living conditions, through progress in terms of conquest of nature — introducing both physical and psychological new parameters, separating man from nature, from the universe and hence not being responsible for an overall harmony by being subservient to the cosmos, but pretending to be the dominant force himself. Thus being good and bad became mere matters of technical feasibility, since moral, spiritual and other dimensions had little to do with material solid practicality of material comforts. Now, all this is outdated in view of some developments in Science which are ahead of the times, ahead of this reductionistic paradigm which alienated man from the cosmos. It is in this context that scientists are moving in both the inner and outer dimensions, science and religion, between matter and consciousness even if physics and chemistry are inadequate to deal with such problems since so far science has no moral dimensions to it (Weber:1986).

Physics has developed wonderfully and become very important, interesting and a useful science. But it is not very self-consistent, and it does not even try to cover the existence of consciousness or life. Also quantum theory and relativity are not really reconciled with each other. More investigations are necessary. The description of the world and its unity by quantum theory is very different from that of old-fashioned physics, that is macroscopic physics and also that of general relativity. But contradictions in physics are noticed in a particular theory or system of logic only when we apply it to a new situation and the theory predicts results that are not compatible with the observed phenomena. And, this may be understood in terms of quantum mechanics that describes probabilities — probability connections between subsequent observations. Sciences thus speak in terms of approximations, and this is good since physics deals with inanimate nature. It has not gone into the study of Consciousness, just like at one time it did not consider itself ready to study microstructures, as atoms and molecules. Earlier physics dealt with magnetism, electricity and mechanics, etc. So today, while it deals with atoms and molecules, nevertheless human beings are more than just that. Yet, sciences do not yet consider consciousness to be part of their study — no more than the social sciences and humanities unfortunately do. Perhaps because consciousness is considered something non-physical, since the definition of physical is restricted just as Newtonian physics considered atomic physics outside physics. Today, even chemistry and physics is incorporated within each other, if not biology or microbiology.

Perhaps new tools and language is necessary to understand consciousness, just as it was necessary to develop a new tool to understand chemistry, i.e., quantum theory. The questions then raised would be different, does self-identity demand consciousness, or does the latter create identity, viz., I know that I am I because consciousness tells me so; is it a product of something, as an emergence of evolution more or less accepted by everyone, or is the quantum of consciousness in every living entity the same in its nature or ability? The mechanical nature of each body may be different. Maybe just as atoms are not products of something, but are certainly state of matter by transformations, so is consciousness a state of being. Maybe it is either a transformation of matter or it is totally a non-material principle. At any rate, in terms of present science of physics and chemistry, a definition and description of matter will not tell us about consciousness; just as one could say that Newton's theory did not describe the emission of energy, heat and light by the sun — maybe it was not expected to, even though the sun was always there. Today one speaks of heat and light as transformations of material energy. Maybe a basic ground work of theories will have to be changed to include a study of consciousness — something new has to be introduced, a new art and laboratory of observation, i.e., consciousness itself becomes a baseline for the art of observation — it is observing itself ! It involves a shift from particular entities, atoms and the rest as discrete entities to relational phenomena of events as Alfred Whitehead suggested. Physics and mathematics is no longer unidirectional in characterising things, these are processes and probabilities. Maybe this is more akin to the processual idea of Buddhists, rather than that of individual *jivas* as living beings as entities, existing separately (Weber: *Ibid.*).

The suggestion is that it is important to live in an open-ended system, as a human-being and not merely as a good scientist; for example, molecular biologists think that the whole of nature of life can be comprehended in terms of molecular biology — this is a mechanistic way of thinking, this is what science is about and that is all that matters. Thus, the open-mindedness of science is limited within established ideas or paradigms — just as many religions also say the same thing, or social scientists who think that the framework or content one is examining is the whole thing itself. Although the rational approach is very useful in many productive ways, it has ignored psychological and spiritual dimensions, especially the area of consciousness — areas often relegated to a waste of time, or stupidity. This narrow vision, extreme specialisation — while at the same time claiming open-endedness — is very neurotic and hence destructive, consequences that are very much upon us in this century. For example, even the role of intuition is not recognised in the work of the scientist himself, or his own creative process of which little is know — not to speak of knowing himself before knowing the universe.

The unity of things, man and nature, consciousness and matter, inner and outer, subject and object — these can only be reconciled not only when there is no separation between one's personal and professional life but also when exploring their unity, and seen as a spiritual odyssey — no separation between creative scientists, artists, humanists and the Sufis, saints, sages and mystics — no reference to conventional scientists and religious figures and institutions. This struggle for harmony, for integration and a search for wholeness is a priority with which nothing else can compare. A coherent vision is possible by searching for deep structures, whether in nature, the area of brain-mind, or mystic realms — this is not possible through contemporary analytical philosophy which has become merely intellectual, ignoring simplicity and unity. The move towards metaphysics from physics, or towards unity, has as yet penetrated only a minority of the researchers in all disciplines. The search for wisdom is as yet suspect, if not outrightly ridiculed. For any search for a holistic perspective, rigorous examination is necessary both in science and the study of consciousness. This is said emphatically since it is erroneously thought that methodology may be dispensed with in this search for wisdom; the objection is to all isms.

The philosophy of science rests largely on empirical methodology; involves formulating one's hypothesis, subjecting it to empirical experiment via carefully collected data that verify or falsify the hypothesis, in order to draw conclusions that will become a theory or perhaps a law — using equation and mathematics which is its handmaiden. Science is thus concerned with concrete details and abstract reasoning, between inductive and deductive ways; it has a very sophisticated structure. However, unless the thing at hand under study is both itself and something beyond itself, it loses meaning or becomes destructive in the long run — as we see science and technology turning into scientism and empiricism. Scientific details only acquire meaning when they glow with another metascientific reality. The collections of sense data about data is not a mere collection but depicts not describes, like poetry and art does a single reality of grandeur and beauty, which may be experienced on multiple levels — only a handful of scientists like Einstein express it publicly. Feeling and experiencing this oneness is, if it must be defined, mysticism. Science, originating from philosophical searches, also arises from the idea of wonder and awe; there is both an ethical and aesthetic side to it. Perhaps now it explains the mystery of being, while mysticism experiences it; the former is limited while the latter in unbounded. Nevertheless, both seek unity, a unified field of existence which forms the link, the substratum. What is this, and how is it tied to the existence of the scientist itself? It is possible that now one is speaking of a realm that is beyond language, schema-symbols too feeble to translate that ineffable domain, of Silence. Nevertheless, it is knowable, communicable even if whatever one says about it becomes an untruth. Like in physics, there can only be approximations of the statements one makes.

Perhaps, one may call science outer empiricism and the inner exploration as inner empiricism, then the common ground is unity, linking the microcosm and the macrocosm, nature and man, the observer and the observed. Max Planck acknowledged it well, "Science cannot solve the ultimate mystery of nature . . . because in the last analysis we are ourselves part of nature, and, therefore, part of the mystery that we are trying to solve." Man, however, is the crucial clue to the mystery himself. From time to time some scientists have realised this, and the relationship between mysticism and science is re-emerging in a modern form of the ancient relationship between the two approaches. But are these two reconcilable: one is quantitative, the other is qualitative; one's methodology is rigorous formalisation, the other's meditation; one's mastery is over gross matter, the other is over subtle matter (of inner bodies and so on) which has its own laws, logic, insight and workings analogous to science. In the latter too subtle matter has begun to appear in the theories of the twentieth-century physicist; it is no longer value-free even if it is cognitive in nature and understands phenomena by piece-meal analysis — precisely its weakness. The mystic's laboratory is the inner one, and of course in this quest he may equally be lost, forgetting the outer particular things. There is thus a relationship between simplicity and multiplicity, the universal and the particular. Viewing it like this, for instance in chemistry in a homogenous solution chromium stays invisible until it is coaxed to reveal itself through some appropriate steps; similarly there is the enigmatic metaphor of creation in the *Svetasvatara Upanisad*, " Like butter hidden in cream is the (pure consciousness) source which pervades all things."

In short, in Indian cosmology, the phenomenal world is the solid, the precipitate which becomes crystallised in space and time by cosmic consciousness in which it floats. David Bohm speaks of the implicate order cosmology, with its schema of dense and subtle matter, referring to a single source underlying the universe. Immanence and transcendence becomes one – divinity in everything – in this model where the finite unites with the infinite. The universe is materialised *Brahman*. Such a reversible equation recalls Einstein's equivalence of matter and energy, and the particle and wave identity of quantum mechanics. One may even go to the extent of saying that it – mysticism – that is pursuing with ruthless logic the Grand Unified Theory – the one that includes the questioner in its answer. Science wants to leave the scientist outside this search.

Perhaps, the dilemma that while it is easier to deconstruct nature and the other exoteric stuff by the mind, the latter as ego finds it difficult to deconstruct and reconstruct itself. For, in both cases in doing this that an enormous amount of energy is released. The binding power which keeps the atom together and the ego in another sense, will only reveal that energy and dimension hitherto undreamt of, so to speak. Like there is no ultimate building block, only transformational energy, so there is no fixed entity as the personality, independent and free. Once this is clear through different methodologies, techniques, the resultant staggering energy is a channel to limitless universal energy – Cosmic Consciousness. In both cases, it is the unfoldment of immense energy – potential in nature and the human realm through the substratum which one was seldom aware of experientially. This is not hair-splitting but atom-splitting and ego-splitting ! Both are arduous paths that cannot be treaded lightly, since both require an attitude of sacredness – otherwise it becomes negative, pathological and destructive as we all well know by now both in physical and psychological contexts.

These states of the release of energy are quantum transformational jumps with all kinds of possibilities; the mystic altered states of consciousness, harmonise the awareness of that individual, as in some ways his awareness alters the subatomic structure of which he is made up of to the deep structures we referred to above. In this sense, the mystic is a true alchemist since he brings the micro and macro levels together; he lives psychologically in the mode of creation, manifestation, dissolution of every particle of subtle matter and energy – he can let go and dies to each moment so that the next moment is afresh and a rebirth. In short, he lives in the timeless present, the **now** – the **presence**.

Scientist too talk of beauty, elegance, the good and true of reality, in this search for the Unity; it is not merely a mechanical search of an equation, or a single comprehensive law, in a conventional sense, bereft of aesthetics. In this sense its search is also spiritual, since behind the intellectual drive of the great creators of science, a deeper force is at work. Without this idea or something like that, if one hesitates calling it consciousness or intelligence, it is difficult to account for the way scientific genius operates, as behind the multiplicity of appearances lies the unity of an intrinsic reality.[7]

All this is not to devalue science, but it cannot answer questions as, what happened before the Big-Bang, what lies beyond the edge of the universe, what started it and why? Mysticism at least points to a direction, i.e., universe originates in consciousness as subtle matter which gives rise to dense matter, but all matter forms a continuum. The subtler the matter – purer the mind – the closer it gets to consciousness and ultimately cannot be distinguishable. But neither matter nor consciousness, even if they form one continuum are, according to the mystics, the ultimate. Both have a source in something which is beyond themselves, and cannot become an object of knowledge – not even in non-ordinary states of altered consciousness when there is unity of space, matter and consciousness, minus the person, or the ego.

In these ontological-experiential states, the distinction between inner and outer space, nature and self, consciousness and matter are lost. If science produces pure energy from dense matter, the mystic way transforms the dancer as the dance itself, as Consciousness is aware of consciousness itself. As is the Zen saying, "The eye which I see is the very eye which sees me". The participatory universe, however, demands a dialogue, in terms of the I-Thou experience of Martin Buber. Dialogue reflects the insights of each partner at this moment in time, and does not negate the fact that another moment may call forth another response. In this sense, dialogue is creativity, exchanging energies and insights, adding something afresh to the happenings of the universe in this encounter. Scientists like John Wheeler, Prigogine, Heisenberg, and others support this view and advocate it. Bohm goes even further to state that meaning is a form of being. In the very act of interpreting the universe we are creating the universe. Through our meanings we change nature's being. What the cosmos is doing as dialogue is to change its idea of itself in its questions and answers, its struggling to decipher its own being (Weber: *Ibid.*).

Conclusion

Correlating matter with consciousness in science, has been a long-standing puzzle. Recent developments since 1970 in cognitive science has attempted to unravel this puzzle somewhat. Especially the developments of quantum physics and chaos theory have shown us that in any strict sense, science cannot predict and control always. Some say that after a certain point in time, in evolution, consciousness comes into play which is qualitatively different than reductionist causes of science. Maybe the hypothesis of an all-pervasive energetic field of quantum zero-point energy is the all-pervasive field, which Consciousness of the esoteric traditions talks about too.

However, all recent attempts basically retain the old tested approach of science, which wants to understand it from down-upwards causation. First one must understand this, and then reverse this approach; direct it towards an all-inclusive holistic one, an up-downwards causation. Implying thereby that the basic stuff of the universe to study is the physical energy, matter, even if it is terms of fundamental particles and their associated interrelationships. It has been a mistake of modern science to assume that ultimately reductionistic scientific causes are explanations of everything. It is not an adequate world-view, since it has resulted in gaining control through manipulation of the physical — and the psychological-cultural implications thereby — environment albeit within that context everything seems to work well. It leading to conflicts, confrontational dualities between science and religion, free will versus determinism, you versus me, and so on.

Of course, these foundational assumptions have been modified with the advent of quantum physics, particularly by the indeterminacy principle and the inherent statistical nature of measurement of the very small. Agreement is spreading among the few that science must develop the ability to look at things, particularly living things, more holistically. There is evidence that everything physical and mental that is experienced is part of an intercommunicating unity, a oneness, and there is no justification of the assumption of separateness. However, within specific contexts, isolating parts from the whole the ordinary concepts of scientific causation do also apply.

In other words, if we include both ways, inner and outer, into account then we know that one reality is to known in two ways that are not separate but interlinked. The epistemological issue involved is our encountering of reality limited to being aware of, and giving meaning to the messages from our physical senses (objective), or does it not also include a subjective aspect in an intuitive, aesthetic, spiritual, noetic and mystical sense? In any case, in normal science ethics and aesthetics (elegance) enters in various ways. In a restructuring of our view of science, of matter, inner explorers may be included. In doing so, science would be more inclusive and this is not to invalidate any of the physical and biological sciences. One may thus be both distancing oneself and be also participatory, in being one with the subject.

The goal of the above discussion is to point out new directions of holistic science, of oneness — Consciousness — as the new foundations and metaphysics, then whole new vistas are open before us. Many anomalies, paranormal phenomena, will begin to fit in this framework, that does not insist on fitting everything into a reductionistic science and that we humans are here solely through random causes, in a meaningless universe; nor that our consciousness is merely the chemical and physical processes of the brain.

Few scientists are willing to question the philosophical issues underlying their work; that they are part of the underlying definition of science — say the objectivist, positivistic, determinist, and reductionist assumptions of logical empiricism. Not that these have not served science and technological development well, less so in biology even though the new gospel is molecular biology; but when the social scientist have aped these approaches it has been a disaster.

Most scientists would assert that science has moved away from all this for over half a century ago. But it is not clear, towards what; and consciousness has not come into the picture yet even though major paradoxes are facing science today, namely:

1. The fundamental nature of things does not appear to be convergent – more and more of fundamental particles are appearing – reductionism is in fact pointing to a wholeness, in their separation these are connected.
2. The fundamental organising force in living systems, from the largest to the smallest, is unexplained by physical principles (homeostasis; intricate flower patterns, butterfly wings, etc., healing, regeneration, ontogenesis, etc.)
3. The problem of action at a distance, or non-local causality, appearing in the far reaches of quantum physics; meaningful coincidences or connections, or Jungian Synchronicity—called paranormal, telepathic, clairvoyant communication; a host of others.
4. The knowledge of the universe is incomplete since there is no place for the consciousness of the observer, as if he is not in it; the notion of free will, volition and other characteristics of consciousness. Going from physiochemical to the consciousness does not work; it is the movement from higher, subtle, to the lower or gross which will take many of these aspects into account.
5. The notion of the self, the concept is not clear and not taken into account even though it is involved in the act of observation.
6. What are altered states of consciousness, which mystics and others know of, but are indicated in ordinary mundane lives also and are sought after by one and all – in aesthetic experience and so on? If atom, and other splitting causes the release of unforeseen energy, the splitting of the ego releases another dimension of consciousness little known in everyday living in a sleep-dream like state.

Given the above puzzles, researchers are moving into new areas to understand matter and consciousness, unthinkable a couple of decades ago. It requires a restructuring of the approach towards a oneness picture, a wholeness science as some would like to call it. This is to say one experiences the world from inside as consciousness, which is the whole also since the outside experienced by the senses is its external manifestation. Evolutionary speaking, evolution is the manifestation of consciousness, not just a single track of separate evolution from times immemorial. Consciousness, thus becomes an agency, in the relevant data which we desire to create for our images and pictures of reality.

This approach thus implies a sensitisation of the observer, whereby he/she is altered and is willing to be transformed in an ongoing dialogue – with whatever – which is the essence of creation and not any rigid stand of authority, expertise that leads to entropy. This transformation happens, if it is true for the anthropologist, psychotherapist and so it would be true for the scientist who wishes to study meditation and altered states of consciousness. Maybe the movement is up and down, like an hour glass or a spiral. This process of conscious awareness, involves unconscious processes, volition and the concept of the self and so on. In scale, depending on the level – where one is placed – that matter becomes consciousness and consciousness, matter. It all is real or unreal – whatever suits one's terminology.

Naturally, in the new approach (e.g., not that bodies have consciousness, but consciousness has bodies) the questions asked will radically change; how does separateness arise, if all is one; does the brain act as a filtering and reductive mechanism? No longer will one ask questions of how to integrate the universe but how does it feel separate; how to explain the interconnections – not through linear processes of the big-bang; of seeking a unified theory involving many different fields (gravitational, electromagnetic, morphogenetic, string theory, etc.) the various energies. Once, following Einstein who took light's velocity to be basic, consciousness becomes the base line and different explanations will follow – a quantum jump ! It will serve us well in individual and societal development as well. Openness to alternative theories in this scheme, explanations and healthy scepticism remains a part and parcel of it. In brief, the new approach of research scientific endeavours include both direct experience of the inner senses and the outer physical ones as a unity of consciousness; and is not based on any principle of exclusion of any human experience.

In short, the view of this paper has been to emphasise the fact that there is an urgent need to change the basic paradigm globally from a mechanistic one to holistic one in the physio-psychic realm. The split-dualistic is built into the very texture of the scientific study of matter, of thought, in all walks of life. Its limitations have to be seen in order that a unified mode is available as has been shown by particle physics, extra-galactic cosmology, through post-Einsteinian physics, and by Heisenberg and others – in the dissolution of solid matter into waves of probability. The shift indicates that Consciousness is not an epi-phenomenon of matter but the very matrix and the Context of all contexts within which everything functions, i.e., it is the way of perception itself.

When one considers the brain-body system separate from the external circumstances, then it is the old approach to considering oneself outside the picture, a mere observer. The mental setup is made up of the socio-cultural world and the individual personality is not a free independent unit with its own will to play as it wishes; this is the belief one works in the world to solve any crisis. It is like repairing a motor vehicle which is constantly involved in accidents without taking into account the fact that the driver is constantly drunk and that is where the problem ought to be looked into. If one leaves the brain-body system out of reckoning in this attempt to rectify matters, then the most important variable is left out. But one plods along as if the individual, this unit, the brain is all right and all one has to do is to cure the socio-economic conditions for the utopia to come into existence.

Now, the organism, the body-brain mechanism itself, is being hard put to understand all these goings on; it is struggling to know this state of affairs of utter conflict and contradiction since in its very depth of being it knows it is made up of all the elements of the universe. It is in fact in all of its activities trying to relate and communicate by its surroundings, the environment. But this conditioning is so deep rooted, as a separate self, as an identity that obviously it causes agony and alienation as well since it seems to give an empty feeling about one's identity. This so-called separate self unconsciously cannot really discover any solid, stable 'me' or an answer to , who am I? In normal life, all one does is to play the various social roles that are based on a reaction-reaction system within the relatedness to the other functionally given. Without the other, there is no separate identity even at the social level.

Nevertheless, since the conditioning is so strong, the brain struggles to search for its real identity and not finding one in what it has learnt within that limited dimension, it is thoroughly exasperated; it goes *berserk* despite trying to maintain some semblance to sanity, it becomes frantic, and it is in despair and totally alienated both within and without. One may ask, since the separate self has always been there, why is the turmoil so great today? Earlier, perhaps by and large individuals functioned within certain stable social setups that were not governed by rapid changes and one's position in society was relatively secure in terms of who's who and what was one's position. This gave a certain kind of stability within the given world-views which were accepted as one's context of existence in the universe. The same has no longer been true, with the beginning of the modern era in the seventeenth century and the rapid growth of industrialization, urbanization and the philosophy of cross consumerism that has become the global way of life, barring some minor exceptions. All socio-cultural boundaries have been eroded, quickly and there is no certitude even in any world-views, unless it is a reversion to fundamentalism as a last ditch battle. The brain has no time to adjust to changes occurring externally in walks of life, not excluding the environmental changes. A new order based on intrinsic equality is a long way off, just like is the case in terms of socio-political and economic equality. The different parts are not co-ordinated, especially psychologically since thought itself is based, as yet, on hierarchy and domination and subordination principles.

Thus nothing is clear even externally, in this age of transition when even the views of the cosmos are far from clear and the old ones no longer provide any adequate answers. Perhaps, these are phase-changes, like what Prigogine (Artigiani:1990) speaks of the time of dissipative structures. One can imagine the state of affairs in the brain, given the enormity of the problem briefly stated above. This is the uncertainty, and the cause of violence, upheavals since every aspects of life is destablised into several contending problems, their solutions, theories, etc. But the more weight one gives to creating artificial identities, old or new formulations, these are still not one's natural or spontaneous creations. These formulations are made more out of a sense of insecurity, clinging to a so-called reinterpreted past. These are reactive attempts which do not create security since it is a reaction to the others who also are against it as mutually dependent enemies.

The inner psyche is still looking for 'who am I?',who one is, and no amount of external solutions, in the absence of the overarching umbrella of Consciousness, will bring about any lasting peace or contentment. The organism somehow knows its true nature, or at least that what is given is not so. But in the present trance-like conditioning one continues to grope in the hope of 'tomorrow and tomorrow' little realising that mirages continuously recede and will never marterialise. The first signs of the awakening of Consciousness is to be aware of this false image, the false changes, this hope against hope, this untruth. This is the first step towards a new dimension which without being stated may bring about the 180[10] degrees transformation that is so imperative in bringing about the shift in Global Consciousness in all walks of life.

Om
That is Whole
This is the Whole
From Wholeness emerges Wholeness
Wholeness coming from Wholeness
Wholeness still remains.

Notes

1. The richest and most fundamental of all complementarities is of course that of matter and Consciousness (mind). Perhaps, Wolfgang Pauli (of the Pauli Exclusion Principle) has stated

the matter most clearly and succinctly. "To us . . . the only acceptable point of view appears to be one that recognized both sides of reality – the quantitative and the qualitative, the physical and the psychical – as compatible with each other, and can embrace them simultaneously . . . . It would be most satisfactory of all if phusis and psyche (i.e., matter and mind) could be seen as complementary aspects of reality."(1955; pp.208-10); quoted by Kothari (1986).

2. The quest for unity has taken on new poignancy in recent years, as the unstoppable sledgehammer of specialization pounds the world into smaller and smaller pieces and as humankind grows more estranged from nature. For example, the Gaia hypothesis, which proposes that the Earth is a single organism, has attracted a devout following far beyond the scientific community. Introduced in its modern version by James Lovelock (1979; 1988), who claims that the earth's atmosphere, oceans, climate, land, and living creatures are part of a giant feedback loop, which attempts to maintain conditions suitable for life (Myers: 1985). Timothy Ferris (1991) is concerned with cosmic unity since he believes that our true connectedness lies far beyond Earth, with the cosmos. Ferris envisions our relationship to the universe as hour-glass shaped. On the bottom side is the inner realm of the mind; on the top is the outer realm of animals, stars, galaxies. His work encompasses brain studies, astronomy, physics, mysticism, the "near death experience", environmentalism, information theory and so on, all in the context of mind's search for unity and cosmic connection.

3. Does unity have a reality beyond its conception? Is it that the mind must impose unity on the inner world of itself ? Could the same be true of the outer world beyond the mind? Could the unity scientists seek exist mainly in their minds? Perhaps, the unity of science consists alone in its method, not its material, as it is not the facts themselves which form science, but the method in which they are dealt with. Order, and reason, beauty and benevolence are characteristics and conceptions which we find solely associated with the mind of man, wrote Karl Pearson (1892), the founder of twentieth-century statistics, in his influential book, *The Grammar of Science*. This is much the same as Einstein said in the journal of Science(1940), "Science is the attempt to make the chaotic diversity of our sense experience correspond to a logically uniform system of thought" (Ferris, *Ibid.*).

4. The theory of quantum physics was worked out in the first three decades of the century by Max Planck, Werner Heisenberg, Erwin Schroedinger and Louis de Broglie, and that theory has been confirmed with great precision by many experiments, including the double-slit one. But no one understands the meaning of quantum physics. If it has not made the new man of science jump from his chair, it has certainly made him wonder what he was sitting on! We have learned that there is no clear line between the observer and the observed. We are connected to nature. We are part of a whole. The physicist John Archibald Wheeler calls the world as we now understand it as a "participatory universe"; i.e., that we shape the properties of the universe by our very observation of it. Not long ago, such a notion would have been dismissed out of hand by every *bona fide* scientist and many philosophers. We are not mere bystanders who probe electrons to see how they move, or who record the level of carbon dioxide in the air, or who build radio receivers to point up instead of sideways. We are part of it (Ferris, *Ibid.*).

5. Another message is that science is done by individuals who bring with them, and are influenced by beliefs. Chance events can lead to predictable outcomes. For example, the decay of a single radioactive atom is the paradigm of randomness, but the behaviour of a large lump of radioactive material can be accurately predicted. Hence, the contingency of evolution does not depend merely on the random nature of genetic mutation. It arises

because mutations have qualitative different effects, and because these effects can be amplified. This amplification of quantum events, combined with the unpredictability of the environment, makes it impossible to foretell the long-term future, although it may still be possible to explain evolution in retrospect. There is no stately Victorian notion of inevitable progress toward the Omega point. Empirically, individual lineages do not necessarily progress: they are as likely to lead to tapeworms, or to nothing at all, as to lead to man. There is no such thing as global progress; only a tendency to get better and better at whatever you happen to be doing, i.e., increasing information transmitted from generation to generation – from RNA molecules duplicating themselves to social animals and animals with language (Mayr: 1990).

6. Cassidy (1990) writes that at the age of 23, in 1925, Heisenberg laid the foundations of quantum mechanics on which all subsequent generations have built. It abandoned the basic notions of the old classic physics, such as that of electrons moving in orbits, replacing them by a much more abstract description. It is true that a year later Erwin Schroedinger published his theory of wave mechanics, which turned out to be identical in content to Heisenberg's quantum mechanics. But we needed both points of view to develop a real understanding of the physical world.

   The Bohm-Sommerfield theory, accepted before Heisenberg's paper, described electrons in the atom as revolving around the nucleus in orbits, like planets around the sun, as in classical mechanics, but only certain selected orbits were allowed. Radiation was emitted when an electron jumped from one orbit to another, and the energy loss of the electron determined the frequency (colour) of the radiation. Heisenberg discarded the concept of orbits which not in principle be observed, this was made more precise later through his uncertainty principle, and he proposed that the physicist should only deal with observable things. This meant concentrating not on single orbits, but on the emitted radiation, which comes from a jump between two orbits, so that talks of two states of the atom at a time.

   Schroedinger's wave mechanics started from a very different approach, but it also gave correct results and appeared at first to be an alternative theory. It soon proved to be the same as Heisenberg's, although expressed in a different language. After a heated discussion the correct view was expressed by Max Born that the intensity of the waves determines the probability with which the electron will be found at a given point in space. Thus physics cannot specify the position of a particle; its position is a matter of chance, with only probabilities being the subject of the physicist's description. This conclusion led Heisenberg to his "uncertainty principle", which has to do with the accuracy with which different attributes of a physical object can be known; the more precisely we want to know the position of a particle, the more uncertain must be its velocity, because the act of observation causes an unknown change in the velocity. (Gandhi: 1990).

7. Science has undergone radical revolutionary changes in its connections not only of nature but also of its own workings. It has come a long way not only from a Newtonian universe, left far behind, but even in terms of Relativity and Quantum theory with the development of "Copenhagen Interpretation". For example: 1. Planck's constant "now renders description of nature inherently stochastic". 2. Heisenberg's principle of Indeterminancy shows the impossibility of a full and complete mnemonic picture of nature". A combination of both these produces a radically new epistemology in which the scientist participates unavoidably in the picture of nature that he produces. 3. Neils Bohr's Principle of Complementarity recognizes the fundamental complexity of nature, "Forever repudiating any monolithic reduction of nature to a single level of reality describable in a single language. At the same

time, application of these ideas to chemistry and biology have revealed the importance of non-material realities, like order and structure".

In short, all these new areas in science, or a new science, talks of randomness rather determinism, complexity replaces simplicity, mind replaces matter, and aesthetic principles replace mechanical impacts. If the old goals of sciences were antithetical to the humanities or for predicting human behaviour, the new scientific "cannons respect the same values as do the humanities, while its descriptive laws may make possible an organizational paradigm that will allow history to rise to significant levels of theoretical generalities". 4. One such example is Ilya Prigogine's thermodynamics, wherein he talks of 'dissipative structures', open systems far from any equilibrium states, as earlier thought. Such a model may apply to the study of history and civilizations. Prigogine argues that dissipative structure's model the process by which matter organises itself into higher and more complex systems. The self-organization of matter, "explains the origin and evolution of living forms and also the emergence and development of the systems in which living forms are organised. The latter is said to include the course of development of eco-systems and even civilizations. The potential of Prigogine's thermodynamics for historian is immense. A science that could track the development of civilization would give us a model for the organization of our data, a way to extract meaning from the cacophony of events, and a device for explaining history". (Artigiani: 1990).

Science has been governed by Newtonian systems and Gallileo's knowledge, i.e., gathering facts to make it a whole which rested on a timeless idealization. It posited a nature made up entirely of matter and forces, forces which act on matter but do not change it, i.e., it is a static concept that does not allow nature to other qualitatively, not dynamic. In other words it was a mechanical model (as followed in history and social sciences) of nature that is indifferent to time, where potential and kinetic energy is constant so that any strictly mechanical alteration is wholly reversible. Thus Newtonian forces leave dead matter substantially the same although the positions may have changed. Newtonian sciences cannot explain the existence of scientists who create it!

Irreversibility is the key to Prigogine's revolution. If nature is irreversible then it is not indifferent to time. Time is a fundamental part of nature, not just a device for measuring nature. This means that with time built into it, a historical nature would be one in which new forms of existence could develop as a result of concrete experiences. These new forms in turn, could constitute wholly new levels of phenomena, dependent in their antecedents but not reducible to them. Dynamics would then become profound, for movement would result in qualitative change leading to increased complexity and new laws of behaviour. This like a science of systematics theory, for it would be the very evolution of a structure over time through experiences that defined the structure. The structure would be self-referential, like a work of art. Science thus absorbs the epistemology of history, for it describes nature existentially as the narrative sum of its experiences. This, in short, is Prigogine's science, rejecting monolithic idealization of nature, but embracing Bohr's Complementarity and develops different languages to describe nature in its several stages.(Aritgiani: *Ibid.*).

Dissipative structures are often thus systems exchanging matter and energy with its environment. " Because it can draw upon environmental resources it can maintain its internal order even though that order is far from equilibrium, therefore it is open to variations in environmental inputs, a dissipative structures is always vulnerable to evolutionary developments . . . .Thus structures follow function and is dependent on environmental fluctuations". In summary, dissipative structures combines freedom with order, stability with change, internal with external factors. Its self-consciously Aristotelian character describes a nature in which dynamics is significant, for now nature not only moves, it changes. Change, growth, and development are now fundamental to nature, like time. But change takes place through a process of evolution punctuated by non-linear departures occurring when a system is driven through a stage of complexity which exceeds its organizational capacities. Further, this leads to bifurcation points – catastrophes endured – continuity and discontinuity, order and transition succeed each other in ways which can never be predicted. All structures are the result of wholly random occurrences, but structures once in existence are far from a state of equilibrium, these can govern their internal behaviour and thereby sustain themselves. All these laws could be applicable to the study of history and social sciences. Prigogine's science is what matter thinks about itself, once matter gets complex enough to think, in the sense what history has not done in the very narration of it!

Prigogine's Bernard instability, of replication, all at the molecular level, all this suggests that the emergence of civilization, like a phase change, is wholly unpredictable event caused by free and creative people as they react to environmental factors. In other words, suggesting that a new civilizational structure would demand greater environmental resources than the simpler organization preceding it. In open systems many variables are involved; in this way boundary-structures being defined by the system itself and thus be defined into higher forms or be crystallised. Details of such aspects will have to be worked out in details. It is therefore a mind-effected, mind-affected world – a snake eating its tail symbol. In many in which mind transforms matter, leaving behind a template that reconstructs the creating mind in any succeeding intelligence encountering it. Works of art are obvious examples of how artist effects his work, the media; the latter effecting the artist too and the viewer as well. One could say in a similar way how technology has effected humankind albeit it was created by it, e.g., cars taking over man's organisation.

In this way a physical record of historical experience survives to program future actions, in a manner quite like the DNA molecule which is also a system of organisation. In humanity's case, its capacity to record and communicate experience symbolically that most affects behaviour. Recent social theorists have developed the idea of a cognitive map to explain the process by which environments and experience are encoded to orient behaviour. The cognitive map is a set of symbols held in the mind that represents the environment and preserves the record of ancestral experiences to deal with environmental challenges, i.e., a data bank and programme constituting the cultural complex relating to one another and their world. The maps are meant to match the environment, and like a thermostat maintains homeostasis; often the map is clumsy and seldom recognized and aware of it, i.e., people are unconscious of it, of how to use it and read it. It is only when systems of values in it are most important like the hexagons of Bernard's instability, then only transformations become possible, i.e., when knowledge and experience fuse into values they undergo phase change. If this does not happen, civilization is unable to match internal changes, and environmental changes, then do enter catastrophe phases. Being conscious of these, one can play the game or be overcome by reactions and chain of events including ways of explaining one's self. There is no meaning of history; there is meaning in history, the meaning people give to their own experiences when they map and thereby order it, i.e., it is not deterministic but self-referential, in order to test their validity. This, in order to create non-linear departures or psychologically quantum jumps which this civilization requires at this crucial juncture both historically and in terms of evolutionary goals. It may be done by self-organization, self-definition, re-definition of cultural values that are not antithetical to nature. This would bring about the necessary radical revolution so necessary for humankind today (Aritgiani: 1990).

References

Artigiani, Robert, 1990. "Thermodynamics and History", In Kishore Gandhi (ed.), *The Odyssey of Science, Culture and Consciousness*, New Delhi, pp. 112-26.

Bouissac, Paul, 1991. "Semiotics and the Gaia Hypothesis: Towards the Restructuring of Western Thought", In *Philosophy and the Future of Humanity*,Vol.1, 2. pp.168-84.

Cassidy, David C., 1990. *Uncertainty: The Life and Science of Werner Heisenberg*, W. Freeman.

de Chardin, Teilhard, P., 1959. *The Phenomenon of Man*, New York.

Ferris,Timothy, 1991. *The Mind's Sky; Human Intelligence in a Cosmic Context,* Bantam.

Gandhi, K., (ed.), 1990. *The Odyssey of Science, Culture and Consciousness*, New Delhi.

——, 1990. "The Synchronization of Science, Culture and Consciousness: The Quest for New Epistemology", In *Ibid.* pp. 21-44.

Heisenberg, Werner, 1959. *Physics and Philosophy — Glifford Lectures*, George Allen and Unwin, London.

Kothari, D.S., 1986. "Science, Culture, and Values", Mimeographed.

——, 1990. "Complimentarity Principles: Physics and Beyond", In *N.R.L. Technical Bulletin*, special issue, New Delhi, pp. 21-24.

——, 1990. "The Perception of Truth in Science and Philosophy", In Gandhi, 1990 *Ibid*, pp.44-63.

Lovelock, J., 1979. Gaia: *A New Look at Life on Earth*,Oxford.

——, 1988. *The Ages of Gaia,* London.

Malik,S.C., 1989. *Modern Civilization — A Crisis of Fragmentation*, New Delhi.

——, 1993. "Holistic Science and Consciousness", *Nature and Man-An Integral Vision* IGNCA Seminar, New Delhi, Mimeographed.

——, 1993. "A Question of Consciousness", *Future of the Mind-Mind of the Future* Seminar, New Delhi, Mimeographed.

Mayr, Ernst, 1991. *Towards a New Philosophy of Biology; Observations of an Evolutionist*, Harvard.

Myers, Norman (ed.), 1985. *The Gaia Atlas of Planet Management.*

Pauli,W., 1955. *The Interpretation of Nature and the Psyche,* edited with C.G Jung, Bolingen, New York.

Pearson, Karl, 1892. *The Grammer of Science.*

Smith, Lester, J., 1975. *Intelligence Came First*, Illinois.

Weber, Renee, 1986. *Dialogue with Sages and Scientists*, New York.

7

Matter and Magic

C.V. Vishveshwara

To quote Punch in the matter of matter,

What is matter?	—	*Never mind.*
What is mind?	—	*No matter.*

That is a light-hearted way of dismissing two of the most fundamental problems faced by scientists and philosophers. Since antiquity, the nature of matter has been studied and speculated with a view to discovering its fundamental constituents. Both theory and experiment carry an aura of magic in their ancient as well as modern versions.

Among the ancient Greeks perhaps the first one to formulate a basic constituent that could take all possible forms of matter was Thales of Miletus in the sixth century before Christ. An important criterion for such a material is its easy changeability which could be extrapolated to embrace different types of matter. Thales identified water, that would take on all the three states of matter readily, as this fundamental building material. Anaximenes, around the same time, conjectured that it was air that constituted all matter in the universe. Heraclitus, in the fifth century, found fire, with its ever changing form, to be the true candidate for this unique position. Earth was added to these three by Empedocles making up the four 'elements'.

Fire provided the energy that could change matter from one state to another consisting of the other three elements. Elements could combine or dissociate because of forces of 'love' and 'hate'.

The theory of Empedocles was strongly favoured by Aristotle who developed it further. Each of the four elements possessed two of the four properties, namely hot, cold, wet and dry. Dry and cold combined to form earth; wet and hot, air; cold and wet, water; hot and dry, fire. The qualities shared in common allowed one form to change into another.

Aristotle's choice had the unfortunate effect of arresting the development of the theory proposed by Leucippus and Democritus. Their atomic theory, surprisingly modern in its conception, had to wait more than two millennia for rebirth and recognition.

The experimental and pragmatic consequence of the theory of elements and their mutability was alchemy. Alchemy reflected the best and the worst in human nature ranging from total dedication and academic pursuit on the one hand to low charlatanism and avarice on the other. Since all matter was mutable, one should be able to change base material into gold. It was believed that this process would be mediated by the legendary Philosopher's Stone. In their quest for transmutation the alchemists supplemented the theoretical basis propounded by Aristotle with the principle of the two contraries. The two contraries were identified as Sulphur, representing fire and lightness, and Mercury, representing water and heaviness. Depending on the proportions of admixture, these two could in principle produce lead or gold which were therefore inter-convertible. Considerable part of alchemical experimentation involved Sulphur and Mercury. Another secondary objective of alchemy was to produce the "elixir of life", panacea to all human ills and the pathway to immortality. Practice of alchemy was widespread extending from Europe to China. On the one hand, alchemy involved a bizarre mixture of pictorial symbolism, allegory, astrology and sorcery. On the other hand, the serious, dedicated alchemists contributed significantly to the progress of science. This included improvements in metallurgical techniques and advancement of medicinal knowledge. Furthermore, they brought great refinement to laboratory techniques like crystallization and distillation. Alchemists' notable achievement was the discovery of new elements, namely antimony, arsenic, bismuth, phosphorus, zinc in addition to alcohol, several acids and alkalis.

Often alchemy is scoffed at for its hopeless fantasy and quackery. Just as astronomy in its early days was aided by astrology, sciences was helped by alchemy. Furthermore, the theoretical basis for alchemy was the unity of all matter, a concept towards which modern physics steadily advanced. Alchemy occupies the shadowy region between antique speculation and logical thought. Within a similar framework in the history of science one finds a towering figure that symbolises the transition from mysticism to modern science, namely Kepler.

Kepler is well-known as one of the giants who heralded mathematical method of science. But it is also known that he was deeply immersed in astrology, theological speculation and matters related to alchemy. Kepler opposed the traditional views of alchemy as championed by the English physician Rober Fludd whose model of the cosmos made links between macrocosm and microcosm through the four elements. The cosmos was in fact divided into four spheres corresponding to the four elements.

Beyond was the Empyrean and way below the Earth, the abode of the devil. Fludd believed that world-harmony could be understood only through the mysteries of alchemy. Fludd was against all quantitative measurements. Kepler sharply opposed Fludd maintaining that quantitative mathematical proof alone was the characteristic of objective science, declaring that "without mathematical demonstration I am like a blind man . . .". His laws of planetary motion were indeed perfect examples of "mathematical demonstration". But one must realize that even in Kepler this mathematicisation was a process of evolution starting from Pythagorean mysticism.

The Pythagoreans believed that the Creator or the Ordering One had structured the Cosmos — the word originally meant Order — as a harmonious whole in concordance with the symmetries and correlations intrinsic to the numbers and their geometrical representations. Stemming from this conception of the universe grew the complex mysticism of numbers and geometrical figures. Specific characteristics were attributed to them and hidden meaning read in their interrelations. For instance, five was considered to be the most important number, the symbol of health and harmony; it was the emblem of love, being the offspring of the union between the first female number two and the first male number three. Its geometric counterpart, the pentagram, exhibited so many intriguing, magical properties that it was chosen as the sign of brotherhood among the Pythagoreans. The secret knowledge originating from the Pythagoreans cascaded down the centuries along diverse channels, such as the cults of Kabbala, Freemasonry and Rosicrucianism. But never did the original geometric mysticism exercise such a profound and far-reaching influence on an individual as in the case of Kepler during his early years that witnessed his quasi-scientific fantasies slowly transmuted into the pure gold of his three laws of planetary motion.

The inspiration that fashioned Kepler's ideas and fueled his relentless explorations had its roots deep within the Pythagorean and Platonic geometric mysticism. He expounded the divine status of geometry in his *Harmonices Mundi*, the Harmony of the World. "Why waste words? Geometry existed before the Creation, is co-eternal with the mind of God, is God himself (What exists in God that is not God himself?); geometry provided God with a model for the Creation and was implanted into man, together with God's own likeness — and not merely conveyed to his mind through the eyes."

God picked as his building blocks of the universe the Platonic solids because of their perfect symmetry. It is an incredible fact, but true, that, although there can be an infinite number of symmetric two-dimensional figures, there exist five — and only five — such solids in three dimensions. In each instance, the solid is bound by faces which are themselves symmetric two-dimensional geometric figures of a particular kind. These are the tetrahedron (made of four equilateral triangles), the cube, the octahedron (eight equilateral triangles), the dodecahedron (twelve pentagons) and the icosahedron (twenty equilateral triangles). Each of these corresponded to a basic element of nature, for example, the tetrahedron with fire, the cube with earth and so on. The dodecahedron, being composed of the magical pentagons, occupied the highest place among the constituents of the universe. This represented the additional fifth element ether (*quinta essentia*) or all of space as we may call it in our modern terminology. While geometry admitted this unique set of precisely five perfect solids, was it a mere accident that nature had decreed the existence of six planets with exactly five intervals in between? Surely, this was a crucial clue to the mystery of the cosmic structure. This explained why there were six planets, no more no less. Would not the five solids decide the sizes of the planetary orbits and the order in which they had been arranged as well? The orbits could be drawn as circles or spheres either circumscribing the Platonic solids or inscribed within them. When chosen properly, the five solids seemed to fit roughly the known orbits of the six planets. Kepler was to remark on this revelation in 'the preface to the reader' of his *Mysterium Cosmographicum*. "I saw one symmetric solid after the other fit in so precisely between the appropriate orbits that if a peasant were to ask you on what kind of hook the heavens are fastened so that they don't fall down, it will be easy for thee to answer him. Farewell!"

This was only the beginning and not the end. Had Kepler ceased his probing at this stage, satisfied by the fruition of his fantasies, his name might not have found a place even in the footnotes to astronomy and cosmology. But, his scientific objectivity drove him to test and justify his model against the available astronomical data. In this venture, he was obliged to replace his two-dimensional spheres by spherical shells in order to accommodate deviations of the orbits from perfect circles — the first step towards the realization of elliptical orbits. Obsessed with the desire to prove the validity of his model, not only did he criticize Copernicus for his inexactitude, but he even dared to accuse him of deliberate cheating. Nevertheless, years of excruciatingly painstaking research finally converged on to the three famous laws of planetary motion. With these laws firmly established, the artificial scaffolding of the universe Kepler had erected could be dismantled and the true order of the cosmos revealed. The planetary orbits were asymmetric ellipses and not the ideal circles of the Greeks. On the other hand, with Kepler's work, Apollonius' *Conic Sections*, a purely intellectual creation, found its niche within the realm of cosmic reality. Plato in his *Timaeus* had described how God had created the planets as the regular keepers of time, and Kepler had now found the exact law that regulated their divine duty. In addition to all this, it was Kepler who introduced, however vaguely and hesitantly, the idea of a force — or 'soul' as he termed it — emanating from the sun and impelling the planets in their heavenly courses. Starting from the nebulous mysticism of an antique era, Kepler had unveiled the true face of the cosmos for contemplation by other giants like Newton.

Kepler's cosmic structure involving the Platonic solids that represented five elements was very much in consonance with Pythagorean-Platonic theories. It reflected the sentiment Pythagoras had expressed:

> There is geometry in the humming of the strings.
> There is music in the spacing of the spheres.

Hermann Weyl commented in his *Space, Time, Matter*: "We are overwhelmed by a feeling of freedom won — the mind has cast off the fetters which have held it captive. Our ears have caught a few of the fundamental chords from that harmony of the spheres of which Pythagoras and Kepler once dreamed."

In a way, matter through the elements had been incorporated into this geometric harmony. But the true picture of the planetary system — the macrocosm — was to be elucidated through Kepler's three laws. Concepts inherent to this system were to find their echoes in the atomic structure — the microcosm. The atomic physicist Arnold Sommerfeld wondered: "Would Kepler, the Mystic who, like Pythagoras and Plato, tried to find and to enjoy the harmonies of the Cosmos — would he have been surprised that atomic physics had re-discovered the very same harmonies in the building stones of matter, and this is even purer form?" The simple Bohr atom, even with refinements, resembled the Keplerian planetary system. Even the wave mechanical model with probability clouds of electron display harmonies that are reminiscent of both types of Keplerian models. Once again one wonders whether Kepler would be disappointed that the atom does not bear exact resemblance to his cosmic order.

Apparently Sommerfeld did not think so. After all Kepler himself had written about replacing geometrical picture by mathematical formalism in his *Astronomia Nova*, "At last, I have brought to life and found true far beyond my hope and expectations that the whole nature of harmonies in the celestial movements really exists — not in the way I thought previously, but in a completely different, yet absolutely perfect manner."

Discoveries made in the realm of nuclear structure, along with atomic theory more or less firmly established the unity of matter — the cherished dream of ages. The forces of 'love' and 'hate' have been replaced by the fundamental interactions of nature. Through them the dream of alchemists has also been achieved — namely the transmutation of elements. The neutron has turned out to be the modern day Philosopher's Stone. Atom smashers are being built with ever increasing size, strength and expenditure. These not only probe the structure of matter deeper but throw light on the unity of the fundamental forces.

The fifth element space had a long history of its own. It was Isaac Newton who for the first time, invoked the attributes of all-pervading absolute space within the context of physical laws. His ideas came under attack on both theological and physical grounds. Bishop Berkeley condemned the 'dangerous dilemma of thinking either real space is God or else there is something besides God which is eternal, uncreated, infinite, indivisible, unmutable both of which may justly be thought pernicious and absurd.' Einstein wrote, "It conflicts with one's scientific understanding to conceive of a thing which acts but cannot be acted upon." Matter had no influence on Newton's space. But, Einstein's general theory of relativity — the new theory of gravitation — completely changed this picture.

The English geometer William Clifford had envisaged 'little hills' on the otherwise flat space and visualized the passage of this spatial curvature equivalent to the motion of matter. This vision in which space, matter and geometry are interwoven was given concrete shape by general relativity. Here matter through gravitation, curves space. On the other hand, there have been attempts to describe the contents and qualities of the physical world, including matter, purely in terms of space and its attributes. "There is nothing in the world except empty curved space" wrote John Wheeler, "Matter, charge, electromagnetism and other fields are only manifestations of the curvature of space."

The grandest application of Einstein's theory lies in the description of the universe as a whole. One arrives at a curved evolving universe that started from a singular state in which density, temperature and space curvature are all infinite. This is the point of cosmic origin near which unanswered questions regarding the nature of matter and the unity of all the four fundamental forces of nature including gravitation remain as a challenge to the theorist. This is the uncharted terrain of modern alchemy.

The magic of new discoveries and the mystery of the unanswered questions hold sway as science probes even deeper into the heart of matter. The quest continues, a saga without beginning, a story without end.

8

Forms of Life in the World of Matter
Reflections on Tribal Cosmology

Baidyanath Saraswati

The following reflections are based on tribal myths of north-east India.[1] Myth[2] may be defined as a body of revelatory knowledge of the unseen reality that flows eternally in time and space. As a self-reflective and self-validating statement of the true nature of the phenomenal world, it is founded in faith that supports all knowledge. Myth, believed and lived from inside, expresses the believers' conviction of truth. It is not an empirical description of the natural phenomena; it is a symbolic expression of the experience of the mystery of cosmic existence.

The Fivefold Order

Tribal cosmogony refers to a fivefold order that sets forth the timeless sequence of creation, preservation and dissolution of the world of matter. Let us discover its fundamental intuition.

First Order is set in 'nothingness': In the beginning there was nothing, nothing at all but water, or clouds and mist, or two eggs soft and shone like gold.[3] In that state of 'nothingness', life was there above the primeval water, hidden deep in the clouds and mist, or in the two whirling eggs.

With such vibration of life, the beginning was not an absolute vacuity.

Second Order causes primary creation of elements from the element of the First Order.

The First creation was asexual: The golden eggs collided and both broke open. From the one came the earth, from the other the sky.[4] Subsequently, creation became a male-female principle: When the sky made love to earth, every kind of tree, grass and all living creatures came into being.[5]

The world was created in phases by a number of vibrant bodies and not by a single creator: The order of creation began with the formless spirits,[6] and then the sun-moon[7] and all the rest. At first there were two or four or eight or nine suns of an unbearable brightness. The radiance of one of them was gradually reduced to the cool and gentle light of the moon.[8]

The early phases of creation were marked by total integration of all that exists; there was no difference between man and non-man.[9]

Every element has its own life. Elements of nature are interrelated.[10]

What activates or transforms matter is the transcendent life, but life itself is not matter.

Third Order causes natural identity and differentiation in terms of colour, direction and form. Smell is another element of the Third Order. It makes communication between the form and the formless possible.[11]

Fourth Order causes the return to primordial state: Water is the self-existing element from which all other elements originate and to which they all return.[12]

Dissolution is a process of regeneration or rejuvenation, not chaos or disorder.

Fifth Order is the order of all orders: It creates the scenario of the world in which everything has its proper place, and everything grows and allows others to grow. It is inviolable.

Cosmic Intelligence revealed itself: The universal knowability lay in the cosmic eggs. Priests of all creatures were born at the beginning of creation.[13] Primordial knowledge came to man from birds and animals.[14]

Not a single event takes place without any cause. As there is a cause, so there is an effect or viceversa. Cause can be found, but not under ordinary condition. Through rituals one may return to the primordial conditions of life represented in such form as an egg (unmanifest), cowrie-shell (manifest water), hen (manifest earth) and rice (life-maintaining substance) to determine the cause.[15]

Consciousness is created by Cosmic Intelligence (Hiranyagarbha). Patterns of cultures are derivative expressions of cosmic forms.

The Pluriverse

This world of matter is continuous with the other world or worlds. There are also transition zones filled by primordial water.[16]

Life in this world is repeated in the other world, in a similar order.[17] Worlds are communicable.[18]

Of the other worlds some are structured up in the sky, and others down below the earth.[19] Earth is the *axis mundi* of the pluriverse.

The Same Life But Different Forms

Four operant ideas emerge from tribal cosmogony: (i) That life, as primal energy, manifests itself from 'nothingness' and is hence indestructible; (ii) that forms of the primordial elements such as water, fire, earth, sky and air are predetermined, and they in turn determine the form of the creatures of the Second Order; (iii) that life is the source of origin of all, but forms are different; and (iv) that the reality of the subtler plane is responsible for the grosser plane.

Transcendental creation is the primal process of bringing the form and the life together. Life is self-existent, and hence indestructible; forms are predetermined. Both are intrinsically related.

The predetermined forms of species are filled by matter, that is, primal elements of earth, water, sky, etc. Each form is thus a microcosm.

Form is natured by life; but life itself is formless. By entering into a form, life acquires qualitative distinctions in terms of species or form.[20] The same life is called by different names.[21]

There are stages in the formless existence of life.[22] What retains the breath of life in man, animal and other creatures is the same; it is often identified as soul or spirit.

The physical form, or the state of matter, can alone be seen growing, weathering and converting into new forms. But the behaviour of life during its transcendental transformation as a formless substance cannot be empirically verified. Transition in matter does not cause transition in life. What happens in the situation is the translocation of life from one form to another and from form to the formless or vice versa.[23] The same life may concurrently be present in two forms.[24]

As a substance, life gives expressions to different forms of matter. In a formless state it performs wide ranging functions: Formation (creation), affirmation (preservation) and negation (dissolution) of elements.

Annotation

The following may be taken as proper annotation for tribal viewpoint on forms of life in the world of matter.

A fivefold order governs the cosmos.

In the beginning there was nothing. The primal 'nothingness' was not an absolute vacuity: As thought comes from the unthought, the manifest comes from the unmanifest. The unmanifest encompasses the vibration of life.

The first principle of the cosmos is "one-two-and many". Creation was originally asexual, but subsequently it became a male-female principle. There is no single creator. A creature becomes creator of another creature. This interrelatedness of creature-creator makes the cosmos the one undifferentiated reality. The world came into existence in phases. The early phases were characterized by total integration of all elements. Creation causes differentiations; dissolution is the return to primordial state of undifferentiation. There is no intrinsic disorder in nature.

The world of matter is continuous with the other world or worlds. Earth is the *axis mundi* of the pluriverse. Source of life is not matter, but what activates, or transforms, matter is life. Life is self-existing and self-expressing; forms are predetermined and transitory. Both are intrinsically related. Transcendent life is the cause; form its effect. Matter fills the form but form itself is not matter. Life expresses the unity of all; but forms are different. The same life exists in a formless state as also in many different forms.

Tribal epistemological thought is characterized by the assumption that patterns of life and culture are derivative expressions of the cosmic forms.

Notes

1. Cosmogenic myths discussed in this presentation are taken from Elwin (1968).
2. Panikkar (1983) has set standard for hermeneutic interpretation of myth. My own initial understanding of myth has come largely from his works, but he is in no way responsible for any unclarity that one may find in the present formulation.
3. Cf. Elwin, *op. cit.* 9-24, see specially the myths of Bori, Hill Miri, Khampti, Nockte, Singpho, and Hrusso (Aka).
4. *Ibid.,* 17, see Hrusso (Aka) myth.
5. *Ibid.*
6. *Ibid.,* 20, see Nocte myth.
7. *Ibid.,* 40-63, see Dhammai (Miji), Idu Mishmi, Kawan Mishmi, Singpho myths.
8. *Ibid.*, 48, 50, 59, 62.
9. There are many stories of marriage of human beings with gods, spirits, animals (real animals, not human beings in disguise or under enchantment) as well as leaves, trees and even fire. *Ibid.,* 108-48. Thus in tribal perception, man is not unique in his origin.
10. The earth and sky are a divine couple and a universal parent. Fire and whirlwind are brothers just as water and mist are brothers. But water and fire have always been enemies. Wind is the friend of fire against water and he fights the rain and drives it before him. (Saraswati, 1992).
11. The medium of interaction between the Ongees and the spirit world is the smell, kept in the ancestral bone which the Ongees wear as an ornament. It is the smell that keeps the Ongees in the island and the spirits in the sky and the sea. (Pandya, 1991).

12. Cf. Elwin, *op. cit.* 15-22, see Gallong, Sherdukpen, Taraon Mishmi, Singpho.
13. The Dafla myth reveals that Tarangum Sung Sung was the ancestor of all priests. There are priests of men, priests of the earth, priests of god and spirits, and priests of tigers and all animals. *Ibid.*, 76.
14. *Ibid.*, 105 (Hill Miri), 213 (Wancho, Singpho, Bori). Tribal myths deny the uniqueness of man in the possession of knowledge.
15. When a Khasi suffers any affliction, he performs his rituals with the aid of Ka Shanam (cowries, rice grains, an egg, or a hen) to find out the cause of affliction (Mawrie, 1981: 32).
16. The Ao Nagas believe that there is the world of the dead souls (Asuyim). In between the world of the dead and the world of the living there is a boundary line. The boundary line is a river called *Longritzu* (bitter water). (Ao, 1980: 64). Miris also believe that their world is not the only one. Other worlds are known to exist and their limits are determined (Hamilton, 1912: 87). Hindu scriptures mention the pluriverse. There are five worlds (*Loka*) up in the sky with *Brahmaloka* as the highest, earth in the middle, and seven netherworlds inhabited by demons and serpent-spirits.
17. According to the Ao Nagas, life in the village of the dead is like life on the earth, except that in the village of the dead there is no sexual intercourse and no social organization (Ao, *op. cit.,* 65). The Apa Tanis make the two worlds similar, even in conjugal and occupational contexts. In the world of the dead called Neli, every woman returns to her first husband, but those who died unmarried may there marry and beget children. Life in Neli is similar to life on this earth: people cultivate and work, and ultimately they die once more and go to another land of the dead. (Furer-Haimendorf, 1953: 37). Tribal eschatology reveals that the ontological experience of life and death is the same. Death brings to man only a new existence. The errant soul moves on in the cosmos from one abode to another.
18. Khasis believe that in the days when righteousness prevailed there was a tree which served as ladder to the original sixteen families for their communication between heaven and earth. This tree grew on top of U Lum Sohpetbneng (the navel peak of the heaven) which is the centre of the world. This tree formed the golden bridge ensuring physical contact between man and god till the time when transgression became the order of the day and this bridge gave way. Thus destroying the communication link between heaven and earth (Mawrie, *op. cit.,* 33-34).
19. Among the Nagas there is a belief that if one leads a good and worthy life upon the earth after his death his soul (*Mangla*) fly away into the realms above, to a higher place of life and becomes a star (Horam, 1980: 60). There is a common belief all over India that the hell is located beneath the earth.
20. The Nagas believe that the soul does not die with the death of his body. If a man has led a bad life he has to pass through seven stages of spirit-life and ultimately transformed into insects like bees, locusts and butterflies (*Ibid.*). The same life but different forms and formless stages.
21. What retains the breath of life in man and other creatures is called by various names (Yalo, Aith, Lumpu, Mangla) which may be placed in the category of soul.
22. According to the Hill Miri, when a man dies his 'soul', the *Yalo*, is carried away by the Wiyu, (spirit) who has caused his death. The *Yalo* retains, or resumes, the human shape of a different order after it has left the Wiyu's house and made its way to the land of the Dead when it becomes an Orum or ghost. (Elwin, *op. cit.,* 303).
23. After death, man's life may assume the form of animal or birds or insects. In a formless state, the same life may exist as soul or spirit of various kinds.

24. In the Naga villages some men are believed to have the soul of a tiger. If the tiger is wounded the man who possesses the soul of that tiger also gets wounded instantly and no sooner the tiger dies the soul of that man departs. Whatever happens to man also happens to the tiger with a common soul. (Personal communication from my Naga students).

References

Ao, P.J., (1980). "The 'Here-After'; Traditional Ao Nagas", In *Religion and Society of North-East India*, (ed.). Sujata Miri, New Delhi.

Elwin, Verrier, (1968). *Myths of the North-East Frontier of India*, Shillong.

Furer-Haimendorf, C. von, (1953). "The after-life in Indian Belief". In *Journal of the Royal Anthropological Institute*, LXXIII: 37.

Hamilton, Angus, (1912). In *Abor Jungles*.

Horam, M., (1980). "Naga Religion: a Case Study", In *Religion and Society of North East India*, (ed.) Sujata Miri, New Delhi.

Mawrie, H.O., (1981). *The Khasi Milieu*, New Delhi.

Pandya, Vishvajit, (1991). "Tribal Cosmology: Displacing and Replacing Process in Andamanese Places", In *Tribal Thought and Culture: Essays in Honour of Shri Surajit Chandra Sinha*, (ed.) Baidyanath Saraswati, New Delhi.

Panikkar, R., (1983). *Myth, Faith and Hermeneutics: Cross-Cultural Studies*, Bangalore.

Saraswati, Baidyanath, (1992). "Cosmogenic Myths and the Forces of Nature", Paper presented at the seminar on Perception of *Bhutas* (Elements) in Oral Tradition. IGNCA, New Delhi.

9

The Panca Mahabhutas

P.G. Lalye

Ancient Sanskrit texts have dwelt on the problem of origin of universe as a problem of cosmogony. While trying to establish that the origin of the gross world is the subtle Absolute Spirit, they have given certain stages of evolution – the transformation real or apparent – of the Absolute into the gross natural objects.

The elemental matter or the five *Bhutas* or *Mahabhutas* as they were termed and, though independent, evolves from some Original cause, are supposed to mix with each other in certain proportion, thus giving rise to the different basic objects of the nature.

The *Brahmanas* (Literature) for the first time, enumerated the five principles. They gave the five names of the *Bhutas*, which were also called five *Purusa*. They were described as constituting the gross manifested universe. Sometimes they are called five *Sattvas* or the primary forms of matter.[1]

The *Brahmanas* went a step further by declaring that the five *Bhutas* or *Mahabhutas* are integrally connected with five senses of human beings. They also declared the whole creation as arising out of 'motion'.

The *Brahmanas*[2] also recognized three aspects of the above-mentioned motion.

(1) *Gati* – Movement from the centre to the circumference
(2) *Sthiti* – This is the controlling centre of *Agati* and *Gati*
(3) *Agati* – Stationery position.

This approach shows that the doctrine of motion, arose out of the concern of the *Brahmanas* for giving an account of the origin of matter having various characteristics.

Later in the *Upanisads* we find a further development of this 'motion'. They have tried to point out the relation between the elements, in figurative matter, (in the spirit of *Bandhuta*) which was a common respectable approach of the *Brahmana-Upanisadic* thinkers. One *Upanisad* says:

The Earth is the first form;
Heaven is the counter form or the ultimate form;
Space (or *Akasa*) is the union;
wind or air is the medium or agency of that union.[3]

There is some discussion about the other categories also.[4]

In some passages five forms of union are described, which try to explain –

(1) Creation as due to actions of divine beings;
(2) Creation due to the power of esoteric knowledge;
(3) Creation due to some union of Cosmic Sex;
(4) Creation due to *Atman*, or man as the Centre.[5]

In the same spirit of *Bandhuta*, of identifying the constituents in a mystic manner, one of the *Upanisads* has dilated upon the *Vaisvanaravidya*.[6] The propounder of that sacred Mystic Lore (*Vidya*) is Asvapati, who has taught that Heaven, Sun, Wind, Ether, Water and the Earth are only the different aspects of *Atmavaisvanara*, who is to be viewed as all-comprehending totality of all these. This is the developed form of more or less identical teaching with the same personnel and the same categories found in one of the *Brahmanas*.[7] Asvapati also points out that the real *Vaisvanara* fire is the cosmic *Purusa*.

The very epithet *Atman* is suggestive, inasmuch as the *Atman* eats, swallows, absorbs the different elements, which constitute the objective world.

Some *Upanisads* describe what may be called the graded creation, in which the five *Mahabhutas* are supposed to have been emanated from the earlier category, one by one. From the undifferentiated infinity, air, fire and other elements were created.[8] Figuratively, the Infinite is thought to be a river of five streams from five sources.[9] It is one of the earlier references to the interrelations of the gross universal objects, the vital air (*Prana*) and the sense functions. There –

(a) the five senses represent the streams;
(b) the five elements are the five sources;
(c) the five *Pranas* represent the waves;
(d) the five sense objects, viz., sound, touch, colour, taste, smell are called whirlpools, as the individual soul gets involved in them.

In the post-Upanisadic period the *Samkhya* philosophy dominated the field. The *Purusa-Prakrti* dichotomy was accepted, along with the doctrine of the *Gunas* and *Bhutas*. It was accepted *mutatis mutandis* by the Epics, the *Puranas*, and the *Smrti* works. While elaborating the *PrakrtiVikrti* doctrines, the sixteen were supposed to be *Vikrti* – which include five senses of cognition, five senses of action, mind and five elements. While describing the stages in the Evolution, the order is given as follows

– *Prakrti-Mahat* (*buddhi*) = *Ahamkara*, the five subtle elements (the *tanmatras*) – the five gross elements – *Akasa*, *Vayu*, *Tejas*, *Ap*, *Prthivi* – the five senses, the five organs of action and the mind. The creation process is also given systematically.[9(a)]

Each succeeding gross element has more properties than the succeeding one because of the larger number of *tanmatras* fashioning it.

In *Karika* 38,[10] it is told that the subtle elements are non-specific. From these five, proceed the five gross elements. These five gross elements are known as specific beings, tranquil, terrific and stupefying.

On account of the Supreme authority of the Nature over everything, the subtle body the (*linga deha*) acts through the connection with the means and their results. The subtle body plays its part with the *Nimittas* (causes).[11]

The divisions of organic and inorganic mental and non-mental are divisions from the object point of view. The *Samkhya* order of creation suggests that every individual is a composite one, so far as the five elements and their transformations are concerned. The creations etc. are applicable mostly to empirical variants of the universe, which are generally categorized under *Prakrti*, (which is also termed as *Svabhava*, *Maya*, in many texts).

Thus, *Prakrti* is the prius of the whole material and psychical order of phenomena. Though *Prakrti* is numerically one singular entity it is by no means a simple homogeneous substance. It is the union of opposites. It consists of three elements viz., *Sattva*, *Rajas*, and *Tamas*, which are by their nature and functions opposed to one another. This opposition is kept in check, when *Prakrti* is in its pure state of equilibrium prior to evolution. *Sattva* is primarily responsible for self-maintenance and self-manifestation of *Prakrti*. *Rajas* is the cause of all activity. *Tamas* is responsible for inertia and restraint of activity. These three elements have different expressions in the material and in the psychical plan.

The order of evolution which occurs in and through *Prakrti*, is determined and justified by a logical necessity. The different stages reached in the course of evolution are also regarded as different categories. The whole process of evolution is summed up in terms of twenty-four categories, of which *Prakrti* is the primal and the initial limit. It is the uncaused cause and (so-called) the first original cause. The final limit or terminus or evolution is furnished by the five gross elements, the five cognitive organs, the five organs and mind. But in between these two limits, there are seven categories, viz., *Mahat* or *Buddhi*, which is the material counterpart and revealer of pure consciousness, the principle of egoity and five superphysical elements (Potentials). These seven categories possess the dual characteristics (*tanmatra*) of being evolutes and evolvents in their turn. The intellect is the first evolute from the primordial *Prakrti* and is the evolvent of the egoity. Egoity in its turn is the evolute of intellect and is the evolvent of five subtle elements – sound, touch, colour, taste, smell and the eleven organs. The five subtle elements are the evolutes of egoity and the evolvents of five gross elements, viz., ether, air, fire, water and earth. These twenty-four categories comprise among them the entire realm of reality. The spirit (*Purusa*) is, however, neither the cause nor the effect of anything else and thus stands apart and aloof from the course of evolution.

According to the *Samkhyas*, the effect must be existent in the cause, because a non-entity cannot be produced. Choice of material implies the previous existence of the effect. Again, production is not arbitrary, production means the manifestation of an attribute, implicitly present in the substance and cessation connotes the relapse of the manifested attribute into the unmanifest state. Causality presupposes determinate capacity of the cause to produce a determinate effect. This capacity can come into play only if there is a relation between it and what is produced. The very possibility of causality implies that the effect must be existent in the cause. *Prakrti* is thus ultimate causal ground of the whole flux of phenomenal order.

The *Guna* domination over the *Prakrti* evolution is quite apparent. The *Tanmatras* possess physical characteristics like penetrability, pressure, heat, capacity for cohesive attraction. They also possess the potentials of the energies represented by sound, touch, colour, taste, and smell.

These potentials are within the subtle matter. They undergo transformations by new groupings before they act as stimuli to the gross matter.

From the *Bhutadi*, different *Tanmatras* are generated, which have only the potential power of affecting our senses. The fivefold classification of the elements is not based on any chemical principle, but from the point of view of the five senses, through which their knowledge comes to us.

The five classes of items are generated from the *Tanmatras*. Sound potential and (*Akasa*) touch potentials and combine with the vibratory particles to generate *Vayu*-atom. The light and heat potentials combine with touch potentials and sound potentials to produce the *Tejas*-atom. The taste potentials combine with light, heat, touch and sound potentials to generate *Ap*-water and the smell potentials combine with the preceding potentials to generate the earth-atom. They possess the qualities as follows:

Akasa	—	Penetrability
Vayu	—	Impact or mechanical pressure
Tejas	—	Radiant heat and light
Ap	—	Viscous attraction
Prthivi (Earth)	—	Cohesive attraction

According to the *Vedanta*, which generally follows the *Samkhya* School, the creation process is dormant in Nature or *Prakrti*. It becomes active or productive when it comes into contact with the sentient, but Inactive *Purusa*. In the evolutes of *Prakrti*, mention should be made of five elements (*Mahabhutas*) and five subtle elements (*Tanmatras*).

This amalgam of the five elements is a point often discussed in *Vedanta* texts. The elements amalgamate with each other in certain proportion. Every element contains half or 50 per cent of its own and the rest of the half is of other four elements generally 1/8 of each (*Pancikarana*).

In the second chapter of *Pancadasi*, it is told that if *Brahman* is to be comprehended, it can be comprehended indirectly through its adjuncts. It is told that from *Prakrti*, dominated by *Tamas*, Five *Bhutas* emanate, by the order of the Almighty. Through the *Sattva* aspects of Ether etc. five organs of cognition emanate. They adopt the properties of their causes, ether and others.

The mind is the activator of all the ten organs. The existential characteristics are to be understood through the *Sastras* and also through deductive reasoning.

All the rules of change as variations are not applied to the Highest *Brahman*, because it is free from *Svagata*, *Svajatiya*, and *Vijatiya* differences. Names and forms are superimposed on *Brahman*.

The *Akasa* is the first *Karya* or the effect of *Maya*. Thus the elements and elemental creations are transitory according to *Advaita Vedanta*. The properties like touch, motion and speed are those of Air. The *Sattva*, *Nistattvarupa* and sound are derived from *Sat*, *Maya*, *Akasa* respectively. When Air is separated from *Sattva*, through discretion, nothing original of Air remains. This is due to *Maya*. The sound is the nature of Ether. The discretion enlightens us and makes us cognize the right or correct properties of Air etc.[12]

Like this by intelligent discretion, the *sat* can be separated from many properties of Fire. All other are false.[13]

Pancadasi gives its own ideas about the mutual amalgamation of the five elements. For example, Air absorbs some qualities from *Sat*, *Maya*, *Akasa* (Ether) and permeates some portion of *Maya*, which in turn permeates some portion of ether. Air occupies some portion of ether; fire that of air. This methodology of mutual amalgamation shows that cause has got a wider canvas than that of Effect. The occupied portion is only about 10 per cent.

The elemental creation is described in the *Vedantaparibhasa* which adopts the "*Samkhya* Theory".[14]

The *Nyaya-Vaisesika* system defines Substance as that in which qualities and actions inhere. There are nine substances — the five *mahabhutas*, time, space, spirit (*Atman*) and mind. The first five are called physical substances and each of them has a peculiar quality as given earlier. There is a psychological sense with the physical sense-organ, which is a part of the physical body. Earth, water and fire are perceptible; air and ether are inferred from the qualities.

Of the twenty-three qualities, air possesses nine, fire possesses eleven, water has fourteen, Earth has fourteen, *atman* has fourteen, time and space five each.[15] The *Tanmatras* have got a peculiar role to play on the physical level. The *Vedanta* and the *Samkhya Yoga* schools believe that the stuff of the gross elements, seen in earthly objects is a transformation of the stuff constituting the subtle elements (*Bhutas*). The psychological senses and their respective objectives are the polarizations of the subtle forms of the elements (*Devatas*) and the subtle elements as such are the manifestations (say *Rasmi, amsu*) of the potentialities of the *Atman* and are co-extensive with the *Atman*. They are the patterned, potential forces of the cosmos.

These elements are the infinite potencies of polarization lying latent. The *Vedanta* position is that these elements are derived — one out of other, while the *Samkhyas* maintain that the subtle elements evolve out of the ego (*Ahamkara*) independently of one another and get transformed into the gross elements, and instead of belonging to the cosmic person, they belong to *Prakrti*. The subtle elements thus can be treated as the transcendental grounds of the substance quality or substance property manifestations. The subtle elements are the evolutes, the potential evolutes, from the attributes according to the *Samkhya* theory.

According to *Nyaya-Vaisesika* school, the empirical world is constituted of the imperishable atoms of Earth, Water, Light and Air. They also enumerate Ether, Time and Space with them. The God is only the intelligent cause, who keeps order in the Nature. The creation is absolutely an *ab ovo* process.[16]

The *Saiva* School explains the phenomenon of creation as follows:

At the time of creation, vibration also termed as *Maya*, starts in the Absolute. In this super vibration, the three *Gunas* are generated. The *Sattva* indicates consciousness, *Tamas* inertia and *Rajas* a combination of both. There the five *Bhutas* are present in subtle form. For vibration some space is required which is provided by ether. It has sound as its property. The vibratory movement is obviously unsteady. It is the nature of wind. When the vibration is in the state of appearance, it is soft, being subtle. Viscosity is the nature of water. The lack of knowledge or consciousness of it is the veritable toughness of the Earth. So, it is said that the *Gunas* and the five *Bhutas* are present in the vibration in a subtle form. Later, the five elements are separated from the *Tamas* and attain distinct nature. The original state of equilibrium of the *Gunas* create agitation among the *Gunas*, when all the *Gunas* become manifest along with their capacities — cognition, activity and substance.

The substance capacity is in the form of five *Bhutas*, which manifests in the following order — Ether, Wind, Light or Fire, Water and Earth.[17]

The Ether (*Akasa*) encompasses in itself, the reality of the *Brahman* and the unreality of *Maya*, as *Akasa* is smaller than *Maya* by one degree. Void, Emptiness and sound are the characteristics of Ether. From *Akasa*, *Vayu* or Air emanated. Air also is marked by *Brahman*, *Maya*, *Akasa* with their real and unreal, sound aspects. In addition, it has got the quality of Touch. Air is less permeative than *Akasa* by one degree and it is unsteady. From Air, Fire is born. It has got all the earlier qualities, with the addition of Form. Fire is less permeative than Air by ten degrees. From Fire, Water is created. In addition to all the qualities of the earlier causes, it has got Taste as the additional one. Moreover it has got two more qualities, Softness and Fluidity. Water is less permeative than Fire by ten degrees. From water, Earth is born. It has got smell as an additional quality. In addition to all those it has got three more qualities, Hardness, Substance and Smell. Earth is less permeative than water by ten degrees.

Though these *Bhutas* are lesser in permeation than the previous ones, they are more and more permeative as far as inertia is concerned. The qualities also increase gradually. They can be enumerated as follows:

Ether	Sound
Air	Sound, Touch
Fire or Lustre	Sound, Touch, Form
Water	Sound, Touch, Form, Taste
Earth	Sound, Touch, Form, Taste, Smell

Maya is one of the bonds of the soul. It provides the soul with the means, locations, and objects of enjoyment called *Bhogyakanda*.

Kashmir Saivism observes that the appearance of the universe in creation is due to the self-limitation of the divine power and dissolution follows from the self-assertion of the same power. *Prakrti* is one of the thirty-six principles which includes the five *Bhutas* also.

Just as light and heat coexist in fire, in the same way universal *Ahmta* and freedom or *Sakti* coexist in *Caitanya*. This freedom is *Maya* which though essentially identical with *Caitanya*, brings out varieties of infinite kinds.

Prakrti with which the lower creation begins is indeed the assemblage of the dispositions and tendencies (*Vasanas*) of all persons with various and beginningless *Karmas*. This *karma-vasana* or *Prakasa* is threefold.

An important *Tantra* text – *Saradatilaka*, shows the origin of the manifested world from Paramesvara to *Nada*.[18] It gives a lucid account of the creation of the universe, in its own terminology.

During creation, the first manifestation is that of *Sakti*, characterized by will which is the first evolute. It is a spontaneous act, like the appearance of the oil out of the seeds. The void is termed as *Maya*. The vision of void is accompanied by an indistinct sound called *Paranada*, which fills the entire state. *Nada* is of the nature of light. Generally *Tantras* recognize that sound and light co-exist.

The next step is represented by the concentration of this diffused light sound into a focus, called *Bindu*. The creative principles are evolved out of this supreme *bindu*. *Bindu* subsequently breaks into three *Bindu*, *Bija*, and *Nada*. In *Bindu* Siva aspect predominates, in *bija* Sakti, in *Nada* both are of equal strength.

It is the *Kala* which breaks the equilibrium of *bindu*.

The causal state of *Brahman* is represented by *Sabda Brahman* or Kulakundalini, figured as a triangle consisting of *Bindu*, *Bija*, and *Nada*.

Matter is regarded as the collective organism or collocation, consisting of the four-fold substratum of colour, smell, taste and contact. The qualities of all the *Mahabhutas* are inherent in the *Paramanus*. The special characteristics of roughness, viscousness, heat, movableness combine together to form each of the elements. The difference between the different elements consists only in this that in each of them its own special characteristics, though present, remain only in a potential form. The mutual existence of material things is due to the quality of earth so inherent in them; the mutual attraction of things is due to moisture or the quality of water and so forth. When the *Prakrti* is disturbed, the three *Gunas*, appear along with their potentialities. The *Tamas* has got power of materialization from which the five *bhutas* emanate. The five elements are permeated by the three *Gunas*. From the *Sattva* emanate Ear, skin, eyes, tongue and nose from the distributory aspect and *Antahkarana* as the unitary aspect. From the *Rajas* the five *Karmendriyas* evolve in distributory aspect, but in unitary aspect, when the elements are indeterminate (*avyakta*) and they are subtle.

The elements become gross and materialized through the process of *Pancikarana*. In that process every element is equally divided into two halves; one half is kept in the self same *bhuta* and the other half is further divided with four equal parts and each is allocated to each of the remaining four.[19]

The doctrine of the five *Bhutas* is more or less accepted by the *Puranas*. The *Puranas*, have mostly adopted *Samkhya* terminology while describing the creation of the matter through evolution. One special mention, however, should be made, regarding the *Purana* ideas about the creation. *Bhagavata*, for example, has mentioned that the Almighty plays a positive role in activating the five elements, senses, mind and the *Gunas*, to fashion out a body for their own purpose. It is told that the five elements got themselves interrelated with (*Samhatya*) each other through Casual relations, and created *Pinda* and *Brahmanda*. The *Brahmanda* origin of the creation is mostly concerned with sentient human beings, the first of which was *Virat*. Various categories and regions emanated from the limbs of *Virat*.[20]

In the *Guna*-graded creation, it is told that *Tamasa* the origin of the five *bhutas*, had some commotion. Then *Akasa* was born, and the creation of the subsequent *Bhutas* took place after the same pattern. This pattern of creation can be illustrated in a tabular form as follows:

The Category	*The Element*	*Cause*	*Quality*
Undergoing Commotion stris Initiated by *Kala* Action (*karma*)	Produced *Karma* *Mahat*	*Rajas-Tamas*	*Jnana* *Dravya* also
	Tamas Ego		called *Ahamkara*

(It is to be understood that the Time created stir in the three *Gunas*, the Nature transformed them and *karma* gave birth to *Mahat*).

Movement in	*due to Accretion in*	*Transformation from*	
Mahat	*Sattva, Tejas*	*Tamas three fold Ahamkara*	
		Vaikarika - Jnana	*Tanmatra*
	Taijasa - Kriya		
		Tamas - Dravya	
Tamasa Ahamkara	Stress exertion	*Akasa*	*Sabda*
Akasa	—	*Vayu*	*Sparsa* and *Sabda*
Vayu	*Kala, Karma Svabhava*	*Tejas*	*Rupa, Sabda, Sparsa*
Tejas	*Tejas*	*Jala*	*Rasa, Rupa, Sabda, Sparsa*
Jala	—	*Prthivi*	*Gandha, Rasa, Rupa, Sabda, Sparsa*
Vaikarika Ahamkara	Movement, Stress Exertion	*Manas*, Ten Superintending deities of ten senses	

Taijasa	Stress, Exertion	Five senses of cognition and five senses of action.	*Buddhi* + *Prana*

We find another reference to *Virat* in the same *Purana*[21]. In a discourse to Vidura, the sage Maitreya reiterates that on observing that *Mahat* and other powers are unable to create anything due to their independent or disintegrated nature, the Lord himself entered into that group of twenty-three. This stimulated the *Adrsta* of the individual souls, and created *Virat* out of those twenty-three principles.

There are certain modern or 'Later' versions *Pancikarana*, mostly effected by the Saint poets of India. Here a specimen is given. It is propounded by Hamsarajaswami of Maharashtra (1805-55).

In the table[22] given below air is divided into five types of *Prana* and each element is connected with *Jnanendriya*, *Karmendriya* and *tanmatra*.

Elements	*Ether*	*Air*	*Lustre*	*Water*	*Earth*	*Function*
Ether	*Antahkaran*	*Vyana* (moving throughout body)	Ear	Speech	Sound	Hearing & Speaking
Air	Mind	*Samana* helping (Digestion)	Skin	Hands	Touch	Touch, giving, taking
Lustre	Intellect	*Udana* (Taking food etc. upwards)	Eyes	Feet	Form	Seeing & Walking
Water	*Citta*	*Prana* (Air inhaled and exhaled)	Tongue	Penis	Flavour	Eating and enjoyment
Earth	Ego	*Apana* (Air passing through lower parts)	Nose	Rectum	Smell	Smelling, excreting

In this running account about the Five *Mahabhutas,* one fact clearly emerges. The Universal categories are indivisible five elements, which themselves emanate in a particular order, the earlier one being the cause of the latter one. Each evolute has certain *Guna*, which itself absorbs some potentials of other elements. The *Akasa* is quite comprehensive and permeating element. It has given rise to a doubt. (The word *Akasa* is generally translated as Sky, ether, space. The *Upanisads* use the word mostly in the sense of Vast space. A question may be put. How can the vast eternal space, equated with the *Atman* or *Brahman*, be deemed to have produced air?).

Akasa is described as permeating, eternal and having sound as quality. In the later works, it is described to have been created from the *Sabda* potential. It is obvious that *Akasa Bhuta* cannot be supposed to be indivisible. The permeating *Akasa* can never be the material (*Samavayi* or *Upadana*) cause of the sound, as there cannot be any harsh impact on the space to produce the sound. Moreover *Vayu* and other elements cannot be produced from the infinite *Akasa*. A way out can be suggested. Just as the atoms of other *Bhutas* are disjuncted at the time of deluge (*Mahapralaya*), the atoms of *Akasa* must also be supposed as segregated. Thus *Akasa* may be taken to be *Mahakosa* whose material cause (*Upadana*) is the *Sabdatanmatra*. It has not the contact with *Sparsa* potential. There is no difficulty in accepting that the harsh impact, as the Logicians believe, is the Contact between quarters, Time and *Atman*, though they do not have *Sparsa* potential.

With the movement in the atoms (termed as *Arambhaka Samyoga*), the gross space is formed. This *Akasa* has got the potential of sound only, as *Akasa* does not have any contact *(Upastambha Samyoga*) with other *Bhutas.*

We may conclude by saying that the term *Bhuta* comes from the root *Bhu* which connotes existence. Moreover, those which are called *Bhutas* are prone to be converted into effect *Karya*. This distinguishes the *Bhuta* from *Sati*. The various schools of philosophy take the word to mean an eternal material cause (*Upadana*). They are also the inherent cause of the qualified substances and so, Time, Space, *Atman*, and mind are not reckoned as *Bhutas*. The five *Mahabhutas* give rise to five subtle elements (*Tanmatras*).

A verse in *Ayurveda* work defines *Bhuta* as follows:

> न जायतेन्यतो यत्तु यस्मादन्यत् प्रजायते।
> सगुणानामुपादानं तद्भूतमिति कथ्यते।

This definition is more succint:

> नित्यत्वे सति गुणवत्समवायिकारणत्वं भूतत्वम्।

The essential qualities of Earth, etc. are manifest in the elements. While those of the other four are unmanifest the senses can cognize (or have cognition of) the special material (*Upadana*) quality, as for example, light (*Tejas*) is the chief material – of the Eye. Light's quality is form; therefore, Eye can grasp form only.

Moreover, a synthesis was sought to be achieved by the *Ayurveda* writers, by recognizing six *Dhatus,* i.e., Five *Bhutas*, with *Atman*. They are advocated to be the cause of the universe. We may surmise that a particular School believed in six principles — Six *Dhatus* This may show the way for bringing about a harmonious blending of various schools.

Thus the *Ayurveda* system may be taken the archetype to carry further research on the scientific aspects of the Five *Mahabhutas*.

A few observations on the Five *Mahabhutas* are given here, for further investigations by the scholars.

The Five Elements — An Interpretation

What are the traditional five elements, 'earth', 'water', 'fire', 'air', 'ether' ? Though they are called 'elements', they are often described as a series of increasingly subtle levels in the appearance of the world. On the one hand, in a progressive enquiry towards underlying reality (as described in the *Brhadaranyaka Upanisad,* 3.6 and 3.8), each element is found to overlie the next (in the above order). On the other hand, in cosmological accounts of creation, the same elements arise in reverse order, as a progression of increasingly gross levels through which reality appears.

Accordingly, from a philosophical point of view, the five elements could perhaps be interpreted as a division of experience into five levels, along the following lines.

Traditional element	*Element of*	*Level of experience*	*Correspondence with modern physics*
'Earth'	Differentiation and particularity	Particular objects	Pieces of matter
'Water'	Change and transformation	Changing forms	Moving configurations
'Fire'	Representation and propagation	Intelligible meaning	Propagation of energy
'Air'	Qualification and conditioning	Relative characteristics	Fields conditioning space and time
'Ether'	Underlying continuity	Continuing background	The space-time continuum

EARTH

When the world is perceived through body and mind, it seems at firrst to be made up of different objects and events. At this initial level, an element of differentiation and particularity appears in experience. This could well be symbolized by the traditional element 'earth': in the sense that earth is found differentiated into particular objects, like clay is found fashioned into different pots (to use the traditional analogy).

WATER

If particular objects are perceived to exist, then how do their differences and particularities arise? How are objects told apart, and how are they formed? Such questioning leads to an underlying level of experience, where change and transformation become apparent: as that element of experience which forms and shapes the world. This could well be symbolized by the traditional element 'water': in the sense that water flows in changing shapes and forms.

FIRE

What do change and transformation show, and how do they take place? What is shown by changing forms, and how are they transferred from one object or one place to another? Such questioning leads to another underlying level, where representation and propagation become apparent: as that element of experience which gives meaning to forms and enables them to move from place to place. This could well be symbolized by the traditional element 'fire': in the sense that fire consumes and illuminates (like meaning consumes its representations to illuminate what is represented), and fire also propagates (by burning its way through things and radiating energy).

AIR

How do representation and propagation work? What represented qualities are shown by meaningful forms, and what characteristic qualities and conditions travel along with forms that move identifiably from place to place? Such questioning leads in its turn to a further underlying level, where qualification and conditioning become evident: as that element of experience which gives relative character to varying objects and localities in space and time. This could well be symbolized by the traditional element 'air': in the sense that air or atmosphere is an enveloping medium of relative qualities and conditions (described, in one traditional metaphor, as that which can be 'felt but not seen').

ETHER

How is experience qualified and conditioned? On what continuing basis are varying conditions and characteristics compared, in different objects and localities differently situated in space and time? Such questioning leads to a fifth level of experience, where a background of underlying continuity is understood: as the background element of experience, which enables characteristics to be contrasted and compared, and which thus enables objects to be discerned apart and related together again. This background continuity could well be symbolized by the traditional element 'ether': in the sense that the 'ether' was conceived to pervade (and thus to continue through) all objects and all localities in space and time.

The above division of levels is very general and abstract; and hence it can be applied in somewhat different ways to many particular fields of experience. In the above table (and the attached chart), an illustration is given of how it might be applied to modern physics, in a way that is naturally a little different from its application to more general or to more subjective experience.

In traditional thought, the *pancikarana* distinction of five elements has in fact been applied somewhat differently in different fields of experience: as for example in the five elements (*panca mahabhutas*) of the external world, in five levels of personality (the *panca kosas*), in five levels of mind (*ahamkara* – ego or personal identification, *citta* – will, *buddhi* – intellect, *manas* – qualitative mind or sensibility, *antahkarana* – the 'inner faculty' or understanding), in five vital functions (*pranas*), in the five senses (*jnanendriyas*), in five external functions of action (*karmendriyas*), in the enveloping spheres of medieval European cosmology (with the sphere of 'earth' progressively enveloped by spheres of 'water', 'fire', 'air', 'ether': all finally enveloped by the infinite reality of 'God'), and in other ways.

The following chart elaborates a little on the previous table, and summarizes some of the ways in which the division of five elements was traditionally conceived in the past and might perhaps be re-interpreted today.

The Five Elements

Traditional name	*Element of*	*Traditional Characterization*	*Level of experience*	*Level of personality*	*Correspondence with modern physics*
'Earth'	Solidity	Differentiation into objects – as clay can be made into different pots	Matter – differentiated into pieces of matter and thus formed into objects	Body and senses	Objects as pieces of matter – with differentiated forms
'Water'	Fluidity	Change and transformation – as water flows in changing shapes and forms	Form relating component pieces, though patterns recognized by similarity with other objects	Practical mind – will and observation	Changing forms of energy – objects as patterns of moving energy
'Fire'	Energetic illumination	Destruction and radiation – as fire consumes its fust and sheds hight on other things	Meaning–of symbolic representations that direct attention to further experience, by representing qualities of other objects	Intellect – formulation and interpretation	Radient energy – propagation of characteristics (like beat and light) in space and time
'Air'	Transparent tangibility	'Atmosphere' or enveloping medium of relative qualities – which can be 'felt but not seen'	Quality–relative characteristics (like not and cold) compared on the basis of common, continuive principles (like temperature)	Emotional Mind – judgement and lutuition	Fields of distnionted characteristics (like heat, hight, energy, mass) – conditioning of space and time
'Ether'	Pervasion	Permeation of the universe – thus continuing through differences of objects and localities in space and time	Continuity – common principles underlying difference and vanation, thus enabling knowledge to continue from past expenence	Understanding – Coordination and comprehension	Space – time continuum – connecting different objects, events and localities

Notes

1. *Taittiriya Brahmana*, 2.2.9. 1-3.
2. *Ibid.*, 3.8.3-10.
3. *Taittiriyopanisad*, I. 3.2.
4. P.T. Raju, *Structural Depth of Indian Thought*, p. 31.
5. It is said that from the *Atman*, the five *Mahabhutas* have come. The very epithet, '*Atman*' is suggestive, in as much as the *Atman* eats, swallows absorbs the different elements, which constitute the objective world.
6. *Chandogya* p. V.11.
7. *Satapatha Br.*, X. 61.
8. *Taittiriya Up.*, II.1.
9. पञ्जस्रोतोम्बुं पञ्चयोन्युग्रवकं पञ्चप्राणोर्मिं पञ्चबुद्ध्यादिमूलाम्।
   पञ्चावर्तां पञ्चदुःखौधवेगां पञ्चाशद्भेदां पञ्चपर्वामधीम। V
   — *Svetasvatara Up.*, 5

9(a). *Samikhya karika*, 22.
   प्रकृतेर्महाँस्ततोहऽ कारङ्स्तस्माद्गणश्च षोडशकः।
   तस्मादपि षोडशकात्पञ्चभ्यः पञ्च भूतानि।।४

10. तन्मात्राण्यविशेषास्तेभ्यो भूतानि पञ्च पञ्चभ्यः।
    एते स्मृताः विशेषाः शान्ता घोराश्च मूढाश्च।। *Samkhakarika*, 38
11. पुरुषार्थहेतुकमिदं निमित्तंनैमित्तिकप्रसङ्गेन।
    प्रकृतेर्विभुत्वयोगान्नटवद् व्यतिष्ठते लिङ्गम्।।४२।।
    न विना भावैर्लिङ्गम् न लिङ्गेन भाविवृत्तिः।
    लिङ्गाख्यो भावाख्यास्तस्माद् द्विविधः प्रवतते सर्गः।।५२।।
12. *Pancadasi*, II. 2-83; also cf. *Vedantasar*, pp. 68-9.
13. *Ibid.*, II. 2-91.
14. *Vedanta paribhasa, Visayapariccheda*
    एत्तैश्य सत्त्वगुणोपेत्तैः पञ्चभूतैर्ज्यस्तैः पृथक् पृथक् क्रमेण
    नेत्रत्वक्चक्षूरसनघ्राणाख्यानि पञ्चज्ञानेन्द्रियाणि जायन्ते।
    एतेभ्यः पुनराकाशादिगतसात्विकांशेभ्यो मिलितेभ्यो मनोबुद्धि अहङ्काराचितानि जायन्ते।
    श्रोत्रादीनां पञ्चानां क्रमेण दिग्वा तार्कवरुणाश्विनोऽधिष्ठातृदेवताः।
    मन अदीनां चतुर्णां क्रमेण चन्द्रचतुर्मुखशङ्कराच्युता अधिष्ठातृदेवताः।
15. एतैरेव रजोगुणोपेत्तैः पञ्चभूतैर्व्यस्तैर्यथाक्रमं वाक्पाणिपादपायूपस्थानि
    कर्मेन्द्रियाणि जायन्ते।
    तेस्तं च क्रमेण वन्हीन्द्रोपेन्द्रमृत्यूप्रजापतयो अधिष्ठातृदेवताः।
    तैरेव तमोगुणोपेतैरपञ्चीकृतभूतैः पञ्चीकृतानि जायन्ते।
    'तासां त्रिवृतं त्रिवृतमेकैकां कारवाणि' इति श्रुतेः पञ्चीकरणो-पलक्षणार्थत्वात्।
    पञ्चीकरणप्रकारश्चेत्थम्-आकाशमदौ द्विधा विभज्य तेषां चतुर्णामंशानां वाटय्वादिषु भूतेषू संयोजनम्।

एवं तेज आदीनामपि।
तदेवमेकैकभूतस्यार्धं स्वांशात्कमर्धान्तरं चतुर्विधभूतमयमिति पृथिव्या दिषु स्वांशाधिक्यात् पृथिव्यादिव्यवहारः।

. . . एवं तमोगुणयुक्तेभ्यः पञ्चीकृतंभूतेभ्यो
भूम्यन्तरिक्षस्वर्महर्जजनस्तपः सत्यत्मस्योर्ध्वलोकसप्तंकस्य
ब्रह्माण्डस्य जरायुजाण्डजस्वेदजोद्भिज्जायाल्यश्चतुर्विधस्थूलशरीराणां चोत्पत्तिः

पञ्चदशी विसयपसिच्छेदे।

16. Cf. *Siddantamuktavali*, *Pratyaksa Kanda*, pp. 30-34.
संपर्शादयोऽष्टौ वेंगाख्य = संस्कारो मरुतो गुणाः।
स्पर्शादयोऽष्टौ रुपवेगौ द्रवत्वं तेजसो गुणाः।।३०।।

स्पर्शादयोऽष्टौ वेगश्च द्रवत्वं च गुरुकत्वम्।
रुपं रसस्तथा स्नेहो वारिण्येते चतुर्दश।।३१।।

स्नेहहीना गन्धयुताः क्षितावेते चतुर्दश।

बुद्ध्यादिषट्कं स्ङ्ख्यादिपञ्चकं भावना तथा।।३२।।

धर्माधर्मौ गुणा एते आत्मनः स्युश्चतुर्दश।
सङ्ख्यादिपञ्चकं कालदिशोः शब्दश्च ते च खे।।३३।।

सङ्ख्यादिपञ्चकं बुद्धिरिच्छा यत्नोऽपि चेश्वरे।
परापरत्वे सङ्ख्याद्याः पञ्च वेगश्च मानसे।।३४।।

स्पर्शादयोऽष्टौ — स्पर्श, सङ्ख्या, परिमाण, पृथक्त्व, संयोग, विभाग, परत्व, अपरत्व.
वायु - 8 + वेग; तेजस् 8 + रुप, वेग, द्रवत्व = 11
जल - 8 + वेग, द्रवत्व, रूप, रस, गन्ध = 14
आकाश, सङ्ख्या, परिमाण पृथक्त्व, संयोग, विभाग, शब्द
आत्मा - 5 above + बुद्धि, सुख, दुःख इच्छा, द्वेष, प्रयत्न, भावना
धर्म + अधर्म = 14
ईश्वर -above 5 + परतत्व, अपरत्व, वेग = 8

17. चेतनानाश्रितत्वे सति निश्चेतना कला। साऽपि द्विविधा, कार्याख्या करणाख्येति।
तत्रं कार्याख्या दशविधा, पृथिव्यप्तेवाखाकाशगन्धरसरूपस्पर्शशब्द लक्षणा. . .।

गणकारिका, रत्नटीका, pp. 10-1.

18. *Ksemraja*, *Parapravesika*, p. 10.
19. *Saradatilaka*, I. 78.
20. यदैतेऽसङ्गता भावा भूतेन्द्रियमनोगुणाः।
यदाऽऽयतननिर्माणे न शेकुर्ब्रह्मवित्तमम्।।
तदा संहत्य चान्योन्यं भगवच्छक्तिचोदिताः।
सदसत्त्वमुपादाय योभयं ससृजुर्ह्यदः।।२।।

Bhagavata II. 5.32-3, *Bhagavata* II. 6.1-11.

21. *Bhag,* III. 6. 1-9.
22. Source: Dr. Kale, *Parandyache Hamsarajaswami* (Marathi), Pune, 1991, pp. 155-56.

10

Samkhya Theory of Matter

M. P. Rege

1. What may count as the *Samkhya* theory of matter is part of the general philosophical theory advanced by it which aims at giving a true account of the nature of all that there is.

2. *Samkhya* divides all things that are there into two radically different kinds: (a) things which possess consciousness or rather are constituted of consciousness (*cetana*); (b) things which are unconscious (*jada*) but are objects of (or for) consciousness.

The latter category includes not only inanimate physical things and physical processes, living things and vital processes, but also minds and mental acts, occurrences like sensations, wishes and feelings. For, one can be as much aware of one's feelings and perceptions of things, as of tables and stones. Thus for *Samkhya*, physical things, organisms and minds fall on one side of the fundamental ontological divide, on the other side of which are to be found only subjects of pure consciousness (*purusa*).

Samkhya dualism may be compared with Cartesian dualism which has dominated later Western thought, according to which the basic ontological division is that between minds which are characterised by consciousness, and material things which are characterised by extension and motion.

3. The totality of *jada* things is called *Prakrti*. *Prakrti* is one, not only in the formal sense of being the all-inclusive set of all *jada* things, but also in the sense that it is one causal system. A *jada* thing exists, in some sense, within *Prakrti*. It is one form of the stuff of which *Prakrti* is composed and is causally linked with other such forms.

4. The ultimate constituents of which *Prakrti* or all *jada* things are composed are *gunas*. The commonest meaning of the Sanskrit word *guna* is quality. However, as used by *Samkhya*, *guna* does not mean quality. A *guna* is rather a substantive entity. But a *guna* is not something which possesses quality. Rather a *guna* is an entity with

its own characteristic expression. A *guna* expresses itself in a certain quale. The total character of a particular thing or process like a pot or a tree or an emotion is the resultant of the qualia in which all the *gunas* which constitute that thing or process have expressed themselves. Everything or process in *prakrti* is composed of *gunas*.

5. *Gunas* fall into three kinds: *Sattva*, *rajas* and *tamas*. For *Samkhya*, a *jada* thing is something which is essentially (a potential) object of consciousness, an object for some *Purusa*. The consciousness of a *purusa* is likened to light. This metaphor needs to be taken seriously. For a *purusa* to be aware of an object is for the object to be illumined with a glow with the light of the *purusa*. The contribution which the component of *sattva gunas* within a *jada* thing makes to its nature, consists in rendering it illuminạble by the light of a *purusa*. The *sattva gunas* are just those *gunas* which are responsive to the light of a *purusa*.

A composition of *gunas* which is capable of being illumined by the light of a *purusa* is a mental phenomenon. It has this nature and capability because there is a preponderance of *sattva gunas* in its composition. When a mental phenomenon which is in itself unconscious (*jada*) is illumined by the light of a *purusa*, it becomes a conscious experience. Opposed to *sattva gunas* are the *tamas gunas*. (*Tamas* means darkness.) *Tamas gunas* resist the light of a *purusa*; they are opaque to it. They thus constitute the principle of materiality. A material thing is one which has a preponderance of *tamas gunas* in it. However, a material thing can become an object for consciousness indirectly even though not directly. *Sattva gunas* in addition to being translucent are plastic. As a mind is predominantly composed of *sattva gunas*, it can assume, because of the plasticity which it possesses, the form of a material thing. A mental formation of this sort when illumined by the light of a *purusa* becomes a conscious perception of the physical object.

The third kind of *gunas*, the *rajas gunas*, express themselves in motion. They constitute the dynamic principle in *Prakrti*. *Tamas gunas* in addition to resisting the light of a *purusa* also resist the force exerted by *rajas gunas*. They make for inertia. As a material thing is mainly constituted of *tamas gunas* it is inert. As against this, even though a mental phenomenon is overwhelmingly composed of *sattva gunas* it also contains a component of *tamas gunas*. A mental state, e.g., a perception of a pot has a determinate nature which it maintains at least for a brief while. This implies that it successfully resists being transformed into another sort of mental state. This is made possible by the presence of *tamas gunas* in it.

Every phenomenon in *Prakrti* is an admixture of all the three kinds of *gunas*, and the proportions in which they are blended in it determine its character. Things cannot be separated from one another by assigning them to different species or sorts, each with a sharp boundary. They rather form a continuous gradation stretching from the most *tamasika* things to the most *sattvika*.

Further, as each thing contains a component of *rajas gunas*, it is continuously changing. The picture of *Prakrti* — 'Nature' — which *Samkhya* presents is not that of a totality of things each of which has its own rigid identity which it maintains for a longer or shorter duration, is endowed with a determinate nature of its own and acts uniformly on other things in accordance with its intrinsic nature. The identity of a particular thing — a material thing or a mind — is akin to the identity of a wave. Nature is like an ocean in which waves arise and subside and are continued in subsequent waves. One may note that this is largely a similar picture to that presented by Buddhism or *Advaita Vedanta*.

6. A human person, indeed any *jiva* (a living organism) consists of a *purusa*, and a mind-body complex to which it is related. The *purusa* is the transcendental element in *jiva*; the mind-body complex falls squarely within *Prakrti*. The mind, the body to which it is linked, and the environment within which the mind-body complex is set and acts, are different formations of the same stuff of which everything in *Prakrti* is composed. The body can function as an organ of the mind, and the mind-body complex can deal effectively with the environment because of their essential homogeneity. Thus, if *Purusas* are excluded the *Samkhya* view of things is monistic and naturalistic.

7. The last point: According to *Samkhya* there is a teleology inherent in *Prakrti*, which has a reference to the purposes of *purusas*. Whatever happens in *Prakrti* happens for the sake of *purusas*. *Prakrti* in its original state exists as an entity which was totally devoid of any specific character. This is so because the expression of every *guna* in it is exactly nullified by the expression of some other *guna* which counters it, so that no specific character emerges as the resultant. From this pristine condition *Prakrti* evolves into the kind of world-order which is familiar to us: a world, consisting, on the one hand, of diverse kinds of material things which change in accordance with causal laws and, on the other, mind-body complexes, each of which is associated with a distinct *purusa*, and by virtue of this association is capable of perceiving things, feeling pleasures and pains, and the desires they prompt, and acting in order to satisfy these desires. It is within such a world-order that the purposes of *purusas* can be effectively served. These purposes are of two sorts: (a) to enjoy diverse experiences (*bhoga*) and (b) to be liberated from association with *Prakrti* (*apavarga*).

The teleology of *Prakrti* has a moral aspect. The diverse experiences which happenings in *Prakrti* provide to *Purusas* are determined by their past *karmas*. And the supreme end of a *purusa* which *Prakrti* serves is his liberation (*apavarga* or *moksa*). The *Samkhya* vision when considered in its entirety is spiritualistic in the peculiarly Indian form of spiritualism.

11

Transmutation
Ancient Indian Concepts and Practices

B.V. Subbarayappa

The early concept of transmutation had perceivably two facets : one of converting the base metals into gold of ever-lasting glitter, and the other of transforming the transient human body into one of permanence with the soul. The *Bhagavadgita* says: "... The soul has neither birth nor death; it is not slain when the body is slain; it is eternally the same... just as a person puts on new garments, giving up the old ones, the soul similarly accepts new material body, giving up the old and decaying ones".

The exalted imperishable status accorded, over the ages, to the soul in the percipience of body-soul relationship had in it the seeds of challenge to make the material mortal body itself immortal. The responses to this challenge, which were varied in different cultures, were often associated with a shroud of mystery. It took some time for the human mind to cast off the esoteric envelope and, as a first step, to conceive of rejuvenation, thus extending the longevity of the material body, but within the concept that the body has birth and death in contradiction to the soul.

In India, the beginnings of such endeavours can be seen in the *Rigveda* wherein *Somarasa* was extolled as an exhilarating divine elixir. Later in the Ayurvedic classic, *Susruta Samhita*, *Soma* elixir, it was claimed, would enable its consumer to live for ten thousand years with a youthful body and supernatural powers. The *Ayurveda*, the Science of Life *par excellence*, has eight divisions and one of them is entitled *Rasayana*, concerned with rejuvenating elixirs and processes for arresting physical and mental decay. There are references in both the *Caraka* and *Susruta Samhitas* to several other compositions with the claim that they would confer on the consumer a long youthful life of thousands of years. These elixirs were mostly herbal and, what is more, certain amount of processed gold was added to some of them to make them more effective. The *rasayana* of the *Ayurveda*, it may be noted, was more in the nature of prolonging the life of the material body than 'transmuting' it into an immortal state. Even so, it seemed to have paved the way for speculating on the immortality of the body.

The concept of material immortality *per se* received its sustenance from a natural phenomenon, namely, the perennial glitter and colour of gold, the anointed king of metals. Here was a metal, it was believed, which had reached the highest state from the other inferior metals and possessed imperishable characteristics. It was supposed that the other metals would undergo transformation, eventually into the immutable gold.

There was a sort of theoretical framework too for such a supposition. The well-known Greek thinker, Empedocles (5th century B.C.) developed a theory of four 'elements': Earth, Fire, Water and Air and the four primary qualities: hot, cold, dry

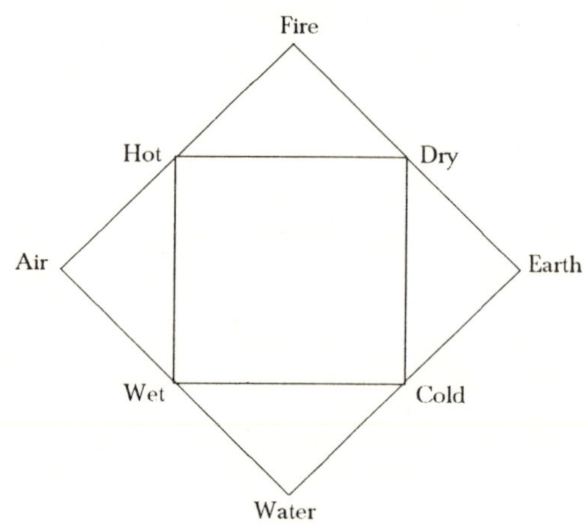

The Four 'Elements' of Empedocles

and moist (wet). Aristotle (384-322 B.C.) conceived of these 'elements' and their qualities as emphasising the unity of matter amidst all the changes. The 'primary matter', a potential one, would become Earth with the pair of primary qualities, cold and dry; water with cold and wet; Fire with hot and dryness; and Air with hot and moist, thus explaining the phenomena of change. These postulates held out the possibility of transmuting inferior metals into silver and ultimately into gold, by changing their qualities. The most perceptible of the changes effected was the colour and the object was to bring about a change in the colour of inferior metals to that of silver or gold. This theory was adopted by the Greco-Roman (Hellenistic) and later the Islamic alchemists in furtherance of their twin objective of the so-called transmutation of metals and the preparation of elixir of life for attaining material immortality. Strange it may seem, the Indian doctrine of five elements which had provided a theoretical foundation for the *Ayurveda* and for the explanation of the phenomenal world, did not lead to concepts of the foregoing type. The Indian five 'elements' had also a metaphysical undertone which often subsumed their physical concepts. Moreover, it was a holistic doctrine and the concept of change was circumscribed by it.

The seed ideas of Indian alchemy, which made their appearance in the fifth-sixth centuries A.D., were at variance with the Hellenistic ones. For, its inspirational source was not in the West, but in the Far East, in the Chinese concepts and practices. Indian alchemy had social compulsions too. The Ayurvedic elixirs and rejuvenating treatment were reserved only for males of the upper castes, (women were excluded), as enjoined by both the *Caraka* and *Susruta Samhitas*. But, to live long in perpetual youth and to experience the best in life have been the goals of all human beings. Such dispositions as these react vehemently against rigid caste-structures and privileges of the few. They go out in search of systems which are conducive to the realisation of their goals. In India, the *tantras* offered such a system and, more importantly, admitted into their fold all – irrespective of caste, creed or sex in an esoteric, but ingenious manner. The tantric concept of *siddhi* evolved certain pathways for disciplined aspirants. And inherent in that concept was the attainment of bodily immortality with even supernatural powers (*animadi astasiddhi*). This was reinforced by the mythical male-female symbolism, the union sublime of immortality.

The Chinese male-female symbolism of Yin and Yang, mercury-sulphur union of cinnabar (mercuric sulphide) to which was attributed extraordinary powers of attaining immortality, found a congenial home in the Indian Tantric milieu. Buddhist pilgrims and the *vajrayana* seemed to have played a seminal role in this alchemical transmission.

Be that as it may, Indian alchemy of both Sanskritic and Tamilian traditions, developed a wide variety a chemical processes for the ostensible transmutation of metals and preparation of elixir of life, in which mercury occupied a prime position. The literature on Indian alchemy called the *Rasasastra* is perceptibly voluminous and methodical in the presentation of a variety of processes whose number is legion. Of these processes, eighteen *samskaras* or complex treatments, which were adopted for the potentiation of mercury, deserve special mention:

Briefly stated, the eighteen processes concerning mercury as the central element, are as follows:

(i) ***Svedana:*** Steaming mercury with a number of plant substances, some minerals, alkalis and salts;

(ii) ***Mardana***: Rubbing steamed mercury in a mortar along with some plant and acidic materials;

(iii) ***Murchana***: Triturating mercury in a mortar with some more plant extracts till it loses its own character and form;

(iv) ***Uthapana***: Steaming mercury again along with alkalis, salts, the three myrobalans, alum etc., and rubbing mercury again in sunlight so that the characteristics of mercury, freed from impurities, are brought into play again;

(v) ***Patana***: Three types, viz. *urdhva* (upwards); *adhah* (downwards); and tiryak (sideways); grinding mercury with alkalis, salts and others, and subjecting the product to distillation;

(vi) ***Rodhana***: Mixing the distilled mercury with saline water in a closed pot to restore the 'vigour or potency' of mercury;

(vii) ***Niyamana***: Continuation of the process by steaming mercury for three days with a number of plant products, alum, borax, iron sulphate, etc., to restrain the motility of mercury;

(viii) ***Sandipana***: Steaming this product with alum, black pepper, sour gruel, alkali and some vegetables substances to 'kindle' the desire of mercury to attain the power of assimilation;

(ix) ***Grasa or Gaganagrass***: Fixation and assimilation of the 'essence' of mica (*gagana*) to the desired extent;

(x) ***Carana***: Boiling this product with sour gruel, leaves of certain plants, alum and others for a week so that mica is fully assimilated;

(xi) ***Garbhadruti***: Heating and treating mercury with the desired metallic substances so that the 'essence' of the latter becomes 'liquified' and the resultant, after cooling, passes through a piece of cloth;

(xii) ***Bahyadruti***: Obtaining 'essence' of minerals or metallic substances also externally;

(xiii) ***Jarana***: Heating the mercurial product with the desired minerals or metals, alkalis and salts so that they are fully digested or assimilated;

(xiv) ***Ranjana***: A complex process involving the treatment of mercury with sulphur, gold, silver and copper as well as salts in such a way that mercury attains colour;

(xv) ***Sarana***: Digesting mercury with gold or silver in an oil-base to increase its ability towards transformation;

(xvi) ***Kramana***: Smearing mercury with several plant extracts, minerals, milk, etc., and then heating it carefully with a view to enabling it to possess transmuting powers;

(xvii) ***Vedhana***: Rubbing the resultant mercury with a few select substances including oil so that it acquires the transmuting power;

(xviii) ***Bhaksana***: Consuming the prescribed quality of the mercurial product which has undergone the foregoing 17 processes, for the rejuvenation and longevity.

(This sequence was rigorously followed by Indian alchemists; but there were variations in the choice of plants and their extracts, salts, alkaline and acidic substances, minerals and other ingredients).

The important, through esoteric, concept which lay behind these extremely complex processes was that the mercurial product, after undergoing sequentially the seventeen processes, was believed to have all the powers of transmutation. At this stage, it was to be tested for its efficacy in transmuting base metals into gold and, if the test was positive, it was to be used for the eighteenth process. The final product, if consumed in prescribed quantity would, it was claimed, rejuvenate the body in such a way that it would make the body as resplendent and imperishable as gold. One could see the ideal of Philosopher's Stone of the medieval European alchemy, in the mercurial product emerging out of the seventeen processes.

There are hundreds of verses in the *Rasasastra* texts which overtly deal with a wide variety of processes, some simple and many complex. Three examples may be cited:

(i) Mercury, cinnabar, pyrites, alum of excellent quality borax, black pepper – each one part – and *sauvarcala* salt in equal proportions to them; six parts of rock salt; powdered iron in the same proportion; and hundred parts of the juice of *Emblic myrobalan*, are to be kept in a stone bowl which is to be deposited in a heap of cow-dung. After one year, a liquid emerges out of it. This (liquid) is divine as well as flawless, and is to be compounded with mercury admixed with pure gold as 'seed'. This compound possesses the capability of transmuting a thousand times its weight of all metals into gold. (*Rasopanisat*, XVI, 241-245)

(ii) One part of the essence of capula (bismuth compound); two parts of mercury; four parts of gold (as seed); and sulphur of equal proportion to that of mercury which is to be mascerated, are to be heated in a closed crucible. Gold and capula of equal quantities are to be blended with this mercury. If this mercury is infused with a hundred times its weight of copper, it makes the latter red and this attains the power of transmuting a hundred times its weight of silver into gold. (*Rasasara*, XV, 19-22)

(iii) One *pala* of powdered seed (gold); one *pala* of pyrites; one *pala* of sulphur; one *pala* of mercury extracted from cinnabar; and one *pala* of borax – all together mascerated with the juices of plants endowed

> with the properties of 'fixation' of mercury. Heated over fire urged by means of a blow-pipe, mercury attains 'fixation' and undergoes colouration with the aid of sulphur. Blended with an equal weight of gold by the *sarana* operation, it is 'killed' by heating in a *puta*. This mercurial preparation transmutes sixty times its weight of silver-copper into excellent gold. (*Rasasara*, XIV,1820)

The technique of effecting transmutation was of five kinds:

(i) ***Lepa Vedha*** (smearing copper or silver foils with a potent mercurial product);

(ii) ***Ksepa Vedha*** (throwing such a product into the base metals;

(iii) ***Kunta Vedha*** (pouring the transmuting agent into them);

(iv) ***Dhuma Vedha*** (subjecting the base metal to the action of the fumes of mercurial preparation); and

(v) ***Sabda Vedha*** (effecting transmutation by the 'impact' of the transmuting agent)

It is well-nigh impossible even to surmise the nature and extent of chemical or other types of reactions that occur in the process of the so-called transmutation, until an experimental verification is attempted from the modern chemical point of view. It would, nevertheless, seem that the colour of the 'inferior' metal like copper, tin or lead, would change into that of gold or silver. The emerging colouration, might be too uniform and intimate enough with the 'inferior metal' to expose, under ordinary conditions, its true colour. The specific gravity and other physical characteristics of the so-called transmuted metal might manifest themselves, as a result of skilful manipulation of the ingredients such as mercury or its compounds, arsenic sulphides, pyrites, sulphur as well as the deliberate addition of the noble metals themselves.

Indian alchemists specially of Tamil Nadu, knew the distinction between the transmuted 'gold' and the real one. A Tamil text (*Amudakalaijnanam* by Agastya) states clearly that if the artificial 'gold' and the natural gold are separately subjected to prolonged heating or calcination, the former gives out ashes and the real face of the metal appears, while the natural gold remains uneffected by this method.

The transmutation of metals and the preparation of elixir of life which were vigorously pursued by Indian alchemists, were more esoteric than scientific, despite their attempts at classification and selection of substances, and the use of a wide variety of apparatus (mostly earthern), for distillation, sublimation, incineration, trituration and the like, which the *Rasasastra* texts describe meticulously and in great detail. To transmute the base metals into the noble one, and to make the perishable body an ever immortal one, were goals ever in sight, but never reached.

It was, nevertheless, a pursuit which was not without a spin-off and that was in the direction of formulating certain mineral medicines. Mercury, sulphur, mica, arsenic and iron compounds, alum, gems and others on the one hand and on the other, metals like gold, silver, copper and its alloy brass, and lead were processed elaborately by using a wide variety of apparatus. Generally it was believed by the *rasavadins* that the minerals and metals would not acquire the desirable iatro-chemical properties unless they were treated with one medicinal plant or the other. The *rasasastra* texts give details of the preparation of a large number of medicines, and their therapeutic effects as well as their dosages. One of the popular preparations called *Makaradhvaja* contains specially processed mercuric sulphide and stimulants like camphor, pepper and cloves. During its preparation a certain amount of purified gold is also added.

The most important medicinal preparations, as described in the *Rasasastra* texts, relate to a class of what are called the *bhasma* of metals and minerals. Although the process leading to the formation of a *bhasma* is one of incineration of the metal or mineral concerned, the original substance is subjected to several processes before it undergoes prolonged heating. Even the heating known as the *Putapaka*, is carried out of several days with extreme care. Various types of *Putas* are mentioned in the texts, recommending a particular *puta* for the desired product, along with its measurement and the quantity of cow-dung cakes or husk to be used for prolonged heating in order to obtain the most efficient composition.

This method is believed to impart extraordinary qualities, both physico-chemical and medicinal, on to the treated substance. A *bhasma* is an extremely fine powder, very light and, when thrown on water, just spreads itself as a thin film on it. Of the *bhasmas*, that of mica, gold and silver are most widely used in minute quantities and are generally mixed with other medicinal compositions.

The *Siddha* (medical) System which is mostly prevalent in Tamil Nadu, appears to have been evolved from the earlier alchemical concepts and practices. Though the System had originally its own ways of preparing certain substances of medicinal value, like *muppu* (a specially prepared mixture of three salts), it assimilated gradually some of the alchemical preparations and developed a number of mineral compositions which go under the names, *bhaspam* (Skt.: *bhasma*), *cendurams* (Skt.: *sindura*) and *cunnams* (probably calcium compounds or earthly substances).

There is no denying that the Indian alchemists had realised the importance of medicinal preparation more than of the transmutation of base metals into gold. In the West, such a realisation came about only in the sixteenth century A.D., as a result of the ceaseless efforts of several thoughtful iatro-chemists led by Paracelsus. But in India, a trend in this direction could be perceived even in the eleventh century A.D. Although the *Rasasastra* is not regarded as an integral part of the *Ayurveda*, some of the medicinal compositions of the former have found a place for themselves in the traditional medical care in India.

References

PRIMARY SOURCES

Rasahrdaya-tantra of Govinda Bhagavatpada: (ed.) Jadavji Trikumji Acarya, Bombay, (eds.) B.V. Subbarayappa *et. al.*, (under publication by INSA) 1911.

Rasakaumudi of Jnanacandra Sharman: (ed.) S.S. Pranacarya, Lahore (1928).

Rasamrtam: (ed.) Jadavji Trikumji Acarya, New Delhi (1951).

Rasapaddhati of Bindu Pandita: (ed.) Madhava Pandita, Bombay (1925).

Rasasanketakalika: (ed.) Jadavji Trikumji Acarya, Bombay (1912).

Rasaprakasasudhakara of Yasodhara: (ed.) Jadavji Trikumji Acarya, Bombay (1912).

Rasarnava: (ed.) P.C. Rayand Harish Candra Kaviratna, Calcutta (1910).

Rasarnavakalpa: (eds.) Mira Roy and B.V. Subbarayappa, New Delhi (1976).

Rasaratnakara of Nityanatha Siddha: edited (annoon) with Hindi commentary, Bombay (1897).

Rasaratnasamuccaya of Vagbhata: (ed.) Vinayak Apte, Poona (1890).

Rasasara of Govindacarya: (ed.) Jadavji Trikumji Acarya, Bombay (1912).

Rasendracintamani of Ramachandra: (ed.) Jivananda Vidyasagar, Calcutta (1878).

Rasendracudamani of Somadeva: (ed.) Yadav Sarman, Lahore (1932).

Rasatarangini: (ed.) Sadananda Sarma, New Delhi (1953).

Rasopanisat: (ed.) K. Sambasiva Sastry, Trivandrum (1928).

The Rgveda: (tr.) H.H. Wilson, 6 vols, London (1860).
(t.) R.T.H. Griffith, Banaras, (1963) (reprint).

SECONDARY SOURCES

Holmyard, E.J., *Alchemy*, Penguin Books, London (1957).

Ray P., (ed.), *History of Chemistry in Ancient and Medieval India*, Calcutta (1956).

Ray P.C., *History of Hindu Chemistry* (2 vols), Calcutta (1902, 1905).

Read, John, *Through Alchemy to Chemistry*, London (1957).

Subbarayappa, B.V., 'Chemical Practices and Alchemy', In A *Concise History of Science in India*, (eds.) D.M. Bose, S.N. Sen, and B.V. Subbarayappa, New Delhi (1971).

Taylor, Sherwood, *The Alchemist*, London (1958).

12

Bhutas
Some Inter-related Themes of Indian Cosmology

P.K. Mukhopadhyay

The expression *Bhuta* is often translated in English as element. We shall see later that these two expressions are not exact synonyms. Keeping that in mind we may for ordinary purposes use the two words interchangeably. The *Bhutas* or the elements constitute one of the most primitive fields of human inquiry known as cosmology. Interest in the themes of this field is most pervasive and abiding. Hardly there is a culture which can claim maturity but did not develop quite early in its history cosmology of some form or other. At the same time it is still one of the developing areas of one of the most developed branches of science. Cosmology has proved itself to be one of those areas of human knowledge which can be said to be a meeting point of speculative philosophy and experimental science, traditional wisdom and modern discovery, theology and mythology on the one hand and secular positivistic inquiry on the other. Two of the most ancient and developed civilizations of human history – the Vedic and the Hellenistic — gifted to the world very rich cosmological ideas and insights. In none of these two cultures science and philosophy seem to be as sharply distinguished as in modern European culture. While the Hellenistic culture was later on completely overthrown or overtaken by or absorbed into the culture of Christianised Europe, the Vedic culture is still maintaining its separate identity. But the cosmological ideas of the Greeks are far more widely known than the contributions the Indian seers and philosophers made in this field. Time has come when the scientists with the right frame of mind may discover useful cosmological insights which did not receive due emphasis in the hands of teachers of Indian philosophy and *Puranas*. Even if much meaningful use of the cosmological ideas of the Indian scholars of the classical age cannot be made, it may be found immensely interesting how in those days the scholars discovered, formulated and tackled the relevant questions and if we can add anything of significance along that line or find any constructive criticism to offer. It is in itself a very rewarding task to see if and how far we can integrate modern discoveries and advances in the field of knowledge into the everchanging and everdeveloping framework of thought which is still continuous with the classical thinking.

In different types of literature of the Vedic culture one finds discussions on or mention of *bhutas*. But we do not have a neat name like cosmology. *Srstiprakarana* (portion of text devoted to the theme of creation) is a necessary part of the type of literature called *Puranas*. Though in almost every system of *darsana* (roughly, philosophy) and in most text books of *darsana* the topic of *bhuta* finds a place, yet it does not seem to be a necessary part of *darsana* in the same sense of the term in which it is a necessary part of *Puranas*. Every distinguishable system of philosophical thought has definite view about *bhuta* and *sarga*. Even those Indian schools of thought which are non-Vedic or anti-Vedic are no exception. In this paper I shall present some of the Vedic cosmological ideas. But for this purpose I shall not reproduce accounts which are available in the *Vedas*, *Upanisadas*, *Puranas* or *Tantras* – which constitute that division of the corpus of the Vedic literature which may be called *agamic* and which is more strongly exhortatory and practical. I would rather draw on accounts available in the other division of the Vedic literature which may be called analytical and empirical and which is more strongly theoretical. One finds faithful elaborations and creative use of the Vedic thoughts and insights in the classical analytical literature which are not direct commentaries on the *Vedas* and *Upanisads* but are works of those philosophical schools which are known as *astika* school because they accept the *Veda* as source of knowledge and truth. Compared to these philosophical works the *Vedas*, the *Puranas* and *Tantras* and even the *Upanisads* often leave their analytical theoretical contents on many matters hidden; this one does not and perhaps cannot hope to find in independent historical and even analytical works of those recent scholars who do not belong to the tradition of the believing theoreticians and practitioners of the Vedic culture. This is bound to happen in every old civilization which in course of history has come in contact with other civilizations and myriad influences from outside as well as stress and strain from within. One respect in which the analytical works of philosophical literature are greater aid in understanding some concepts of the *Vedas* is that in such literature the relevant concept is presented and discussed in its proper perspective of a network of other concepts. The concept of *bhuta* for example is found much more clearly in its relationships to such other concepts as *kala* (time), *dik* (space), *samkhya* (number), *kriya* including all form of physical motion and movement, *karanata* (causality), *sarga* (creation), 'chaos' or a state prior to or after the creation) and the like. It is in the context of these other concepts or in relation to them that one can hope to discover the rich theoretical potentiality of the concept of *bhuta*. Such analytical elaborations of ancient ideas or of views adumbrated in ancient literature go generally by the name philosophy considered as fairly good synonym for the Sanskrit term *darsana*. One difficulty is it seems that in recent times particularly in the community of British and American philosophers it is believed that philosophy is necessarily non-science or pseudo-science, it is taken as speculative (in somewhat derogatory sense perhaps) or analytic whereas science, at least natural science, is necessarily empirical and factual. Besides in European theoretical tradition it seems that cosmology is either scientific or mythological. But just as science-philosophy dichotomy is generally unknown in India at least in the sense in which it is familiar in contemporary West so also the account of *bhuta* and *sarga* we are going to derive from or reconstruct along the line of classical Indian philosophical schools is not mythological; if it is not scientific it is philosophical. It may incidentally be noted that to translate *Purana* as mythology is inaccurate, similarly inaccurate it seems to translate the word science as *vijnana*. In this sense it is sometimes used in modern Indian languages as Bengali but not in classical Vedic literature. As translation of modern European science the word *vijnana* does not seem to have any currency in old literature.

Philosophical schools or *darsana sampradayas* of India including the Vedic or *astika* schools differ more in their account of *sarga* than in their theory of *bhutas*. There is a large amount of agreement also. In the second section I shall note some of these points of similarities and dissimilarities between some Indian schools of thought. In the next section I shall reconstruct some of the more specific and salient features of the old *nyaya* and modern *nyaya-vaisesika* schools which are best known for their rigorous analytical approach at least to theoretical questions.

Vedanta paribhasa is a widely read elementary text book of *Advaita Vedanta*. First two lines of the invocation verse with which the book begins read:

> (I) *yadavidyavilasena bhutabhautika srstayah*
> *tamnaumi paramatmanam saccidanandavigraham.*

Tattvacintamani of Gangesopadhyaya is the major source book of *nyaya* which marked the beginning of modern age in the history of *nyaya* school. This book makes many references to God or *Isvara* at different places and stages of its development. Among these are

> (II) a. *yah srstisthitivilayakarmani tanute*
> and
> b. *jagatnirmatrpurusadhaureyasiddhi*

The first of these passages occurs in the invocation verse with which *Tattvacintamani* begins and the second occurs in the first sentence of the last section of the second or *Anumana* part of the book in which Gangesa developed the *nyaya* analytical theory of inference. In (I) or according to the representative view of the *advaita vedanta* in the matter *srsti* or creation of the universe has within its scope both the *bhutas* or the elements and *bhautika*, meaning things created out of *bhutas* or elements. In other words (I) bears evidence to the fact that according to some Indian schools of thought creation is of two types (i) creation of (all or some) *bhutas* themselves and (ii) creation of the *bhautikas*. One common point between the views (I) and (II) is that creation of anything presupposes existence of some stuff which is either the constituent and continuent cause of the created or some other kind of cause of it. The distinction between these two types of cause is not very important so long we confine ourselves to what may loosely be called material creation but what is more strictly speaking creation of matter, whether at the macro level as when a clay jar is produced, or at the micro level as when first two units of some *bhuta* are combined and a matter having the simplest structure is created. Unless stated otherwise, by *bhautika srsti* we shall mean here the creation of matter out of *bhutas* or out of some material parts (*avayavas*) which they are themselves created out of *bhutas* or of material parts which are and so on. That *bhautika srsti* presupposes ultimately the existence of *bhutas* is admitted by the advocates of both (I) and (II). Since it is also admitted that creation of anything presupposes some pre-existing stuff, the followers of the view (I) would not only accept that the creation of type (ii) presupposes ultimately the existence of *bhutas*, they would also admit that the *bhutas* are not the most basic or primordial stuff of creation. For creation of type (i) there must be some more basic form of matter than the *bhutas*. We owe it to the *Samkhya* philosophers that this more basic stuff out of which the *bhutas* are themselves created is *tanmatra*. Corresponding to five types of *bhutas* there are five *tanmatras*. Important point to note is that the followers of the views (I) and (II) do not disagree as to the denotation of the term *bhuta*. *Samkhya* and *Advaita Vedanta* philosophers for example do not mean to say that the upholders of the view (II) especially the *Naiyayikas* are wrong, when they think that *bhuta paramanus* are not created; they too are created and as such are not the basic stuff of creation or *bhuta* in the true sense of the term; and the basic stuff are the *tanmatras* out of which are produced both the *bhutas* and *bhautika* things. To put it otherwise, the advocates of the view (I) do not mean to say that *paramanus*, say, are not *bhutas* but *tanmatras* are *bhutas*. They on the other hand admit *bhutas*, but since in their opinion these *bhutas* are also created substances and every created thing presupposes existence of more basic stuff they admit still simpler constituents of creation viz., *tanmatras*.

Be that as it may. Unlike the *Samkhya* and *Advaitavedanta* philosophers who subscribe to the view (I), the *Naiyayikas* and the *Vaisesikas* understand by *srsti* type (ii) creation only. This difference among the *astika* schools may be taken as difference in interpretation of relevant passages of the *Veda* and also of other texts and passages of *agamic* literature. Whereas in *agamic* literature *sarga* has been talked about and almost all the different views about *sarga* later developed by the theoreticians in the analytical literature were adumbrated, philosophers of the group unholding the view

(I) came to believe that *srsti* necessarily means *bhautika srsti* or creation ultimately out of the *bhutas*. While the *Advaitavedantins* believe that these *bhutas* are also created, the *Samkhya* philosophers maintain that the *tanmatras* out of which the (*mahabhutas* are created did not themselves exist there always, not at least in the form of *tanmatras*.

Thinkers upholding the views (I) and (II) however agree among themselves on one point and that is this. There is or has been such a thing as creation. Even though in matters of technical details creation is to be understood differently. These philosophers agree that the universe or *jagat* was created and this creation of *jagat* as a whole is in addition to such creation as manufacturing of a clay jar by a potter or conceiving of a human baby. But there is a third view (III) *na kadapi anidrsam jagat*. According to this view, advocated by some *Mimamsaka* philosophers, there never had been a state when no universe was there or *jagat* was yet to be created. This difference between the two groups of philosophers lead to another difference among them. Their commitment to the view that the universe was created at a certain point of time committed the advocates of the views (I) and (II) by implication to the view that there had been a state prior to the state of creation of the universe. This is the state of *pralaya* or roughly speaking, chaos. The upholders of the view (III) consistently with their other views deny a state of cosmic *pralaya* — a state marked by future possibility of *jagat* as a whole. Those who believe in a state of cosmic *pralaya* often believe in cycles of creation and chaos. In their opinion every cosmic creation is preceded necessarily by a state of cosmic *pralaya*; they also believe that all but one state of cosmic creation ends with the advent of a new state of cosmic *pralaya*. The state of cosmic creation, which ends as it must but does not end in such cosmic *pralaya* as is marked by the future possibility of creation, is known as last creation, and the state of *pralaya* in which this creation terminates is called *mahapralaya*, which is defined as or is marked by the absence of every created positive thing. In the opinion of the majority of Indians though the cycles of cosmic creation and dissolution has a final termination, there is no first beginning. Ignoring this point which is of great theoretical importance for the Indian thinkers some Western physicists of recent time tend to argue what the Indians call the cycles of *srsti* and *pralaya* or cosmic creation and cosmic dissolution is essentially the same thing or the anticipation of the energy — matter exchanges of quantum physics. For our present purpose it is not necessary either to support or criticize the attempt to find a link between some classical thoughts of India and some discoveries of modern science. I have written something elsewhere about what should better be our stand in such matters. It may, however, be reiterated that the usual way in which cosmological accounts are classified, viz., that such account is either scientific or mythological — does not seem to be adequate. In fact the cosmological account we are going to reconstruct following the cue to be found in the analytical literature of the Indian philosophical school of *Nyaya* is not only not mythological, it is not even just speculative. It is not for that matter that we know today as scientific cosmology of astrophysics. The *nyaya* theory of *Bhautika srsti* is scientific in the sense of not being purely speculative. It is better to call it analytical in a broad sense. For without ceasing to be rigorously analytical it successfully combines in it various strands and considerations such as theological-anthropomorphic, structural-analytical and empirical-causal.

The first point to note about the *nyaya-vaisesika* theory of *bhautika srsti* or cosmic creation is that it is not a theory of material or physical creation in the narrow sense of the term. It includes creation of least complex matter such as a dyad formed out of just two simplest and smallest units of matter and also things like a clay jar and its colour on the one hand and such organic matter as a human body on the other. Further the process of creation includes both physical and chemical transformations. The second point to note is that the ultimate stuff and material component of *bhautika srsti* or the *bhutas*, are not theoretical abstractions or constructs but are believed to be actual existents. Among many actual and possible questions relating to the *bhutas* two deserve to be especially discussed. In the first place the two notions and expressions of *bhuta* and *paramanu* are to be distinguished. This is also very much necessary if one wants to introduce the English expression element as synonym of either or both. It is required of a *bhuta* that it should be structurally simple (*suksma* and *niravayava*) unit of matter (*jada dravya*); it is not further needed that it should be the smallest or infinitely small (*paramanu-rupa*). Nor it is a part of the meaning of the term *bhuta* that it must be a constituent part of some actual or possible created matter in the sense in which the constituent material part of a created matter is necessarily smaller in dimension (*parimana*) than the matter thus created. Thus structural simplicity of a *bhuta* is not to be confused with infinitesimally small dimension of it; it is to be understood rather as unanalysability. A *bhuta* cannot be structurally, physically or conceptually broken into further simpler units of matter (*avayava*).

The second important point for discussion in the *nyaya* theory of *bhautika srsti* is how *bhutas* combine and what sort of combination of what *bhutas* can amount to creation. Unlike philosophers of some other Indian school the *naiyayikas* hold that *bhutas* of anyone of the five types cannot combine with the *bhutas* of any other type; at least one *bhuta* of one type, say, *prthivi* or earth cannot combine with another *bhuta* of another type, say, water or *ap* in a way in which two *bhutas* of one type, say, of earth or water can combine. This tenet of *nyaya-vaisesika* school has a far reaching consequence; however complex internally and structurally a particular material substance may be, it is *eka bhautika*. But every created substance must have more than one or *aneka* material constituents and hence ultimately *aneka bhuta* as its constituents. If thus every created matter must contain *aneka bhutas* and also must necessarily be *eka bhautika*, then the *bhutas* must be distinguished both quantitatively numerically as well as qualitatively. *Akasa* is a *bhuta* and it is numerically one. It, however, differs qualitatively from any single *bhuta* of any one of the other four types of *bhutas*. Such qualitative difference is not there between any two *bhutas* of the same single type. Thus whereas any two *bhutas* of one qualitative group or kind such as *prthivi* or *tejas* are merely numerically quantitatively different, two *bhutas* of two qualitatively different kinds such as *prthivi* and *tejas* differ both numerically and qualitatively. In other words there necessarily obtains quantitative and numerical difference between two *bhutas* irrespective of whether or not they belong to the same class, and qualitative difference obtains only when they are of two different kinds. Be that as it may, one necessary implication of the view, that all created matter is *eka bhautika*, is that not only one element or *bhuta* cannot be changed into another *bhuta*, but no substance of one *bhuta* can be changed into substance of another *bhuta*. What it meant for the project of alchemy seemed to have been well understood in the classical period of *nyaya* also. On this theory it becomes easy to classify substances into various *bhuta* classes. Each substance belongs exclusively to one of the five *bhuta* classes; it is *prthivi* or *parthiva* or it is *tejas* or *taijasa* and so on. But those who believe that almost as a rule a created matter whether organic or inorganic is *aneka bhautika*, in fact *pancabhautika*, we need a principal to decide when a *pancabhautika* substance is *parthiva* and when it is *taijasa* and the like. To simplify the matter one principle is that of preponderance; a created matter is grouped in that *bhuta*-class, the number of constituent of which class is the greatest or most preponderant. Exact measure of preponderance has also been worked out in the theory of *Pancikarana* about which we have written elsewhere. A *pancabhautika dravya* is *parthiva*, as fifty per cent of its constituent *bhutas* or one part of it, if it is evenly broken into two matching parts, is *prthivi*.

The theory of *eka bhautika dravyas* of the *naiyayikas* should be carefully understood. The *naiyayikas* do not deny that a gross material body whether organic or inorganic does contain more than one kind of *bhuta* or *bhautika dravya* as constituent. Thus a normal and common material substance of the macro world contains usually all the five *bhutas*. So far in a loose sense all types of *bhuta* are found in a state of conjunction or combination in the body of one gross substance. But suppose in such a substance *S* there are two *prthivi* or *parthiva* elements and also constituents which belong to other four *bhuta* or *bhautika* class, how are we to decide whether the substance is *parthiva* or *jaliya* and the like? A human body is a case in point; it certainly has as constituent water, air, fire, *akasa* and *prthivi*. How does a *naiyayika* decide that the organic matter called human body is *parthiva*? We shall return to this soon. But we must first clarify a bit further what type of material or physical substance the *bhutas* are and what are other types of substances.

All the actual and possible things that may be found to be there in the universe or constitute it have been broadly divided into seven fundamental kinds or seven *padarthas* by the *naiyayikas*. Of these the first is called *dravya* or substance which again has been subdivided into nine classes: *ksiti* (earth), *ap* (water), *tejas* (fire), *marut* (air), and *vyoma*, *kala* (time), *dik* (space), *atma* (soul), and *manas* (internal sense-organ). There are various ways or principles of classification according to which these substances may be classified or grouped. By choosing different principles at the same time we may even produce cross divisions of these substances. One important principle according to which these are distinguished into different groups is whether or not a substance is available in a form in which it is created. Each one of these nine substances is available in eternal or uncreated form. But the first four are also found in created form. The fact that the first four substances are available both in created and uncreated forms and that in their uncreated form they are not only partless but can themselves form parts of created substances make this distinction most important from the point of view of the theory of *bhautika srsti*. In their uncreated or eternal form these substances are known as *paramanu*. So whereas there are five *bhutas*, there are only four types of *bhuta paramanus*. The fifth *bhuta* or *akasa* is only available in the eternal and uncreated form. Hence so far as this *bhuta* is concerned there is no distinction between *nitya* and *janya*. The other *bhutas* are available in the *nitya* or *paramanu* form and in the *janya* or created form. Strictly speaking no *bhuta* is itself caused.

A created substance is necessarily created ultimately out of the (*nitya*) *paramanus* of one of the four *bhutas*. When a substance is thus created we call it an instance of *janya bhuta* of the respective type. *Eka bhautika* substances are really the only *janya bhutas*. Now since every *janya dravya* is *eka bhautika* and since the model of creation is combination of *paramanus* of respective type, there must be admitted indefinite number of *paramanus* of each of the four types. The number of *paramanus* to be admitted in the case of any single *bhuta* or substance of anyone of the first four is related to such other questions as whether the *paramanus* can really be partless, and this in its turn is related to the question whether the *paramanus* can really combine to create a *bhautika* substance of the same *bhuta* kind. In addition to these we shall not have a fully worked out rational and analytical theory of *bhuta* and cosmic creation till we can clarify the nature of the combination, its effectiveness and possibility which is supposed to create a whole universe out of tiny bits of matter known as *bhutas*. One thing is clear: if *bhutas* are to combine to produce a *bhautika* substance and only the substance that can be produced is *bhautika*, every *bhuta* must be an actual or possible constituent of some *bhautika dravya*. But by the principle that *paramanus* of different *bhutas* cannot combine, combination of *paramanus* or *bhutas* means necessarily combination of *paramanus* of one *bhuta* only. Unless therefore a *bhuta* is numerically many or at least two, it cannot enter into effective combination that can explain creation. A *bhuta*, which is numerically one, cannot participate in any *bhautika srsti* as constituent of created substance. *Akasa* or *vyoma* for this reason cannot be the constituent of any *bhautika* substance and it cannot combine with any substance in the sense or in the way in which two *paramanus* of anyone of the first four *bhutas* can combine. But for all that, *akasa* is counted among the *bhutas* and it is also admitted to be capable of combining with other *bhutas* and substances in some sense.

Now the uncreated *bhutas* which admit of numerical difference and are numerically many are *paramanu* in nature. What about the *bhuta* which is even numerically one? The *naiyayikas* hold that this *bhuta* is infinitely vast or is ubiquitous. By contrast the *paramanus* are minutest parts of *bhautika* substances. Thus while part of the meaning of *paramanu* is that it is the simplest material constituent or *avayava* of the smallest ever substance to be produced, being material part of a substance is no part of the meaning of *bhuta*. *Bhutas* are therefore available in two forms, infinitely large (*vibhu rupa*) and infinitely small (*paramanu rupa*); the former type of *bhuta* cannot be constituent of any created matter also because a constituent matter must be smaller than the matter it constitutes. But since *akasa* is not smaller than any substance it cannot be a constituent matter. Nor for that matter can it be a constituted substance; a constituted matter must ultimately be the result of the combination of numerically distinct *bhutas* of the same kind, i.e., *paramanus* of the same single *bhuta*. But since there are no two even numerically distinct *akasas*, there cannot be *janya akasa* constituted by smaller bits of *akasa*. All these matters of detail deserve to be separately discussed. But that is not possible within the limited length of hence I shall discuss as many of these points as possible together, though that is not the way to ensure clarity or accuracy; paradoxically enough attempt to save space in this way often makes certain amount of repetition unavoidable. The terminological clarifications achieved so far may be remembered. We cannot use interchangeably the two expressions of *bhuta* and *paramanu* and none of these expressions can be used as synonym of element. We shall see how inaccurate it is to translate *paramanu* as atom.

Paramanus of any one *bhuta* is believed to be indefinite in number. But whatever may be their exact total number it remains permanently fixed. The total number of *bhutas* is also fixed; we know the number is five. But the number of individual *bhautika* substances such as clay jars and of kinds of such substances, e.g., *ghata* or *sarira* (organic matter of, say, human body) is theoretically speaking infinite. Any two *bhautika* things and any two *paramanus* of two distinct *bhutas* differ both numerically and qualitatively. Two *paramanus* of any single *bhuta* differ only numerically. *Paramanus* are actual or possible constituents of some *bhautika* substance. The number of *paramanus* which constitute any given *bhautika* substance is finite. From this point of view the universe though created is not one *bhautika* substance as a clay jar is. For then the total number of *paramanus* in the universe would have been finite. The universe is regarded as the totality of effects including all the created substances, and ultimate material constituents total of all the created matters is *bhuta* including *bhuta paramanu* the number of which is, we have seen, infinite. We shall soon return to the question why the number of any single created substance is indefinite rather than infinite. But let us first note another feature of the *paramanus* and the consequence of that so far as the theory of *bhautika srsti* is concerned.

Any two *paramanus* of the same or different *bhutas* are independent of each other. The same is true of any two *bhutas* also. Anyway, two *paramanus* may or may not stand combined; and even when they stand combined they do so contingently, i.e., they may fall apart again. The *paramanus* therefore can remain unrelated and once they come to be related they can become separated later; and once separated they can recombine. When two substances are contingently combined in this way the *naiyayikas* say they are combined or related by way of conjunction, i.e., the relation that binds together any two substances – whether two *paramanu bhutas* or two *bhautika dravyas* or two *abhautika dravyas* or any permutation or combination of them – thus contingency is called by the *naiyayikas samyoga*; we translate this as relation of conjunction. There are other relations like inherence the relata of which are not so contingently related. The contingent relation of conjunction presupposes that the terms to be related by its means must previously be in a state of disjunction. In other words this relation presupposes or implies a prior state of disjunction between the items which now stand conjoined. It is also true on *Nyaya* theory that any state of conjunction between any two substances must be followed by a state of disjunction or loss of at least effective conjunction.

Though there are no two sorts of conjunction yet we must distinguish between the conjunction which bind together two constituent substances – whether two *bhuta paramanus* or material parts or *avayava dravyas* constituted ultimately by the *bhuta paramanus* – within a single substance constituted by them from the conjunction which obtain between two substances which are not constituents of the same (gross) substance. At the macro level also we distinguish between the conjunction which hold together the threads of a piece of cloth and the conjunction that obtains between a book and a table if we happen to place the former on the latter. The threads are so conjoined as to bring into existence another substance with an identity of its own. Such substances are called *avayavin* and they alone have proper parts or *avayavas*. Where the conjunction between certain substances fail to bring forth an *avayavin* the conjunction accounts for there being a mere collection or heap of matter. When a conjunction or set of conjunctions is effective in bringing about an *avayavin* or *avayavi dravya*, that is, a new substance with its own identity, it is called effective conjunction or *dravyarambhaka samyoga*. But when the same *samyoga* or conjunction (same because as conjunction, all the conjunctions are the same) accounts for a mere collection we must distinguish it as ineffective. It is clear that here being effective means being causally effective or effective in bringing about a new single substance rather than only a collection of a (the same) number of substances.

We are now in a position to answer a question which we left unanswered. On *Nyaya* theory every created substance is necessarily *eka bhautika* by which is meant that any such substance is created ultimately through effective conjunction of *paramanus* of one *bhuta* only. When in a gross created substance at the macro level, such as, say, an organic human body, we say all the *bhutas* are somehow present, what we mean is that in such a gross body different *bhautika* or created substances are present as parts not in the sense of *avayavas*. An organic body is not strictly speaking a single substance, nor again it is a mere collection of many unassorted substances. A body has a unity but not the identity of a single *avayavin*. What are ordinarily called parts of a body can hardly be said to be the *avayavas* of the body. Thus the eyes of a human body are not the *avayava* of the latter. For the eyes are *teja dravya* or belong to the class of substances made out of the *paramanus* of the *bhuta* known as fire, whereas the human body is *parthiva*; and no two *paramanus* of two different *bhutas* or of substances, created through effective conjunction of *paramanus* or parts of two different *bhutas*, can be proper parts or *avayavas* of the same single *eka bhautika dravya*. The eyes of a body are not even strictly speaking *upadana* in the sense of *samavayi karana*. They are better called *angas*. Thus *anga* of a created or gross substance is to be distinguished from the *avayava* of it. We need so far to distinguish between three types of situations. Two *paramanus* of the same *bhuta* may stand effectively conjoined as parts of an *avayavi dravya*. Two *paramanus* of two different *bhutas* or a number of bricks or a number of human bodies may be made into a heap in which these substances stand conjoined though not effectively. These are two extreme cases where terms conjoined stand respectively as intimately related and barely related. Conjunction, which obtains between the limbs of a body, or between certain limbs and the body of which they are the limbs, seem somehow to fall between the two extreme cases. A human body is called *deha indriya samghata*.

The conjunction between a body and the sense-organ is also causally effective — it is what makes sense experience of the soul possible — only it is not effective in the sense of bringing about another substance; in other words conjunction between a body and its sense-organ is not an instance of *dravyarambhaka samyoga*. Another instance of causally effective *samyoga* which is not *dravyarambhaka* is the conjunction between *manas*, not as the internal sense-organ but as the last of the nine substances, and soul. Like the conjunction between the *deha* and sense-organ this conjunction between soul and *manas* is effective in bringing about experience of sentient creatures like man. But there are instances of conjunction which are not effective in either of these two senses; take for instance the conjunction between *kala* and *ghata*. So far as we the finite beings are concerned, such conjunctions cannot even cause awareness of them as object. But in the case of a heap of unassorted substances the conjunction, which accounts for this heap, is not effective in bringing about a new substance, or causing an experience, except of itself and as the object of the experience concerned.

An effective conjunction, which causes a new unit substance to occur, i.e., *dravyarambhaka samyoga*, obtains between either two *paramanus* of the same *bhuta* or two gross matter parts or *avayavas*, provided they are created out of the *paramanus* of the same *bhuta*. One question is why do the *naiyayikas* admit two types or levels of *dravyarambhaka samyoga*? Since much *samyoga* between two created matter, which are *avayavas* of the same *avayavi dravya*, presupposes necessarily and ultimately *dravyarambhaka samyoga* between *paramanus*, we could, it seems dispense with one of these two types of causally effective *samyogas*, which account for the material creation in the narrow sense of the term.

In the *nyaya* conception creation through combination is a process rather than an one-time single event or occurrence. If even all the actual-effect substances were created as a result of effective combination of the simplest material constituent or *paramanus*, then they would be produced in one go. In that case there would not have been a good rational explanation to why created substances do display different structural complexities. But once these complexities are hierarchically arranged, and we admit two types of *dravyarambhaka samyoga* and the corresponding two levels of creation, which may respectively be called, risking a small inaccuracy, micro and macro level creation — creation out of *paramanus* and creation out of smaller and less complex *avayavi dravyas* — we can account for what is experientially evident, namely, that substances of different structural complexities are there, and that the substances of higher and higher or more and more complex structures are produced gradually. But there seems to be a theoretical or conceptual difficulty here. If both *paramanu dravya* and *avayavi dravya* can be constituent or *avayava* of respective higher-order created substance, then the distinction of *dravyas* into those, which are *avayavin* and those which are not *avayavin*, becomes rather unnecessary complication. If on the other hand this distinction is to be maintained on independent and rational consideration, then the *nyaya* theory of gradual creation with level distinction should appear to have both rational and empirical support in its favour.

We shall argue in favour of the *nyaya* theory rather negatively. We shall show why we cannot say that no *avayava dravya* must itself be an *avayavin*, or that every *avayavin* must be an *avayava* of some actual or possible *avayavin* of higher complexities. If this can be shown then it will be demonstrated that there must be two types of *avayava* and two types of *avayavin*. If every *avayava dravya* were itself an *avayavin*, then it would itself be the result of effective combination of two or more *avayavas*; so far as each of these *avayavas* is itself an *avayavin*, it must be made out of further *avayavas*, each of which must be an *avayavin* of lesser structural complexity. If this logic is followed then every created substance will admit of being broken into parts or substances of lesser and lesser structure *ad infinitum*. Every finite structure would be infinitely divisible. Apart from logical paradox of such a position the predictable observable consequence of it will be empirically disconfirmable. The predictable consequence of infinite divisibility of every created matter is that all material structures will be of same size. There will be neither measurable nor visible difference in size between a mountain and a mustard seed. Since the thesis of infinite divisibility of created matter is both logically inconsistent and empirically false, then the opposite thesis must be true. Analysis of matter must stop somewhere. The logical and physical end point of the analysis or breaking of a finite or created matter, in our language, *avayavin* or *janya dravya*, must be a unit matter which is not further divisible; it is *antya avayava*. However simple a structure must be the number of the *avayava* into which it can be broken, must be more than one. The number of *antya avayavas* into which any finite matter gets divided is usually very large. Be that as it may, the *antyavayavas* could not be *antyavayavas* if they were themselves *avayavins*. For then analysis of matter would not terminate with them. This therefore is the reason why we must admit some *avayava* or constituent matter, which are themselves not constituted by other matters of smaller structure. As such these are simplest and not further analysable matter. Though these *antyavayavins* have no *avayavas* of their own, they are themselves *avayavas,* i.e., constituent material structure or unit matter which are parts of other matter. These other matters by contrast have parts or *avayavas*, and as such they are *avayavins* or constituted matters; and since to be constituted in the sense of being brought about by effective combination of parts is to be caused, the *avayavins* are necessarily created matter.

There are a few theoretical problems here. A theory of creation is designed to explain the phenomenon of creation. But the phrase 'explanation of creation' is ambiguous in many ways. A theory may begin by accepting the phenomenon of creation, not just as a fact of experience but also as the starting point of theory building. For such a theory explaining creation may consist in answering the question, "What are the conditions which must have been realised in the past, as otherwise there could not have been the universe as we see it today?" If such a presupposition is granted, then we can begin by actual existence of structured and created matter and arrive at simplest matter, which is *paramanu* by physically and/or conceptually analysing or breaking matter till the end. If *paramanus* are arrived at in this way, then in the same act in which we prove the existence of such simplest matter as *paramanu*, we also prove that it is an *avayava* and hence *antyavayava*. But if in spite of granting full objective and experiential reality to the phenomenon of creation, one does not make its reality a presupposition of the theory of creation being developed, then explanation of creation cannot start from the acceptance of *avayavi dravyas*. It would not be a part of the meaning of simplest matter that it is *avayava* or *antyavayava*. We now see that the two parts of the meaning of *paramanu*, (i) that it is the simplest matter or that it is not an *avayavin*, and (ii) that it is *avayava* or *avayava* of the least complex matter to be first created, are not analytically or necessarily related. So the question remains, though it did not surface because of the particular approach we adopted above, wherefrom comes the necessity for the partless and simplest units of matter to combine effectively? It is in its ability to answer this question posed in the way we have done just now that the utility and strength of a theory of creation seems to lie. Some theories which begin with this perspective takes the existence of matter or primordial matter or stuff to be a presupposition and limit of scientific explanation. The question under reference gains further strength in the *Nyaya* school of thought from the fact that the *naiyayikas* do not admit that everyone of the simple unit of matter is an *avayava*. They admit among the *bhutas akasa* which is as much partless as any *bhuta paramanu*, but *akasa* is not a constituent or part of any actual or possible created material substance. To put it differently, its being a *bhuta* or its being partless and hence structurally simple may not be enough to qualify or compel any unit of matter to be an *avayava*.

To return to the question we were discussing, why must one or must a *naiyayika* admit two types of *avayava* – one which is both an *avayava* and an *avayavin* and the other which is only *avayava* but not also an *avayavin*. It was argued that if infinite divisibility is an unacceptable position, and therefore if we are to accept only finite divisibility of gross or structured matter, then we must admit *paramanus* which are not *avayavins*. It was perhaps hoped that to be able to show this is to show that there are or must be admitted to be such matter, which are not *avayavin* but are nonetheless *avayava*. Then some doubt and critical points were raised to the effect that there may be other reasons for admitting uncreated and even simple substance, such that it would not necessarily follow that such substance, is an *avayava*. Thus the proof given so far in favour of the existence of partless substance, which is in itself part of some other substance, is not fully satisfying. Leaving this question unanswered and postponing another question to be raised shortly we may address ourselves to the other proof.

Let us admit for the present that we have proved that there are *avayavas* which are not *avayavin*. Let us now see if we can prove that there are *avayavins* which are *avayavas* also. There does not seem to be any necessity for a structured substance to be the part of another material substance. But if there is no logical inconsistency or empirical disconfirmation against the hypothesis that every *avayavin* must also be an *avayava*, then that may be thought to be enough. But we must remember that the *naiyayikas* do admit certain *avayavins* which according to them are not *avayava* in relation to any actual or possible complex matter. These they call *antyavayavin*. Secondly the pattern of proof we decided to offer compel us to find if and what argument may be there, why we cannot say that every *avayavin* is an *antyavayavin*. If we cannot find any such argument, then we may have to end up so far with only two types of substance — the *bhuta paramanus* on the one hand, which are *avayavas* but not *avayavins*, and on the other the *avayavi dravyas* which are not *avayavas*. In that case there will not be two types of *avayava* but only one type. We have argued earlier if no *avayavin* were *avayava*, then every unit of matter of every degree of complexity would be constituted in the same way, directly by the *bhuta paramanus* standing in effective conjunction. Every created thing would be caused simultaneously. One way in which we can avoid this and make the observed succession among created things theoretically possible is to propose the hypothesis that material substances of higher, and more complex structure do not emerge till the substances of immediately lower degree of complexity are produced. If this is not to be a gratuitous assumption but a reasoned position, it is to be founded on some sound principle. One way of founding it in this sense is to make it a matter of causal necessity. If higher structures are causally dependent on lower structures, then gradually higher structures will be produced only temporally successively. Since at this level of creation of material substance 'causing' means effective combination of parts, gradually higher structures will be produced as a result of combination of preceding complex structures. The latter therefore must be parts or *avayavas*; and as complex structures they are *avayavins* also. So some *avayavins* are also *avayavas*. The question remains, why cannot all *avayavins* be like this or be *avayavas* themselves? Why there has to be higher limit of *avayava*? Why there must be *antyavayavin*? We shall leave this question unanswered here and say in conclusion that we have found, if not conclusive yet adequately convincing, argument why there should be *antyavayava* or *bhuta paramanu*, and why every *avayavin* cannot fail to be an *avayava*, or why every *avayavin* cannot be an *antyavayavin*. If however *antyavayavin* is at all admitted, then we find that matter would be available in four different forms. These four forms are, as the *naiyayikas* call them, (a) *antyavayava* e.g., *bhuta paramanus*, (b) *avayavins* which are also *avayavas* such as threads of a piece of cloth or pot halves, (c) *antyavayavins* such as a clay pot or jar or a piece of cloth, and lastly (d) the *bhuta dravya* which is neither an *avayava* nor an *avayavin*. *Akasa* is a case in point. This *akasa* is similar to *bhuta paramanus* in respect of being partless. It resembles *antyavayavins* insofar it never constitutes as part of another material body. It is easier to find a justification why *akasa* cannot be an *avayava*. No infinite substance can be a part of another material body, or we would have to admit a body which has a dimension greater than that of an infinite body. But this argument is not available in case of *antyavayavin* like a jar or earthenpot which has only a finite dimension. Existence of *akasa* renders another simpler and more neat classification of nine substances impossible. If *akasa* like other *bhutas* (or as it is more usual to call them *bhuta paramanus*) were *avayava* of some material body, or if it were not considered as a *bhuta*, then we could divide substances into those which inhere (in other matter which would be its part), or are *samaveta* and those which do not inhere or are not *samaveta*. Then *asamaveta dravyas* could be divided into *bhutas* and those which are other than *bhutas* according to the principle, the former cause as constituent some created material body, while the latter type of *asamaveta dravya* do not form part of any other matter. All *samaveta dravyas* in that case would be *bhautika*, though all *asamaveta dravyas* would not be *bhutas*. As it is, while all *bhautika dravyas* are considered by the *naiyayikas* to be finite in dimension, *abhautika dravyas* whether *bhuta* or not include both the variety. Among the *bhuta dravyas akasa* is infinite, whereas other *bhutas* (or *bhuta paramanus*) are finite; among *dravyas* that are neither *bhuta* nor *bhautika manas* is finite but all the rest are infinite.

We have seen why we cannot accept the hypothesis of infinite divisibility of any complex bit of matter. But it has been pointed out that the other thesis of finite divisibility is not free from difficulty. In fact the Bauddha philosophers have argued that the *nyaya-vaisesika* conception of *paramanu* is inconsistent. But the way they argue brings it out clearly that they find fault not so much with the conception of a matter which is partless or simple, as with the conception that a piece of matter can be both partless and combine effectively with other (partless) matter to create or cause a material body having minimal complexity. They seem to argue that if *paramanus* were partless, then their conjunction could not constitute a larger material body. If parts to be combined are not infinitely small but have (however small) finite dimension, then we can distinguish between conjunction with one part from the conjunction with another part or matter. It can be visualized this way. We place a book *b* on the table or bring it in conjunction with the table then we place another book *b** on the first book. Because *b* has a finite dimension, it relates while it keeps separate the two — the table and the book *b**. We can say now that the book is the seat of two conjunctions or is conjoined with two substances on two sides of it. We could hardly say this if the *b* did not have any finite dimension or different sides so to say to be conjoined with different substances simultaneously. Greater the number of things with which a thing is simultaneously and directly conjoined, greater is the dimension of it. In other words a substance gains in dimension by the number of direct simultaneous and distinguishable conjunctions of which it is the seat. But the direct and simultaneous conjunctions to be distinguished, the thing which is the seat of these conjunctions must have finite dimension or parts. Different bodies parts or units of matter should be conjoined with different parts of the same thing; the thing must have different distinguishable points in its body where different particles of matter can touch it. This line of argument shows that if *paramanus* are to cause higher structure of matter to emerge through effective combination among themselves, then every single *paramanu* must have at least, as they say, six different points on its surface so to say; or it must have six parts or *sad amsa*. It is believed to be a very strong way of arguing against the notion of matter, which is the partless part of another matter which has not only a part but also a larger dimension, consisting in greater number of distinguishable and countable parts. The *nyaya* reply to this objection is very subtle and extremely beautiful. The *naiyayikas* question a number of assumptions which remained unnoticed behind the Bauddha criticism. The Bauddhas have assumed that increase in dimension of material body is to be explained only in terms of addition of parts of lower dimension. This assumption is weak as it makes very difficult to take infinite magnitude to be objective. For infinite body on this view must be an infinitely divisible body. In other words the line of argument the Bauddhas offer to disprove partless *paramanu* has the consequence of making it necessary that every infinite substance is infinitely divisible. The weakness of this position is well-known from the time of Zeno or even before. Their second assumption that the only way to distinguish the direct and simultaneous conjunctions of which a certain body is the seat is to refer those conjunctions to different distinguishable parts of that body. It has been shown by the *naiyayikas*, how without referring them to different parts of the substance which is their seat, these conjunctions can be distinguished in terms of different direction or *dik*, which are related to the body in question, not as distinguishable parts of it but as what may be called different *avacchedakas*. A single partless *paramanu* can have different conjunction in different *dik avaccheda*. These are important points of technical detail which however we cannot discuss in this paper.

13

Indian Cosmology
Reflections in Religion and Metaphysics

A.K. Chakravarty

The exact origin of astronomical studies in India is not known to us though it is fairly clear that it eventually formed part of ancient Vedic people. The earliest text on this subject now available, *Vedanga Jyotisa*, aims at determining the most suitable time for performing a *yajna* in consideration of the luni-solar-stellar situation at that time. The subject was based on so crude astronomical parameters that its failure could not escape the notice of any sky-watcher, till then it was never questioned by anybody perhaps because of its association with religious *yajnas*. This scheme of astronomy survived for some 2000 years.

In later India, these parameters were scraped, scope of astronomy was extended to include natural phenomena, like, eclipses, identification of planets and formulations of their motions, etc., till then astronomers often invoked metaphysics to explain cosmological facts. It occurs to us that the general people of that period in that class-ridden society was more interested in earning *punyaphala* through religious functions than acquiring pure knowledge. Astronomers could not or did not ignore this sentiment and so, to honour this sentiment, they found it necessary to blend religion and metaphysics with cosmology in an astronomical background. Science in ancient times had to be supplemented by speculative materials and was thus mixed up with myths and metaphysics.

The period of the 5-yearly cycle in *Vedanga* and *Jain Jyotisa*

The *Vedanga Jyotisa* (*VJ*) is essentially a guidebook for finding positions of the sun and moon in the asterism divisions (*naksatras*) at *parvas* (new or full moon), the beginning or ending moment of a *parva* in the day, the *tithis* and *naksatras* in which the solstices occur and above all, the description of a 5-yearly cycle (*Yuga*). We shall consider this *yuga* in further details in a later section, for the present we state that the text itself says (*Yajuṣ* 2, 3) that *yajnas* are to be performed in proper time, and astronomy is the science of time. One who knows this science of time also knows *yajnas*.

Now, major part of this text is obscure or corrupt in form. We give one specific illustration.

Yajus 12: *Duheyang parva chet pade. . .*

A straightforward translation of it is: If a *parva* ends in a quarter of a day, then *duheya* it. But, according to Tilak, "there is no verbal form as *duheyang* or even *duheya* in sanskrit". As shown in § 3, the astronomical contents of the *VJ* appear to be earlier than the period of Vedic Aryan and hence the presumption is that the text contains certain words and expressions inherited from an unknown earlier language. Hence the commentator Somakara often fails to make a clear sense of many words in the text. Many modern scholars, tactly assuming that it is a textual corruption try to suggest what the original word could have been. We cite two examples only.

Tilak suggests here *dyu heyang* (day to be omitted) to make the meaning: if a *parva* ends in a quarter of a day, then that day is to be omitted, i.e., no *tithi* rites (like fasting, bathing, etc.) should not be performed on that day.

Dixit's emendation makes the meaning: if a *parva* ends in a quarter of a day, observe *tithi* on that quarter.

It is now almost impossible to know what the original author intended to say. Only this much is obvious that the verse gives an instruction on *parva* rites should a *parva* end in a quarter of a day.

We have stated that astronomy was used as a science of computing times for *yajnas*. Time's role was to be auspicious or unauspicious for *yajnas* and had no other role like recording chronology, etc. Chronology has been recorded in contemporary period through a history of genealogical tables as we find in the two great epics and *Puranas*. In *Ramayana*, (*Bal.*, 70) Vasistha gives the chronolgy of Rama in the ancestral order from Manu, Iksvaku and so on up to Dasaratha and in reply Janaka stated his ancestral order from Nimi to himself.

We construct the following story on origin of the science of astronomy in ancient India.

The Aryans had been performing *yajnas* since their settlement in India. It is a separate branch of studies as to whether they formulated these *yajnas* of their own or they brought these ideas from elsewhere. Our present concern is that they performed various *yajnas* on different seasons for different purposes and also observed *tithi*-rites on *parvas*. When such functions multiplied in number, the task of maintaining the order or sequence of such functions became somewhat technical and it became necessary to detail a section of priests to specialise in computing times for *yajnas*. Astronomical literature as it comes down to us owes its birth to meet this need of the priestly class, and so it is more connected with *dharmasastras* than astronomy proper, and accordingly this subject was named *Vedanga,* i.e., a limb of the *Vedas*.

The very basic principle of *VJ* is that the solsticial colour passes through the star β-Delphini. A little of spherical astronomy shows that this was indeed the situation around 1500 BC and so astronomy appeared as a separate subject around this time.

Then rises a pertinent question: Whether the *rsis* followed the same 5-yearly cycle in earlier period for computing times for *Yajnas*. The following example shows that the answer is in the affirmative.

Theory of the 5-yearly cycle

According to *VJ*,

$$62 \text{ lunations} = 62 \times 29 \frac{32}{60} = 1830 \text{ days}$$

$$5 \text{ solar years} = 5 \times 366 = 1830 \text{ days}$$

Hence, 62 lunations fit into 5 solar years. In practice, the practical *yajnic* year is a lunar year of 12 lunations. A cycle begins from a new moon at winter solstice. In the time of composition of *VJ*, this solstice was identified with the star β-Delphini. Hence the text says: Cycle begins from the winter month Magha when the sun, moon, Dhanistha (β-Delphini) are in conjunction at *Uttarayana* (winter solstice). After two years each of 12 lunations, one lunation is intercalated at the middle of the 3rd year, then at the end of the 5th year one more lunation is intercalated at the end of the year. After these 62 lunations the sun and moon again come at conjunction with Dhanistha at the winter solstice and the cycle is repeated. The shift of winter solstice from Dhanistha due to procession can be detected even by naked eye in a hundred years or so. Identification of this solstice by various other stars are also found in early Brahmanic literature. The principle is that a *yuga* begins from a new moon at winter solstice and so solar year is, in fact, tropical year and not sidereal.

The correct values of the above parameters are:

5 tropical years = 1826 days 5 hours app.

62 lunations = 1830 days 21 hours app.

Thus, the cycle is bound to collapse unless provisions are made for periodic corrections. We give a specific illustration.

From standard tables (say, Tables of the sun by N.C. Lahiri) we get that on 22nd December, 1900, the tropical longitude of sun was 270° 14' and it was a new moon day. This day was the beginning of a 5-yearly cycle. From the same table, we further get:

(a) The 62nd lunation ended on 27th December 1905. The first *yuga* closes and the second *yuga* begins on 27th December, 1905. But the intervening period is not 1830 days, the luni-solar conjunction is not at winter solstice.

(b) The 3rd cycle begins on 1st January, 1911, 10 days later than first cycle. The date is not winter solstice day.

(c) Similarly, when the seventh cycle begins, the month is not winter month and also, as above, the date is not winter solstice day.

The calendar totally collapses. But it did not collapse and survived for some 2000 years. The *VJ* does not say anything about how this derangement was stopped. If it is there in the *VJ*, it is hidden in obscurity.

We propose to show that the priests had some domestic methods connected with *yajnas* to keep the cycle running in order. They extracalated these accumulated days by practical observations, i.e., sky-watching.

Brahmanic literature contains description of *Satras*, i.e., annual sacrifices. "The *satras*, which lasted for one year were nothing but an imitation of the sun's yearly course" (From Dr. Haug). Such descriptions are found in *Taittiriya Samhita*, *Tandya Brahmana*, etc. The following extract is quoted from *Taittiriya Samhita*: (English Translation by Tilak).

> Those who are about to consecrate themselves for the year (sacrifice) should do so on the *Ekastaka* (day). The *Ekastaka* is the wife of the year; and he (i.e. the year) lives in her (i.e., the *Ekastaka*) for the night. (Therefore they) practically sacrifice (by) beginning the year. Those who sacrifice on the *Ekastaka*, sacrifice to the distressed (period) of the year. It is the season whose name comes last. Those that sacrifice on the *Ekastaka*, sacrifice on the reversed (period) of the year.

The *Ekastaka* is defined to be the 23rd *tithi* of the month of Magha, and corresponds to the 23rd day of the moon which can be easily recognized as it is the dichotomized phase of the moon. The word distressed (*artam va ete*) has been interpreted by Sayana to mean that the old year has ended and a new year has started by this *Ekastaka*, i.e., visibility of the half-disc moon. Sabara maintains that the word reversed (*vyastam va ete*) means a change in *ayana* and consequently means that a new year has already started by that time (*ayanaparivrttih vyastasabdena ucyate*). Thus both the commentators agree that the visibility of a half-disc moon after winter solstice indicate that the new year had started from the previous first day of the moon and that the month was

Magha, the *Ekastaka* was the 23rd *tithi* of the month. The following table will clarify the above discussions.

First Cycle begins on 22nd December 1900
half disc moon seen on 12th January 1901
Second Cycle begins on 27th December 1905
half disc moon seen on 18th January 1906
Third Cycle begins on 1st January 1905
half disc moon seen on 24th December 1910

In the last case, there has been an accumulation of some 10 days and the *yuga* is heading for a collapse. But the half disc moon is seen on 24th December 1910, just after winter solstice. This day is therefore an *Ekastaka* and so constitutes the 23rd *tithi* of Magha. Thus Magha commenced on the previous new moon, on 2nd December 1910. By this criteria of *Ekastaka*, the excess days are extracalated and the 3rd *yuga* is reckoned from 2nd December 1910 and not from 1 January, 1911.

The priests of the *yajnas* knew the science of time, and they kept the *yuga* in order.

Antiquity of Vedic Astronomy

Brahmanic literature contains sufficient references to stellar phenomena. We consider some such references purposely selected to trace the origin of astronomical studies by Vedic Aryans.

The *Taittiriya*, *Kathaka*, *Maitrayani Samhitas* and the 19th book of *Atharva Veda* contain a list of 27 stars/star-groups (the last two mention an additional name, *abhijit*, making a total of 28 stars.)

The *Satapatha Brahmana* says that the *Krttikas* do not shift from the east. The *Krttikas* rise in the east and the seven sages (*Ursa Majoris*) rise in the north.

Svati (α Bootes) is an outcast (for being far away from other stars) and is ever traversing the northern way.

The *VJ* itself estimates the length of the longest day as 14 hours 24 minutes.

We give the astronomical significances of the above statements in plane language for the general reader. A command over spherical astronomy is necessary for understanding the mathematical proofs of our analysis.

The *krttikas* can rise in the east and may not shift from the east if the central and brightest star of the *krittika* group, η-Tauri lies on the equator. This was indeed the situation around 3000 BC.

Around 3000 BC α-Draconis was the pole star (within tolerable limits of accuracy) and β-UM had the highest co-declination. A straigh-cut meaning of seven sages rising in the north is that the seven stars were circumpolar or at least β-UM touched the horizon at rising. This hold true at a place above 30°N latitude.

Exactly similarly, Svati can be seen to rise and set at a place below 40°N latitude.

With proper allowances for refraction, the length of the longest day can be 14 hours 24 minutes at a place of latitude 33° N.

In short, the above observations were made around 3000 BC from a latitude-belt of 30° - 40° North, and there was no Vedic settlement in that region of India at that period. It is indeed an interesting course of study as to how Vedic Aryans collected all these data and included these in their literature. From the viewpoint of Vedic Aryans, these observations were no longer true, as till then they recorded all these data without any verification. Thus from evidences in Brahmanic literature it appears that Vedic Aryans got ready at their hands a course of astronomy before settling in India.

Jain Cosmology

As Brahmanism declined with rise of Jainism and Buddhism, the *yajnic* aspect of *VJ* lost its importance. When the Jains developed their astronomy and cosmology, they adopted the parameters of *VJ*, but the cosmology developed by them is so unconventional to Indian tradition that we totally fail to understand what prompted these astronomers to develop this theory. According to the Jains, there are two sets of sun, moon and asterisms; while one set works, the other set rests behind the Meru mountain.

The concept of a Meru mountain at the north pole, also called Sumeru mountain, is found in the *Mahabharata*, *Puranas*, Jain Cosmology and in Aryabhata. Using the Aryabhatiyan scale for *yojanas*, the dimensions of Meru are:

Mahabharata : 193 km inside the earth's surface, 1017 km above.
Puranas : 193776 km inside the earth's surface, 823548 km above.
Jains : 12111 km inside the earth's surface, 1198989 km above.
Aryabhata : Cylindrical in shape, of height 12 km and diametre 12 km

Many of the present researchers have found out some inner meanings in these descriptions of the Jain Meru and have traced astronomical depth there. But in developed astronomy we also expect developed astronomical literature and terminology. Brahmagupta bitterly criticised this cosmology as a fantasy. We are also unable to connect this cosmology with Jain traditions on religion and metaphysics.

The Jains borrowed at least the 5-yearly cycle from Brahmanic tradition, but later Brahmanic tradition totally ignored Jain astronomy.

The Siddhantic Period

Astronomical literature in India took a comparative scientific turn around 300 AD., and this literature is now called siddhantic astronomy. They identified the planets and formulated laws governing their motions, computed the times of beginning and ending of eclipses from a scientific viewpoint through mathematical approach, and till then, as we shall see, they were obsessed with the doctrines of *dharmasastras*, the priests and *pandits*.

We can easily guess the literacy and science consciousness of the general public in the caste-ridden society of that period. The ruling castes were then more interested in religious *punyaphala* and security of life and property because of political uncertainty of that period. The priests and *pandits* took full advantage of the first sentiment, the horoscopic astrologers that of the second, and both of them used astronomy as a common platform.

Perhaps astronomers also realised that in such a background a mathematical description of astronomy cannot be presented unless these common sentiments are properly acknowledged, or may be that due to inherent tradition, they also developed some obsessions for the *dharmasastras* from which they could not fully recover. We shall see next that many of the celebrated astronomers made statements which cannot be correlated with the beauty of the mathematical equations they developed for planetary motions. Astronomy continued to develop with three distinct objects: its application to *dharmasastras*, to horoscopic forecastings, and the science proper.

When asked to account for the circular orbits of the planets, Aristotle replied that circles are most natural curves and motions of planets are taken for granted. Hence planets move along natural curves by nature. He did not invoke any super power or metaphysics to account for this motion. But Aryabhata, and for that reason even Bhaskaracharya II in the twelfth century replied that a super wind, *Pravaha vayu* drives the planets in circular orbits. The Suryasiddhanta further says that the gods of *ucca*, *manda* and *pata*, holding reins attached to the planets, guide the planets once to the east and then to the west by pulling these reins.

Now, this concept is of Vedic origin. We are told in the *Mahabharata* (*Santi*, 329) that while Vedavyasa was teaching *Vedas* to his son he said that seven *Vayus*, winds, are constantly blowing through the universe and each *vayu* is doing a specific job. The *Abaha*, also called *Apana*, causes the luminaries to rise and set, *Pravaha* also called *Prana*, causes activities in man. It seems that in later hands these *Vayus* changed their original duties and *Pravaha* was assigned the task of moving the luminaries including the sun, moon, planets and stars.

The concept of a universal wind as the prime cause of motion of the planets cannot be correlated with the mathematical depth of the equations of epicycles. Either astronomers invoked this idea to appeal to the religious sentiments of their students and followers, or they could not overcome their own religious sentiments.

The convention in science is that when a new theory is developed, the earlier theory becomes a history, and improved and refined parameters replace the earlier crude ones. Ptolemaic model became history after Copernicus, and the eccentric circles of Copernicus became history after Kepler formulated his laws of planetary motions. But in Indian astronomy the situation is different. Each astronomer founded a school of his own, and these schools co-existed irrespective of their merits or defects. Even when the Aryabhatian parameters were found defective, the school founded by Aryabhata continued to exist. Puranic or Sastric traditions were perhaps invoked to appeal to the religious sentiments of the followers to found such schools.

We are told in *Mahabharata* (*Santi*, 312) that Rsi Yajnavalkya gave the following description of cosmology to his disciple:

> Ten thousand *Kalpas* make a day of Lord Narayana and a similar period makes a night of the Lord. He created Brahma in a golden egg. After one year Brahma created the universe consisting of the earth and the sky.

Astronomers adopted this theory of cosmology in a slightly modified form. According to Aryabhata, one day of Brahma is made up of 1 *Kalpa* which measures 4,35,45,60,000 years. Aryabhata subdivided this period into *manu*, *yuga* and quarter-*yuga*. The *Kalpa* we are passing through began on a Thursday.

Brahmagupta bitterly criticised Aryabhata arguing that these subdivisions do not follow the *Smrtis*, and further, the *Kalpa* should begin on Sunday. As Aryabhata has violated the *smrtis*, his entire astronomy is incorrect.

Vateswara (904 AD) questioned the correctness of Brahmagupta's astronomy on the ground that the latter violated *smrti*'s doctrine that the moon should be beyond the sun.

Dharmasastras in Astronomy

The astronomical parameters differ only slightly in different astronomical texts. For our present discussions, these differences will not matter much and so we follow the *Suryasiddhanta*. According to this text,

$$1 \text{ Lunar year} = 29.5305 \times 12 = 354.366 \text{ days}$$
$$1 \text{ Solar year} = 365.2587 \text{ days.}$$

Thus one lunar year lags behind the solar year and one lunation has to be added after 3 years to fit the lunar year into the solar one.

Astronomers have called this intercalary lunation as *adhika* month, and have asserted that this month is to be added to the lunar year. They have attached no religious or metaphysical property to this month, nor have they assigned any preferred or privileged position to it relative to the other months.

But priests and *pandits* of *dharmasastras* have outwitted the astronomers by capitalising this *adhika* month. A vast literature has been developed on the suitability or otherwise of this month for performing religious rites, and total authors on this literature outnumber the astronomers. We give below a short account of the literature on this month.

In an ordinary year of 12 lunations, the 12 new moons are most generally distributed uniformly over the 12 Zodiacal signs, i.e., one new moon falls in each sign. But when a lunation is intercalated and the year consists of 13 lunations, then two new moons must occur in one Zodiacal sign and so two lunations are to be designated by the same name. We call such a case as sign with two new moons. The situation becomes complicated in extreme cases when two signs contain two new moons each. In such a situation, there must occur a sign void of new moon. The earlier tradition that the only role of time in astronomy is to be auspicious and unauspicious for *yajnas* was carried forward by the priests and *Smarta pandits* in selecting which months in such cases are auspicious and which are not.

We take the specific instance of such a case. The year 1370 Bengal San (commencing from 15 April 1963 sunrise and ending on 14 April 1964 sunrise) was an intercalary year, i.e., contained 13 lunations. The distribution of these lunations over the signs are shown in the following diagram: (We have drawn the relevant portion only and also the diagram is not to scale. Our aim is to point out the problem and so we have used the conventional Bengal school of *Panchang*).

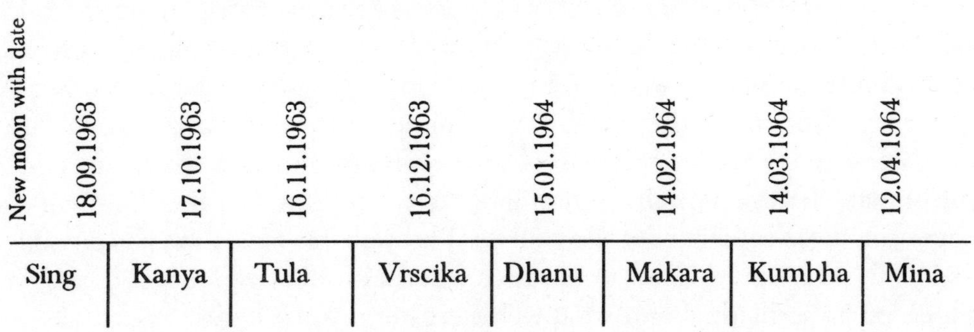

From the point of view of astronomy proper, the months are to be named as.: . . . *Asvina*, *Karika*, *Agrahayana*, *Pausa*, *Magha*, *Phalguna*, *Caitra*, *Adhika* month. No month can claim any preferred or privileged position over another. This is what true science demands. But *dharmasastras* capitalised the situation to their benefit.

If the lunations are to be fitted into signs, the lunations are to be named as:. . . *Asvina*(1), *Asvina*(2), *Karika*, *Agrahayana*, (*Pausa* missing in the order), *Magha*,

Phalguna, *Caitra*(1), *Caitra*(2). *Dharmasastras* now became directly involved in this distribution of months as to the order in which monthly religious functions are to be observed. Monthly rites due on *Asvina*, and *Caitra* cannot be repeated twice each and also those for *Pausa* cannot be abandoned altogether. There are almost as many directives as there are celebrated *pandits* and the literature on this subject is perhaps richer than the science of astronomy itself.

Metaphysics in Astronomy

In all astronomical texts, the planets are celestial objects only and nothing more. The only metaphysical property attached to them is that the 7 planets in the order Saturn, Jupiter, Mars, Sun, Venus, Mercury and Moon are the Lords of the 24 hours (*hora* in text) of the day reckoned from sunrise at Lanka by turn and also, these planets in the order Saturn, Sun, Moon, Mars, Mercury, Jupiter and Venus are the Lords of the seven days of a week reckoned from Saturday (*Arya - Kala* 16). The *Romakasiddhanta* has further defined Lords of the years and for the 12 months of a year as well. Varahamihira comments here that he will explain the astrological aspects of all these in his *Horatantra* after examining the views of *munis* on this subject.

Babylonian astronomy also contains an exactly similar idea. The seven planets were identified with the seven Babylonian gods and these gods watched the world for 24 hours a day, one god for 1 hour, by rotation and the order of the planets in this task is the same as stated in Aryabhatiya. In this order, the 1st hour of the successive days from Saturday onwards are watched by Saturn, Sun, Moon, Mars, Mercury, Jupiter and Venus.

This part of metaphysics in Indian astronomy is undoubtedly of foreign origin. It is now known that weekdays, and weeks of 7 days each are of foreign import in India around third century AD, and along with the week system the whole metaphysics of planetary connections with weekdays was adopted in Indian astronomy. But VM together with other *munis* also, celebrated among them were Parasara and Bhrgu, assigned some more additional powers to the planets through which these could control human destiny as well. A rich literature developed in the hands of these astrologers on these capacities of the planets. Through this literature, it is possible, as claimed by these *munis*, to know in advance when a particular planet will cast evil or good look on an individual and what will be result of such looks.

It is now believed that the original works of Bhrgu are now lost and what now circulates as *Bhrgu Samhita* is not the original work.

Parasara is a legendary figure. His name is found in *Mahabharata* and other ancient literature. But astrologer Parasara is of much later period, and cannot be earlier than fifth or sixth century AD.

The *Horasastra* of Parasara (IV.12) states that the sun should be corrected for *ayanamsa* to ascertain the equinoctial day at beginning of Mesa. But the concept of *ayanamsa* in Indian astronomy first originated in the fifth-sixth century AD.

We quote below some forecastings from this text to illustrate how easily these appeal to the sentiments of an average man:

> IX.59: If Jupiter or Moon stays in the 7th house of any person's horoscope, he will get a beautiful and faithful wife. If sun be in the 7th house, his wife will be unfaithful.
>
> VI.7: If a *dhuma* planet stays in the *lagna* of an individual he will be weak, poor and unfaithful to his wife.

The author cautions the reader that one who disbelieves all these things will suffer in the *Raurava* Hell.

It is perhaps impossible to ignore or overlook these metaphysical and religious aspect of astronomy or its application for such purposes. Earlier astronomers perhaps took resort to puranic and sastric traditions to give due weight to this sentiment. Even in the present age also, when science consciousness has greatly developed among the general people, *panchang* reformers do not ignore this sentiment.

A movement for reforming Indian *panchangs* by using modern astronomical tables replacing the age-old traditional and obsolete parameters developed in India by the mid-nineteenth century and such reformed *panchangs* started appearing by the late nineteenth century. The reformers claim that such *panchangs* are scientifically correct and that these are aimed at creating science consciousness among the general people.

Now, a scientist must have an all-round scientific viewpoint. A mathematician or physicist may not know the latest techniques in bio-science, till then a true scientist is supposed to believe in the broad outlines of bio-science inasmuch as an elephant's head cannot be amputed on a man's body or that eight additional hands also cannot be amputed on a human body. But scientific *panchang*-makers continue to print such photos in their *panchangs* aimed at preaching science proper. Modern science has not yet discovered any experimental device by which it can measure the amount of *punya* gained or lost if a sacrificial he-goat is beheaded at the proper moment or not, but they claim that only their timings are correct. They surely do not preach any science thereby however scientific their *panchangs* may be. This is done to appeal to the religious sentiment of the general people. If this is the position at this present time, we can guess the situation in the initial stage of development of the science of astronomy. It was out of necessity that metaphysics and religion were blended with astronomy.

14

Creation of the Universe and Evolution of Life

Arshad Hussain

It is a well-known fact that Muslim scholars have made a significant contribution to science, philosophy, mathematics and medicine, etc. during the last few centuries. As a matter of fact, they began to take active interest in all the branches of learning from the beginning of the Abbasid caliphate (750-1258 AD) of Baghdad. Thus Baghdad of those days became the central point for the scholars of the Muslim world. Among those scholars, Ibn-i-Sina is very famous for his work on philosophy and medicine. His work attained worldwide recognition, some of them were translated into Latin and taught as textbooks in Europe.

Ibn Sina, known in Europe as Avicenna, was a celebrated central Asian Philosopher, scientist and physician. His full name was Abu 'Ali al-Hussain bin 'Abdullah bin Sina. This great encyclopaedist, poet and critic was born at Khormethan near Bukhara in AD 980/370. But according to the *Encyclopaedia of Islam*,[1] he was born in Afshana near Bukhara which was his mother's home. His father 'Abdullah had migrated from Bulkh of Bukhara where he became an official of the Samanid administration. His father paid full attention to his education. At the age of ten years, he attained a good knowledge of the *Qur'an*, general literature, Indian calculus (Arithmetic) and algebra. His extraordinary intelligence and memory helped him in overtaking his teachers at the age of fourteen. He did not learn natural sciences or medicine from any teacher, in fact, famous physicians were working under his direction when he was only sixteen. He felt some difficulty in grasping Aristotle's *Metaphysics* which he overcame only with the help of al-Farabi's commentary. He was called on by the Samanid Prince Nuh bin Mansur for his treatment who was suffering from a severe illness. At this time he was hardly seventeen. Having cured the Prince he was allowed to make use of the splendid library of the Samanid princes in Bukhara which benefitted him immensely. He consulted there many books which he could not study before. At the age of eighteen he had mastered all the then known sciences. He was only twenty-one when he wrote his first philosophical book which established his reputation as an outstanding thinker. His father died soon after and he was forced to enter the administration to earn his living.

He was a minister several times and his advice was always listened to. Political intrigues and court rivalries forced him to go into hiding on several occasions. In this period he earned his living by medical consultations.

He was imprisoned, escaped from the prison and then lived the last fourteen years of his life in relative peace at the court of Asfahan, and died at Hamadan during an expedition of Prince 'Ala'ud Daulah in 428/1037. He was buried there and a monument was erected on his grave when (Hijri) millenary of his birth was celebrated in Iran in the year 1331 Shamsi/1952-53.

The UNESCO had taken decision to observe during 1980-81 the 1000th birth anniversary of this great intellectual giant of the Orient.

* * * * * * *

The treatise entitled *Dar Haqiqat wa Kaifiyat-i-Silsilah-i Maujudat wa Tasalsul-i-Asbab wa Musabbat* was written by Ibn-Sina in Persian language in the form of question and answer, so that, according to the author, it may be easily understandable. It consists of nine questions which have been answered in detail. The manuscripts of the treatise are known to be extant in the following libraries/private collections.

1. Personal collection of 'Ali Asghar Hikat (Iran).[2] It was scribed in 603 AH/1207 AD. Among the manuscripts known so far it is the oldest one. It consists of 42 pages and written in Naskh script.[3]
2. Personal collection of Sayyed Muhammad Mishkat of Iran. He was a professor in Tehran University. This manuscript written on coloured paper in Nast'aliq script consists of 15 pages with 14 lines on a page. It was scribed by Ibn-i-Muhammad Yusuf Muhammad 'Ali in 1198 AH/1784 AD.
3. Library of Masjid Sepah Salar (Iran),[4] the Ms. is bound with other Mss. bearing No. 2911. It is very beautiful, gilded with gold and scribed in 1092 AH/1681 AD.
4. Kitab Khana-i-Saltanati.[5] The Ms. was written in 1095 AH/1684 AD in Nast'liq script and the paper used in it was manufactured in Daulatabad. It was scribed by Muhammad Hussain of Khatunabad.
5. Kitab Khana-i-Mulk (Iran).[6] The Ms. bearing No. 34/35 was scribed in Nasla'liq script in 1311 AH/1894 AD by Muhammad Ibrahim bin Muhammad al Hussain al-Tafrisi.

Further I would like to mention here that Dr. Musa 'Amid, a professor in Tehran University edited this treatise in 1331 Shamshi/1952-53 AD providing valuable information about the author and his work in hand. However it needs more comprehensive preface on the original text.

In this treatise the author describes how the creation of the universe started, how the sun, the moon and other planets came into existence, what the reality of fire, air, water and the earth is, what the process of the production of minerals was; what the substance was which converted into a plant; how the process of evolution reached to the stage of a monkey and then a man. The author has belief in the existence of God who created all things but not in the direct way but he adopted for it a procedure with which I would deal in the following pages but first of all contents of the book is being given:

1. What was the cause of fundamental existence of God.
2. What is the difference between the fundamental existence of God and existence of other beings.
3. What is the reason for the creation of the universe.
4. What was the reason behind the appearance of God.
5. Thus when God, who is ever empowered and distinguished with wisdom, was in favour of creating, then what is the wisdom in it that the universe should be pre-existent when the cause arises caused and becomes necessary.
6. What is the first thing which got the effect of the existence of God.
7. Since primary wisdom and authority is with God, who created the reason, why did the reason invent other beings instead of remaining in its simple form.
8. Just as reason itself is not visible but in the form of psyche (Nafs), the psyche came into existence which was the effect of the reason. Psyche too is not visible in its own self and it does not have knowledge, the context demands that it should also appear. Thus it is necessary that something should also be produced from it so that it may appear in it, as it was said about reason otherwise it will be unwise.
9. What was the first element which came into existence and what shape did it adopt when it got mixed with the nature (*Tabi'at*).

In the forthcoming pages we shall discuss the last question No. 9 which in fact is relevant to our subject. The author says that before the creation of the world there was nothing but one point, comprising four things, *viz.*, the elements, the reason, the nature and the psyche. These were in their simple (uncompounded) form. All heavenly and earthly bodies were concentrated at one place and there was no separate existence in any form in the universe. The first thing to appear from this point (*Nuqta*) was reason (*'Aql*), which aroused nature (*Tabi'at*). At this juncture, the nature (*Tabi'at*) set in motion which created the units of space, i.e., length, width and depth, and surface and body also came into existence. Then the sensation (*His*) appeared in entity.

Though the elements get the above three units and motion from the nature and its movement, yet the main function is performed by psyche because the nature has no power of understanding. Had the psyche not joined it, it would neither have divided into the three units nor have remained in a fixed quantity, it would rather have been in the shape of a large lump with no end. In other words, the work of the nature was to set motion in the point. The nature also aroused the psyche and other things which were in a dormant and constant condition. Now began the work of psyche. It was the psyche which started division and seperation.

The author goes on to say that from the purest part of the point the body of the uppermost heaven came into existence and that the substance of reason and psyche were combined with it according to its purity (*Safa*). Similarly the other heavenly bodies came into existence combined with reason and psyche until there appeared the moon, the lowest heavenly body.

Now the remaining matter was dominant with impurities which could not form any other heavenly body. The nature joined this matter and set it in motion. The motion produced utmost heat in it, and the heat created porosity. When the porosity reached its utmost limit, it produced a hot and dry substance called fire.

The portions of matter which had fallen at the farthest distance from the moon remained motionless. Thus due to the maximum immovability coldness was produced and the utmost coldness led to the creation of density and density produced a substance cold and dry, called Earth.

Then there was something between these two substances fire and earth. Some was semi-adjacent to fire and some was semi-adjacent to the earth. And the one adjacent to the fire became hot but porosity was not produced in it because it was not a great heat rather it was a hot substance which was moist and it is called 'air'. The other half which was adjacent to the earth got cold by the coldness to earth, it could not become dense because there was no great cold, thus the substance formed was cold and moist. It is called water. These are the four natural elements.

Here completes the creation of the uncompounded world and begins the process of reversion (development) leading to the stage of change in the Earth.

The first change brings about act of mixing in the four elements. The characteristic of Psyche is that it appears in the matter only when the process of motion and change begins. Thus psyche was not perceptible in the first stage of the creation of skies and appeared at the later stage. In the same manner, psyche is not perceived in the very beginning of the process of reversion, and it appears in the brightest or purest thing that evolves from the mixing of elements and the stabilization of the mixture. Likewise began the creation of minerals. As the process of reversion (development) advances, this matter becomes brighter and brighter so much so that it becomes gold and ruby (jewels). The addition of psyche is more than clay and stone in it. When this process reaches its last stage, coral comes into existence, which is the best kind of minerals. The creation of minerals reaches its perfection here and the creation of plant begins with coral which was in water.

It is the coral which leads to the beginning of the world of plants, as stated above. When the purity and brightness of coral increased, psyche joined it at this stage and spirit of developing psyche appeared in it. First of all there appeared wild vegetation, or the process of plant development continued and culminated in the formation of palm or date tree which is the only tree having animal characteristics. It became brighter and purer until the effect of psyche produced the spirit of feeling in it. The first creature which came into existence as the result of this development was shell and mother of pearl. It had some sort of feeling and mostly the feeling of touch. It would drift away from its place no sooner than it is touched. Thus began the animal kingdom from here. Its inner purity and brightness increased with the development of its creative stage. This development increased gradually and attained the form of monkeys which is the most perfect form of animals. The monkey shares numerous characters with Man. Reversion or development process continued until man comes into existence. This is the real description of the earthly creation.

Notes

1. See Vol. III p. 941.
2. *Encyclopaedia of Islam*, Vol. III, p. 941.
3. See Dr. Musa 'Amid p. xvi.
4. See Dr. Musa 'Amid, p. xvii.
5. *Ibid.*, p. xviii.
6. *Ibid.*

References

Daira-i-Ma'arif Islami, Lo Pakistan.

Encyclopaedia of Islam, 1971. London.

Hammond, Robert, 1947. *The philosophy of Alfarabi and Its Influence on Medieval Thought*, New York.

Nasr, S.H., 1976. *Islamic Science – An Illustrated Study*, London.

Majid Ali Khan, 1978. *Islam on Origin and Evolution of Life,* Delhi.

Musa Amid, Dr., 1950. *Risala dar Haqiqat wa Kaifiyat Silsila-i-Maujudat wa Tasalsul-i-Asbab wa-Musabbat*, Tehran.

15

Concept of Matter in Unani Medicine

Hakeem Altaf Ahmad Azmi

Since time immemorial, man has been consistently pondering over the secrets of his Universe, particularly the primary and principal source for the creation of all things including man.

The fathers of Unani medicine have acquired all knowledge about the matter and its constituents from the Greek philosophers. It was believed in Greece that the whole universe has been created by gods and goddesses. But in the sixth century B.C. this idea was challenged by a group of philosophers. They did not refute this idea openly but forwarded quite a different view about the creation of the universe, i.e., creation of the universe by nature (matter) itself.

But before explaining the concept of matter in Unani medicine, I think it necessary to define matter as propounded by Greek and Arab physicians/philosophers.

Definition of Matter

Its literal meaning is to expand and to enlarge. In a more wider sense, it implies a substance out of which a thing is made and sustained by it.[1] It is also said to be an abode (*Mahall*) in which it is transmigrated.[2] Some philosophers have signified it a fundamental which accepts the bodily form (*Surat-i Jismaniah*).[3]

Today, scientifically, it means that which occupies space and with which we become acquainted by our bodily senses.

Broad Division of Matter

Matter has travelled a long way before coming into the present form. Accordingly it has been divided into the following four kinds:[4]

1. First matter (*Maddah-i Ula*): It is directly or indirectly connected to the creator of the universe. It is like a wave flowed from the ocean of light.

2. Matter in aggregate (*Majmu'i maddah*): Out of which the heavenly bodies have been formed. It is a determined luminous form of the first matter.
3. Four essential elements (*'Anasir-i Arba'ah*): water, fire, air and earth.
4. Bodily compounds (*Jismi murakkabat*): Like wood and stone etc.

Since this topic, more or less, deals with the third kind of matter, the other kinds of matter have also been touched to some extent, therefore, the forthcoming discussion is centred round it, and I proceed accordingly.

Constituents of Matter

When the Greek philosophers saw the material world around them and pondered over it, they found it divided into four forms: liquid (water), fiery (fire), solid (earth) and gaseous (air). From this observation they came to this conclusion that matter consists of four constituents: water, earth, fire and air. But the question arose which constituent has the status of primary substance, to which other constituents owe their origination. This issue was discussed and debated at great length by the Greek philosophers, but they had different opinions as briefly mentioned below:

WATER AS PRIMARY SUBSTANCE

The propounder of this theory was Thales of Melitus (585 BC).[5] He was one of the seven wise men of Greece.[6] According to Aristotle (d. 323 BC) he thought that water is the original substance out of which all other constituents are formed, and he held the view that the earth rests on water.[7] Thales is said to have travelled to Egypt and thence he brought this idea to Greece.[8] Despite revolutionary change of mind, Thales could not get rid of the old religious belief that all things are full of gods.[9]

EARTH AS PRIMARY SUBSTANCE

Phrekides, a Greek Philosopher, was of the view that earth was primary substance. He argued that if anything is detached from its natural place by any artificial means, it ultimately returned to its original position after the effect of that means vanishes. This experiment proves that earth is the original substance.[10]

AIR AS PRIMARY SUBSTANCE

Anaxemanes (494 BC) is reported to have said that air is the fundamental substance and other constituents of matter are changed forms of this substance. Accordingly fire is rarefied air; when condensed, it becomes first water then, if further condensed, earth and finally stone. He also thought that our soul is air and it holds us together and that it encompasses the whole world and that the world also breaths.[11]

FIRE AS PRIMARY SUBSTANCE

Heraclitus (500 BC) believed fire to be the primordial substance out of which everything originated. He said that this world which is the same for all, neither made by any god nor by any man but it was ever, is now, and ever shall be an everliving Fire, with measures kindling and measures going out.[12]

He also advocated that everything is in a state of flux. There is nothing that can be called a constant and unchangeable being. I quote here some of his phrases:

> All is and all is not. We are changing but have
> changed. You cannot step twice into the same river
> for fresh water are ever flowing in upon you.[13]

His another worth-mentioning doctrine is the idea of mingling of opposites. In accordance with this concept, by strife opposites combine to produce a motion which is a harmony. There is a unity in the world, but it is a unity resulting from diversity.[14]

After some time, old controversy again arose about the primary substance. Some philosophers came forward and challenged "one substance theory". They expressed view that the two substances instead of one are the basic source of all creation. Some held water and earth and some held water and fire as the primary substances. But later on this theory was also replaced by three and finally by four primary substances. The theory of four substances got supremacy and it is still prevalent.

Theory of Four Substances

The propounder of this theory was Empedocles (440 BC). He rejected the theories of one, two and three substances. He said that primary substances are four in number, i.e., water, earth, fire and air. When these four substances are intermingled in a proportionate manner, things are created.[15] These primary substances are everlasting and unperishable.

He also explained how things come into being and then perishes. He said that there are two forces operating in this world, love and strife. By love, primary substances are brought together and thus things are formed and by strife they are disintegrated into original substances. These two opposite forces are eternal but compounds are perishable.[16] He called these opposite forces as divine eternal force.[17]

The theory of four substances was further augmented and elucidated by Aristotle who compounded it with four qualities: hot, cold, dry and wet.[18] He postulated a fifth substance also called "quinta essentia" from which all heavenly bodies are made.[19]

Theory of Atom

Democritus (420 BC) is credited to have rejected the theory of four substances. He believed that everything is composed of atom which are physically, but not geometrically, indivisible; that between the atoms there is empty spaces; that atoms are indestructible; that they always have been, and always will be in motion; that there are an infinite number of atoms.[20]

Theory of Innumerable Substances

Anaxagoras (500 BC) like Democritus was against that concept in which matter has been divided into four substances as mentioned above. He was of the view that primary substances are innumerable. Every substance contains a portion of other substances. When this portion in a particular substance is accumulated in a greater quantity it is named after it.[20]

According to this notion, the concept of life and death has no real meaning. Life is nothing but the assemblage of necessary primary substances and its disintegration is called death.[21] Chakbast, a great Urdu poet, has rendered this idea in the following couplet:

زندگی کیا ھے عناصر مین ظہور ترتیب

موت کیا ھے انھی اجزاء کا بریشان ھونا

What is life? It is an arrangement of elements in a particular order and the disintegration of these elements is termed death.

Anaxagoras was the first Greek physician who put forth the idea that mind, a non-physical entity, played very important role in the creation of the universe. It enters into the composition of all living things and distinguishes them from dead matter. Mind has power over all things that had life; it is infinite and self-ruled, mixed with nothing; it is the source of all motion; it causes a rotation, which is gradually spreading throughout the world and is causing the lightest things to go to the circumference and the heaviest to fall towards the centre.[23]

Conclusion

The concept of matter in Unani medicine has been constantly changing as described in the foregoing pages. Most of the physicians were materialist in their outlook and assumption. In their view the world has been created from matter (four primary substances). But some physicians mostly Arab, believed that every living thing comprises both matter and non-matter, i.e., mind and/or psyche (Nafs).

When this notion is compared to the concept of matter in our modern scientific age, we find some resemblance between the two. Now, matter is regarded as a condensed form of energy and it can be reconverted again to the same. It means that matter has no independent existence, only energy is the real entity and that the universe is nothing but the expansion of the energy.

In conclusion we can say that the approach of Unani medicine towards matter and the creation of the universe is reasonable and accommodative having belief in both matter and mind simultaneously.

Notes

1. Sayed Sharif Jurjani, *Kitab al-Ta'rifat*, Beirut.
2. Ibn Rushd, *Maba'd al-Tabi'iyat*, Hyderabad Dakan, 1947, p. 12, See further *Kashshaf-i Istilahat al-funun (Al-Thanawi)* Beirut 1968, p. 1327.
3. *Urdu Da'rah-i M'arif-i Islamiah* (Urdu Encyclopaedia) vol. 18, p. 239.
4. Bertrand Russell, *History of Western Philosophy*, London 1957, p. 44.
5. Ibn Nadim, *Mohammad b.Ishaq, Al-Fihrist*, Urdu translation by Mawlana Mohammad Ishaq Bhatti, Lahore, 1969, p. 575.
6. Bertrand Russell, *op. cit.*, p. 44.
7. John Willium Draper, *The History of the Intellectual Development of Europe,* London, 1864, vol. I, p. 91.
8. Bertrand Russell, *op. cit.*, p. 44.
9. Abdul Latif, Hakim, *Tajdeed-i Tib*, Tibbi Academy Aligarh, 1972, p. 32.
10. Bertrand Russell, *op. cit.*, p. 47.
11. *Ibid.*, p. 62.
12. *Ibid.*
13. *Ibid.*
14. *Ibid.* p. 74.
15. *Ibid.*
16. John Willium Draper, *op. cit.*, vol. I, p. 119.
17. *Encyclopaedia Britannica Micropaedia*, 1974, (15 ed.) vol. III, p. 846.
18. Bertrand Russell, *op. cit.*, p. 229.
19. *Ibid.*, pp. 85-91.
20. *Ibid.*
21. *Ibid.* p. 81.
22. Alfred Weber, *History of Philosophy*, Urdu translation by Khalifah 'Abdul Hakim, Hyderabad Dakan, 1938, p. 37.
23. Bertrand Russell, *op. cit.*, p. 82.

16

Ancient and Mediaeval Biology
Looking through the Magnifying Glass of the Modern

Pushpa M Bhargava

Chandana Chakrabarti

Our presentation would be about 'living matter'. Biology is the scientific study of living matter; therefore, our talk would pertain to biology.

Our objective would be to try to understand and evaluate the past – that is our knowledge in biology from the pre-Mohenjo-daro-Harappa period till the end of the last century – against the background of what we know today. In other words, we intend doing reverse history – that is, looking backwards from today's vantage point.

Our approach would involve, first, looking at the nature and the structural elements of today's knowledge in biology: what are the basic rules and generalisations that have emerged. We would then look at how much was, in our evaluation, known about these structure elements, rules, basic tenets and generalisations in our past. Thus, if we were to make a map of biology today, with the knowledge that we have as of now, we would like to know as to how much of this map was filled in our past till the end of the last century. In this way, we should be able to identify our successes against the background of today's knowledge and ask the question: Could our ancestors have done better given the tools they had? We would then analyse our failures and ask if they could have been avoided. We would, finally, like to determine – within the highly circumscribed limits of our competence – if the story of biology in our country can be correlated with the changes in our social, political, economic and cultural scene over the centuries. The larger objective would be to learn lessons from history so that we do not repeat the same mistakes in the future but derive inspiration and strength from our real and established accomplishments of the past in the process of building our future.

The Structure of Modern Biology

We today know that all biological systems, without an exception, can be fully described in terms of four parameters: chemistry, biochemistry, morphological structure and function. The chemistry of living systems would tell us what they are made of. We today know a great deal about the 'chemistry' – that is, the chemical constituents – of living systems, and our dictionary of these constituents is becoming increasingly complete so that it is becoming exponentially more difficult to discover new constituents. In this process, we have also learnt that living systems need to take in from the environment a very small number of what we call nutrients and make from this small number literally millions of different chemical species that are found in the living cell; even the simplest of cells that we know today probably contain several thousand different chemical species. The 'biochemistry' of the system is essentially a description of the set of reactions that allow the system to synthesize its large number of chemical constituents from the small number of nutrients it needs to take in from the environment, and then to get rid of them when they are no longer needed. This is where the excitement was at the turn of this half century but, today, the dictionary of biochemistry is already very comprehensive.

By 'structure', we mean the looks of the system at various levels of resolution from the naked eye to X-rays. There is considerable excitement in this area in biology even today, and there is little doubt that new structures are awaiting discovery. The 'function' of living systems is essentially a description of the capabilities of the system through the manifestation of which we generally identify a particular living system or organism. Thus, movement is a function and we say that animals can move but plants do not. The ability to respond to the environment is also a function, and so on. We shall give a more detailed list of some of the functions that living systems perform a little later.

Chemistry, biochemistry, structure and function of the living systems thus represent four structural elements of modern biology. It turns out that there are enormous similarities which all living organisms from simple micro-organisms to an elephant show in regard to all the four structural elements. It also turns out that the chemistry of all living organisms shows the greatest resemblance; this resemblance declines as we proceed from chemistry, through biochemistry and structure, to function. The above unity and the hierarchies that we have just mentioned in this unity, together, represent another basic tenet of modern biology that we have come to recognise today.

Then, we know today that life evolved from the non-living on our planet somewhere between 3.5 and 4.5 billion years ago, and that the Darwinian evolution acting on this primitive life, led to the evolution of the various species that inhabit our planet today or have inhabited it in the past. The prime principles that have governed this evolution are that of chance that allowed random mutations to occur, of the necessity of perpetuating (through reproduction) the change that these mutations led to, and of natural selection during evolution when there was competition between species. One of the most striking conclusions that modern biology seems to point towards is that all of us who are living today, and all our ancestors, have been the progeny of a single woman who lived in Africa nearly 200,000 years ago! In other words, we are all cousins 20,000 generations apart!

As we shall see later, our ancestors recognised the unity of all life – even of the non-living and the living – but they did not recognise the hierarchy in this unity that is represented by evolution in the temporal dimension.

The last generalisation that has emerged in modern biology, we would like to mention, is that all aspects of living phenomena, without an exception, have a physico-chemical basis. In other words, all properties of life must be explicable in terms of laws of physics and chemistry. We did not recognise this in the past.

Let us now look into some details.

Our Success in the Past

A. CHEMISTRY OF LIVING SYSTEMS

Today, we know that the living and the non-living worlds represent a continuum and that the living world is regulated and controlled by the same laws that hold true for the non-living world. In our ancient tradition, the relationship between the living and the non-living has been ambivalent. On the one hand, we have believed in "dust thou art to dust returnest", implying that living objects were related to the non-living. On the other hand, we have had the all-pervading concept of soul as making living things different – a concept which is incompatible with today's knowledge in biology.

One cannot, however, blame our ancestors for this ambivalence. In order to understand the chemistry of living systems, we needed the knowledge of chemistry as it developed after the Renaissance in Europe, which not only never happened in India but did not even touch our science till this century. Therefore, we doubt if anyone could have done better during the ancient or the early medieaval period in India. (What, of course, is disappointing is the continuation and uncritical acceptance of this ambivalence today.)

B. BIOCHEMISTRY

As regards biochemistry, it is a science of the twentieth century, most of its major advances have been made only in this half century. It is largely concerned with the mechanism of synthesis of the large number of chemical substances that living systems have from the small number of nutrients that they need to take in from the environment, and with the fate of the chemical constituents of the living systems. It is also concerned with the relationship of the chemistry of a system with its structure and function. Since laws of chemical combinations are only a few hundred years old, there was no way for precise biochemical knowledge to be arrived at in the ancient or even the mediaeval times. Yet, there were important inferences arrived at regarding phenomenon such as metabolism.

One such inference was the need for nutrients to undergo change in the living system to enable them to perform the various functions that were recognised. One of the conclusions was that life and biological processes are dependent upon the production of heat inside the organism. "This body-heat comes out of food which also nourishes and maintains the organism through its metabolic transformations. Ingested food and drink pass into the stomach and become minutely dispersed by the digestive fluid present there; their assimilable contents then turn into a sweet, frothy, mucus-like fluid. This process of digestion, carried out by *agni* (digestive fire), continues until the fluid becomes acid, issues out of the stomach and excites the secretion of thin bile. At this stage it is an assimilable, nutritive fluid known as *rasa*, which is pumped by the heart through 24 major channels and permeates the entire system. *Rasa* constantly moistens, nourishes, maintains and irrigates the organism by processes which were not completely understood".[1] Mostly today's state-of-art, and incorrect only in detail!

C. STRUCTURE OF LIVING SYSTEMS

Our ancestors were extremely acute, accurate and perceptive observers. It is this acuity of observation that laid the foundations of ancient Indian science. Nowhere is this capacity so explicit, as in the case of observations that related to the structure of biological systems.

(i) Animals

Detailed knowledge of various internal and external organs of the body and its various systems was acquired during the Vedic period. For example, in *Atharvaveda*, there are references even to Fallopian tubes and to the relationship between testicles and semen. We were aware of not only bones but also cartilage and ligaments. In the *Caraka Samhita* (believed to have been put together somewhere between fourth century BC and fourth century AD, probably around 100 AD) the total number of bones in the human body has been stated to be 360. As we know the total number of bones in the human body to be 206 today, the chances are that all of them had been identified by Caraka's time.

Susruta's description, even before Caraka, of the anatomy of the human body, within the limitations of the human eye, is breathtakingly comprehensive and analytical. The basic difference between vertebrates and invertebrates was clearly recognised: "some beings stand mainly with the support of skeleton and others with muscles".

(ii) Plants

Parasara (first century BC to first century AD) gave the details of the internal structure of leaf. His description refers to innumerable small compartments, cell sap and possibly cell wall.

The *Brhadaranyakopanisad* (1000-600 BC) compares the human being with a tree as follows: "a man is indeed like a mighty tree; his hairs are its leaves and his skin is its outer bark. The blood flows (from the skin) of the man, so does the sap (from the skin) of the tree. Thus blood flows from a wounded man in the same manner as the sap from a tree when it is chopped. Flesh within corresponds to the inner bark; his nerves are as tough as the inner fibres of the tree; his bones lie behind his flesh as the wood lies behind the soft tissue. The marrow of the human bone resembles the pith of the tree".[1] Surely, there is an element of both realism and poetry in these analogies! Susruta, too, gave a more or less detailed account of different parts of a plant, with a tendency to compare the plant parts with those of the human body.

(iii) Classification of plants and animals

Classification of plants and animals into manageable categories came naturally to our ancestors. Some 740 plants and over 250 animals seem to be referred to in our ancient literature, which were classified in many different ways, for example, on the basis of their medicinal property, domestic utility, or morphological features. The first attempt to classify animals in some rational way is found in the *Chandogya Upanisad*, where classification was based on their mode of origin and development. In this classification was also a group comprising of organisms that was born out of heat and moisture of the earth, such as stinging gnats, mosquitos, lice, flies and bugs. It is interesting that all those that were small and apparently caused some damage or discomfort were thought to arise spontaneously out of the scum of the earth! It was only in the later half of the last century that the theory of spontaneous generation was finally buried by Louis Pasteur, so our ancestors did not do badly at all!

The most elaborate classification of plants was by Parasara who based it largely on morphological considerations such as floral characteristics. He classified plants into families some of which clearly represent families of today, for example, Leguminosea, Crustacea, Cruciferae, Cucurbitacea, Kapucynacea and Compositae. The tragedy is that such classification was not improved upon subsequently. Unfortunately, also the relationship between various classes was not analysed. If that had been done, subsequent to Parasara, perhaps a more systematic classification might have emerged many centuries ahead of Linnaeus. The importance of dealing with many parameters at a time in classification was clearly not recognised.

D. FUNCTIONS PERFORMED BY LIVING SYSTEMS

Some of the important functions that we know today to be manifest in living, biological systems are:

Eating and drinking
Capacity to change the environment
Recognition
Death
Adaptation and survival
Organisation
Regulation
Growth
Response to external stimuli
Disease
Ageing
Evolution
Instinct
Rhythms
Energy transduction
Change
Pattern formation
Similarities and dissimilarities (that is, heredity)
Social behaviour
Communication
Conversion of food to energy
Reproduction
Defence
Morphogenesis and differentiation
Ability to convert disorder to order (without disobeying the second law of thermodynamics!)
Locomotion
Compartmentalisation at various levels
Reception, storage, collation and recall of information through the five senses

A significant number of these functions performed by living systems were observed accurately and recorded in detail in the ancient times. Udayana (tenth century AD) recorded, in plants, the phenomena of life, death, sleep, waking up, disease, transmission of specific characters from one generation to another, and movement towards what is favourable and away from what is unfavourable.[2] The recognition of the six basic tastes — sweet, sour, salty, pungent, bitter and astringent — was surely remarkable.[1]

Knowledge that has stood the test of time was arrived in ancient India (and subsequently all through our history) not only by direct observation but also by drawing inferences. This was nowhere more obvious than in regard to our understanding of several functions that biological systems perform. Let us look at some examples.

The conclusions arrived at in regard to the reproductive process, both in animals and in plants, in ancient India were truly impressive. Although there does not appear to be enough evidence of the knowledge of sexuality in plants in the Harappan culture, sexual reproduction in higher plants as well as in higher animals is mentioned in the pre-Buddhistic *Kathopanisad* as being similar.[3] Seeds and flowers were believed to be produced by the cooperation or union of different sexes. Pollen was believed by Amara to be analogous to the female menstrual fluid. In the *Brahmanas* — a constituent of the *Vedas* — there are many references to conception and to child-birth.[4] As has been already mentioned, the testicles were recognised as being responsible for the production of semen. It was also recognised that the semen should get amalgamated with the contribution of the woman in her womb; unless this happened, pregnancy could not be established.

Garbhopanisad gives a detailed and fascinating description of the day-to-day and monthly development of the human embryo through its various stages, from conception to delivery. Susruta gave the best time for conception from the fourth to the twelfth day from the date of the beginning of the menstrual flow: precisely what is recommended for a 22-day menstrual cycle today! Imagine the amount of information he must have collected to arrive at this conclusion and that too how, and in what kind of a culture! (May be our today's perceptions of that culture are inadequate.)

The role of the umbilical cord and the navel was amazingly well recognised [2,4]. "The *dhamanis* in the foetus take their rise from the umbilical cord, thus bringing nourishment from the mother" [2], and the navel in the foetus was rightly stated to be the source and origin of the entire vascular system. To continue the quotation, "The embryo is held at the navel. It grows without taking food, that is, there is no effort made on the part of the embryo to take food and no food is specially served to it. The food in its final form, is assimilated automatically and directly into the system of the embryo. The child is nourished of its own accord as it were. The mother is not conscious of the nourishment given to the young one below her heart". Could it have been said better?

The animal body was recognised to be sustained and nourished by blood which was "conveyed through a large number of channels to every part of the body".[5] Existence of capillaries was recognised in numbers that were impossible to count. It was stated that urine is formed by draining of the waste or refuse matter in the body by water. The water content of the urine was correctly concluded as derived from the drinking water and from the moisture of the food taken in. Urine was, therefore, thought of as a body fluid which served to eliminate waste metabolic products not required by our body.[5]

The growth of a plant was recognised to depend on soil, water and season [2]. It was recognised that light had something to do with the process of manufacture of food by plants and storage of energy in their body [2,3].

Caraka made another highly perceptive and logical statement when he said that diagnosis of a disease should depend on (i) theoretical knowledge of the possible causes and symptoms of diseases, (ii) meticulous observation of the patient's symptoms and complaints, and (iii) inferences based on previous experience.[6]

One of the most remarkable deductions made in the history of Indian medicine was in regard to small pox. In fact, the impression that all of India was in a state of rapid decline in the late eighteenth century, is certainly argued against by the fact that inoculation against small pox was practised in the subcontinent at this time, and long before it became generally acceptable in Europe.[7] It was unknown in Europe till 1720, when the wife of the then British Ambassador in Turkey, having got her children successfully inoculated, advocated its introduction into Britain.

The farmers of the Vedic period were aware of the possibility of improving the fertility of the soil by rotation of crops – a concept that developed in the West very much later.[8,9] Rice was grown in summer and pulses in winter.[10] References to rotation appear in *Rgveda* and *Yajurveda.*[11,13] Thus rye-grass and cloves were grown with wheat, barley or oats, and beans with peas.[7]

The ancient cultivators knew how to select the seeds and what to sow when and where; they recognised the need of replenishing the nutrients of the soil by manures.[3,11-15] The later Vedic agricultural farmers seemed to be fully conversant with the use of organic matter such as appropriately processed cowdung, [12,14] bones, blood, and plant products such as the straws of barley.[3,16] These manures are today known to contain nitrogen, phosphorous and potassium.

From 300 to 200 BC onwards, the early stages of the germination of seeds and the factors governing germination (such as proper season, good soil, water, vitality of the seeds, and proper care) were clearly recognised. Kautilya's *Arthasastra* mentions the effect of temperature on germination; it gave specific conditions required for germination of different kinds of seeds.

Although there was much emphasis on vegetarian food, eating of meat was far from prohibited. The food value of the flesh of a large number of animals was discussed [for example, in *Sutra-Sthana* (800-300 BC)[1]], and cow was not yet "in the venerable company of the Gods and *Brahmins*" but was merely regarded as just another animal. In other words, there was no restriction on the eating of beef. Qualities of beef are stated in *Caraka Samhita* as follows:

> The flesh of the cow is beneficial for those suffering from the loss of flesh due to disorders caused by an excess of *vayu*, rhinitis, irregular fever, dry cough, fatigue, and also in cases of excessive appetite resulting from hard manual work.[1]

We had learned how to determine the age of animals from sequential changes in their teeth[17], and we knew how to train animals and to exercise control over them.[17] Cattle breeding appears to have been one of the important aspects of animal husbandry practice in ancient India. Salihotra's work on horses appears to be most comprehensive, consisting of 16,000 *slokas* in 120 chapters. It can be taken to be a complete guide to the science of horses, from breeding and grooming to care in health and disease.

Surgery was, perhaps, the most illustrious branch of ancient Indian medicine. Susruta divided surgery into eight branches: incision, excision, scarification, puncturing, exploration, extraction, evacuation and suturing. Actually, fifteen different methods were described for the extraction of a foreign body loosely or firmly embedded in the tissues; they were practical, reasonable and highly innovative, a magnet being used for iron particles.[18]

More than 100 surgical instruments made of steel were described by Susruta.[2,9,19] Indian doctors in the ancient period achieved such perfection in plastic surgery that European surgeons of the nineteenth century borrowed several methods from them. Susruta also discovered the art of cataract-crouching which was unknown to surgeons of ancient Greece and Egypt.[2] Limbs were amputated, abdominal operations performed, fractures set, dislocations, hernia and ruptures reduced, and haemorrhoids removed — all with an amazing rate of success.[2] Susruta was, in fact, the first to advocate that dissection of dead bodies was indispensable for a successful student of surgery.[6] The earliest of rhinoplasties appeared to have been performed in India in 1600 BC and there are still families that practise the same method today. The practical secret of rhinoplasty operation spread from India through Arabia and Persia to Egypt and from there to Italy.[20]

E. USES

The Indus valley people understood the qualities of wood, nor did the strength, durability and preservative power of the various timbers escaped their notice.[3]

Garments were dyed with the juice of Lodina flowers, madder and indigo, starting from somewhere between 800 and 300 BC. Silk was known and used to make clothes.[10]

The art of perfumery was highly developed.[21] People knew the technical art of distilling essence from natural sources, and our ancestors had arrived at formulations using different proportions of various aromatic substances to get various notes of perfume. Basavaraja has given a list of nine aromatic ingredients from which as many as 72 perfumes could be obtained by combining them in various proportions.

F. VALUE SYSTEMS

Today we recognise that the practice of science generates and sustains values. Therefore, one would expect that the generation of scientific knowledge in the ancient times also led to the establishment of certain values and value systems. This indeed is true. Let us look at some examples.

In the Vedic period, agriculture had become virtually the universal occupation in India. It had developed to such an extent that there was plenty of produce. It was probably for this reason that hospitality came to be regarded as a cardinal virtue.[8] "He who possessed of food hardens his heart against the feeble man craving for nourishment, against the sufferer coming to him for help, and pursues his own enjoyment even before him, that man finds no consoler".

Ayurveda demanded an elaborate moral and ethical code for the physicians. According to Caraka, friendship towards all, compassion for the ailing, devotion to professional duties, and a philosophical attitude towards cases with a fatal ending, are the four cornerstones of medical practice. There is much here to learn for our present-day doctors.

Where We Failed

It should be obvious from what we have said above that our ancestors possessed a substantial body of knowledge in the area of structure and some functions of living systems; this would not have been possible had it not been for their capacity and desire for acute and extensive observation, the power of reasoning, the ability to arrive at inferences and conclusions, and to learn from trial and error.

This empirically acquired knowledge was put to good use and, therefore, it set up a tradition that allowed India to remain at par, if not gain supremacy with the rest of the world till the beginning of the Renaissance in Europe.

However, our analysis of documented information also shows that, alongside this knowledge that had stood the test of time, there also developed a body of knowledge – perhaps, better called beliefs and ideas – about biological systems that has since then proven to be wrong and shown to be based on fallacious principles or assumptions. Many of these erroneous beliefs and ideas have, unfortunately, not been discarded till today, and have consequently acted as a drag on us; they often exercise a greater hold over the minds and hearts of our people than the tradition of knowledge that has stood the best of time and has been found to be compatible with what was discovered later.

We believe that any objective documentation of the history of the development of science, culture and philosophy in India would be incomplete and of little use, if it is not accompanied by an analysis of the evolution of such ideas and beliefs and their sustenance in an unchanged form even today, when we have much evidence to the contrary. Only if we do this analysis and shed whatever we can be reasonably sure to be wrong, we cannot but accelerate the pace of progress in the country. It is not scientific either to glorify or condemn our past wholesale. We must isolate facts from myth and dogma to appreciate what our ancestors were able to accomplish, and then build on it.

There were beliefs and ideas developed and propagated in our past that have proven to be partly right and partly wrong and those that have turned out to be wholly wrong. Let us first look at some examples of the former: the ones that were partly right and partly wrong.

1. Susruta in his treatise has given a remarkable description of the foetus at various stages of development. He has also prescribed the care that needs to be taken during pregnancy. All this has been found to be fairly accurate. Yet, the same Susruta attributes the reasons for congenital defects that, for example, dwarfs and hunch-backs suffer from, to the fact that the mother's desires during pregnancy were left ungratified or repressed. There were several other speculations about cause and effect during pregnancy that can today be said as being far away from truth. Both Caraka and Susruta also believed that the fertilised ovum (or the foetus) developed by palingenesis and not by epigenesis. In other words, all the organs were potentially present in miniature form in the fertilised ovum or the seed and they unfolded in a certain order during the growth of the foetus. Even Sankara shared this view. We now know that this is not true.

2. Caraka and Susruta believed that diseases were caused by a disturbance in the equilibrium of the three Ayurvedic humours, and that this disturbance was often a direct cause of the disease. They also recognised several remote causes, both external and internal, for example, entry of toxic materials from outside, errors of living, natural decay from old age, and climate or weather, that could play a role in the manifestation of disease. While they were right about the remote

causes, their perception about the direct causes is totally untenable.

3. There is a mention in the *Mahabharata* that plants are sensitive to heat, cold, sound of thunder, and odours, and experience pleasure and pain. While one can substantiate the fact that plants are temperature-sensitive, and one could perhaps stretch one's imagination to include odours by thinking of the possibility that poisonous gases could have a deleterous effect on plants, current scientific evidence does not substantiate the suggested sensitivity of plants to the sound of thunder (or to music to which claims were made subsequently), or their capacity to experience pleasure or pain as we understand it.
4. It is stated that children born with the 'best factors' available are destined to be handsome, virtuous, long-lived, generous, beautiful and responsible in their conduct. While the statement does imply recognition of hereditary factors, it hardly takes into account the influence of environmental factors in the manifestation of genetic abilities.
5. In the *Agni Purana*, it is stated that the sex of the child is determined by the position of the foetus which is not true. Susruta on the one hand has given a remarkably accurate description of the safe and the unsafe periods in a woman's menstrual cycle, but he has gone on to make the erroneous statement that the child is male, if conceived on even days and female if conceived on odd days beginning from the day of the cycle. He also says that sex is determined by the strength of the sperm or the egg; thus the progeny is male if the sperm is stronger and female if the egg is stronger; when the strength of both the sperm and the egg match, the offspring is supposed to be a hermaphrodite.
6. Caraka mentions three types of medicinal stuff — animal, plant and mineral — which is fine. But in the detailed list, he erroneously includes excreta, wine, sperm, hair of all the animals that were commonly used then, and minerals such as gold, silver and lead.

Now a few earlier beliefs that have proven to be wholly wrong.

(1) According to Susruta, the intervention of a superior agent was absolutely essential for the origin of life on our planet. We today understand the basic sequence of events that led to the origin of life on our planet some 12 to 15 billion years ago and in that sequence there is no place for any superior agent.

(2) In the *Upanisads*, evolution on earth is explained as follows: ether

sprang from earth, air from earth, fire from air, water from fire, earth from water, herbs from earth, food from herbs, seed from food, and men from seed. This, of course, is a far cry from what we know today about evolution.

(3) Our ancient postulate that five physical elements — ether, wind, water, fire and earth — constitute the human body is, of course, totally untenable.

(4) The theory of spontaneous generation of lower forms of life such as maggots and worms, is deeply rooted in our ancient culture. Pasteur disproved this theory dramatically in the last century.

(5) The food that we eat was stated to contain five classes of nutrients: the earth-compounds, the aqueous-compounds, the *tejas* compounds, the *vayu*-compounds and the *akasa*-compounds. The earth-compounds were postulated to form the hard matter of the body, the *tejas*-compounds to provide the metabolic heat, the *vayu*-compounds to serve as sources of the motor-force in the organism, the aqueous-compounds to furnish the watery parts of the body, and the *akasa*-compounds to contribute to the fine etheric essence that was considered to be the vehicle of conscious life. These concepts do not relate at all to our knowledge of nutrition as of today.

(6) In the *Brahmanas*, Caraka says that the offspring derives its softer tissues like skin, flesh, navel, and intestines from the mother, and harder tissues such as bones, blood vessels, veins, etc., from the father. This erroneous belief, perhaps, satisfied the male ego!

(7) It was believed that mother's nutrition could affect the sex of the child. For a male child , *ghee* and milk were recommended, and for a female child, oil and beans. Another example of male chauvinism!

(8) In the *Agni Purana*, heart was considered to be the seat of consciousness, and the centre of our nervous system. It was only in the Tantric writings between the eighth and the fourteenth century AD that the seat of consciousness was transferred from the heart to the brain. It was even proposed that one pair of *dhamanis* going from the ear to the head was engaged in conducting sensory currents pertaining to sound, smell and taste. Perhaps, this was so because all the sensory perception was lost with the stopping of the beating of the heart. Today, we know that in a clinically alive person, the heart could still be beating, in spite of all the sensory perceptions being lost. Susruta also stated the precise location of the soul in the body! The soul or *jiva*

was supposed to reside in the upper cerebrum but could traverse the whole cerebrospinal axis up and down. There is no place in modern biology for such a concept of "soul".

(9) The Indian traditional medicine, contained in the *Ayurveda*, arose from the notion that a body remained healthy if there was equilibrium between the three humours, *vayu*, *pitta* and *kapha* present in our body. These three humours were stated to govern and activate the entire gamut of biological processes from conception onwards. The description and characteristics of these three humours in *Susruta Samhita* does not even remotely correspond to our knowledge either about the body or about its functions as of today.

(10) In the Atharvavedic period, there appears to have been two kinds of healing arts: (a) that depended largely on incantation of magical verses and on sacrificial practices; and (b) that were based on empirical or rational use of herbs and other medicaments. Thus, herbs were used in combination with spells, and this had the support of *Upanisads* and *Sutras* as far back as 800-300 BC. There were specific *mantras* (a *mantra* is a specified sequence of words which, when recited, is professed to have a special effect) for curing particular diseases. There were *mantras* addressed to Surya for diseases of the heart and jaundice. There were *mantras* to increase the power of and to cure diseases of the eye. One would not be exaggerating if one says that this was unmitigated nonsense.

The supremacy of magico-religious medicine during the Atharvavedic period was also evident in our ancestors' belief in the wonders of the amulet that was looked upon as a weapon, or an instrument that protected the wearer against misfortune or disease. Amulets were used for virtually everything, from curing diseases to obtaining a male child.

If the above-mentioned magico-religious element had been shed, and our ancient system of medicine had confined itself to adhering to and relying upon empirical observation which could then be modified as the database increased, perhaps the evolution of medicine in India and, consequently, around the world, might have taken a different course.

(11) The beliefs that were codified in our ancient writing, regarding the position of a pimple determining the immediate fate of an individual, make amusing reading. Thus, "pimples appearing on the hands,

fingers and belly lead to the acquisition of wealth, fortune and grief, respectively; on the navel, to finding food and drink; those beneath the navel, to loss of wealth through theft; on the pelvis, to wealth, on the thighs, to the procurement of a vehicle and a wife; on the knees, to loss on account of enemies; and on the ankles, to trouble while travelling and during confinement".

(12) It seems likely that Manu's belief in the caste system that led to his systematising the entire system and has been at the base of many of our present-day problems was deeply rooted in his erroneous perception of the hereditary transmissibility of characters.[22]

(13) Our ancient literature is replete with examples of scientifically untenable male chauvinistic statements. Here are translations of two such *slokas*[19] (note the part in italics):

When (at the time of coitus) the blood (of the woman) exceeds the sperm (of man), a female will be born; when the sperm exceeds the blood, a male; when both are equal, a hermaphrodite. *Hence, one ought to take tonics that increase one's sperm.* A man ought to have sexual union with his wife when the Kendras and the *Trikona* houses are occupied by benefics, when the Moon and the *Lagna* are conjoined with benefics, when malefics are posited in the 3rd, 6th and 11th houses and when there are planetary combinations *ensuring the birth of a male.*

Why the Erroneous Beliefs?

First, although our ancestors were obsessed with the desire to find answers to questions and to be exhaustive, they were armed only with an acute sense of observation. They did not even have the simplest form of aid such as a magnifying glass to help them in their endeavour. Therefore, wherever observation by itself was enough, they did extremely well – even to the extent of drawing valid inferences following trial and error.

Secondly, there was a lack of democratisation of knowledge. Knowledge became the privilege of particular castes and families, with the caste system becoming more and more rigid with time. Further, knowledge was treated with great secrecy and was handed down only to a chosen few. Instead of being written down in books and given a wide circulation, the art was taught by the preceptor to the disciple, in most cases by the father to the son, so that where there was no son, the knowledge may have died with the father.

Thirdly, there was a lack of tradition of questioning. In fact, referring to the *Susruta*

Samhita, one commentator says that a wise phyisician was not expected to raise any theoretical questions about the properties of a drug which were already known through traditional knowledge and practical experience. A physician was expected to rely on what was traditional, rather than act on theoretical reasoning, or take into account new knowledge and experience. Therefore, many untruths remained unchallenged and often got attached to vested interests over a period of time. This was a clear step towards stratification of knowledge; what is particularly interesting is the kind of logic that is used to justify it. It was probably on account of the above that there have been few changes in the practice of *Ayurveda* since its inception: contrast this with the modern system of medicine!

Fourthly, the mixture of truth and myth got further amalgamated with religion and dogma. When this happened, truth ceased to stand on its own merit and, instead, sought the sanction of religious authority. Gradually, the distinction between truth and myth got lost.

Fifthly, there was very little inflow of knowledge from elsewhere, excepting during the Moghul period and the subsequent European period.

Perhaps, language too played a major role in stratification of knowledge and consolidation of untruths. The observations were often written in poetic verses in Sanskrit, with great economy of words, and one could give the written material various interpretations whose meanings hardly overlapped. Therefore, in many cases, the true meaning may have been distorted if not lost with the passage of time. Then, in course of time, Sanskrit became more and more rigid with Panini's prescriptions, while other languages started evolving and absorbing more and more. Sanskrit no longer remained the common man's language; therefore, the wealth of information contained in this language became inaccessible to a vast number and became stratified.

Finally, the tradition of experimentation was lacking in our ancient and mediaeval culture – even in Gautama's *Nyaya Sastra*. Experimentation to test a hypothesis based on observation on analysis of existing information is the key to all modern scientific inquiry and progress. In the West, the experimental tradition based on the scientific method took root in the thirteenth century and flowered after the Italian Renaissance, of which the Industrial Revolution was a logical follow-up. This did not happen here. Wherever we did experiments such as in relation to surgery – for example, in dissection – the knowledge gained has stood the test of time.

Conclusion

To sum up, we believe that, in biological knowledge, India was far ahead of most of the then civilized world up to, say, 1000 A.D., or even 1500 A.D – that is, for some 4000 years of documented history. However, after this period, the knowledge of biology in Europe progressed by leaps and bounds while our knowledge remained static. Thus, the advantage we had of history, culture and tradition (e.g., of no ban on dissection) were lost.

Our forefathers in the ancient and the mediaeval period did all that was humanly possible. However, they tried to do more and in that process gave us untruths which, in the social milieu in which they were generated and sustained, came to be stratified, amalgamated with truth on one hand and with myth, legend, magic and religion on the other. If we can separate the myth and dogma from truth, and reject what is not compatible with modern science, we would be in a position not only to have a better appreciation of what our ancestors were able to accomplish, but also lay the foundations of a systematic and rapid development of modern biology in India by providing a new motivation. We have no doubt in our minds that one of the reasons for the lack of this development has been the hold of obscurantism and religious authority on the minds of our people, partly derived from what has been said in our scriptures.

Acknowledgements

We are grateful to a large number of friends and organisations that have helped in collection of the information presented in this article. They include Prof Anil Gupta of the Indian Institute of Management, Ahmedabad, Dr Irfan Habeeb of NISTADS, New Delhi, Dr A. D. Bag and the staff of the library of INSA, New Delhi, and Prof A. S. Kolaskar and Prof Khubchandani of Pune. We would also like to acknowledge with grateful thanks the pioneering work of Shri A. Rahman, the two D. P Chattopadhyaya's and Dr B. V. Subbarayappa that stimulated our interest in this area.

Notes & References

1. D.M. Bose, S.N. Sen and B.V. Subbarayappa, *A concise history of science in India*, Indian National Science Academy, New Delhi, 1971.
2. B.N. Seal, *The positive sciences of ancient Hindus*, Motilal Banarsidass, Delhi, Varanasi, Patna, 1958.
3. R.N. Kapil, "Biology in ancient and medieval India", In *Indian Journal of History of Science*, 1970, *5*(1), 119-39.
4. R.S. Shivaganesha Murthy, "The *Brahmanas* on medicine and biological sciences", In *Indian Journal of History of Science*, 1970, *5* (1), 80-85.
5. P. Ray and H.N. Gupta, *Caraka Samhita, A scientific Synopsis*, Indian National Science Academy, 1980.
6. P. Ray, "Medicine, as it evolved in ancient and mediaeval India", In *Indian Journal of History of Science*, 1970, *5* (1), 86-96.

7. P. Dharampal, *Indian science and technology in the eighteenth century*, Academy of Gandhian Studies, Hyderabad, & Bharatiya Manisha Peeth, New Delhi, 1983.

8. G.P. Majumdar, "Origin and development of the science of agriculture in ancient India", In *Proceedings of the 13th All India Oriental Conference: Technical Sciences*, 1946, pp. 113-16.

9. Susantha Goonatilake, *Aborted discovery: Science and creativity in the Third World*, Zed Books Limited, London.

10. Vishnu Mittre. "Biological concepts and agriculture in ancient India", In *Indian Journal of History of Science*, 1970, 5(1), 144-61.

11. *Indian Council of Agricultural Research Report on Agriculture in Ancient India*, New Delhi, 1966.

12. G.P. Majumdar, "The history of botany and allied sciences in India", In *Archives International d'Historie les Sciences*, 1951, 14, 101-33.

13. S.P. Ray Chaudhuri, "Some aspects of agriculture practices in ancient India (3250 B.C. - 800 A.D.)", In *Bulletin of National Institute of Sciences of India*, 1962, 21, 107-17.

14. A.K. Bhattacharjee, *Agriculture in the Vedic Age*, Bharatiya Vidya, 38, pp. 47-51.

15. J.C. Luthra, "Ancient wheat and its viability", In *Current Science*, 1936, 4, 489.

16. D.P. Chattopadhyaya, *History of science and technology in ancient India*, Vol II, *Formation of the theoretical fundamentals of natural science*, Firma KLM Private Limited, Calcutta, 1991, reviewed by R. Temple in *Nature*, 1991, 353, 28 (also see the inset by PT).

17. S.K. Kalra, "Possibilities of relating modern veterinary science literature to the growth of relevant knowledge in ancient India", In *Indian Journal of History of Science*, 1987, 22(2), 141-57.

18. P.V. Subramanya Sastri and M. Ramakrishna Bhat, *Brhatsamhita of Varahamihira* (6th century) (English translation with original Sanskrit version), Reprinted, New Delhi, 1982, pp. 255-621.

19. R.C. Chakravarty, "Surgical principles in the Sutrasthanam of the Susruta Samhita: Management of retained foreign bodies", In *Indian Journal of History of Science*, 1970, 5 (1), 113-17.

20. C.A. Alvares, Homeo Faber: *Technology and culture in India, China and the West, 1500-1972*, Allied Publishers Pvt. Ltd.

21. *Indian Journal of History of Science*, 1987, 22, Various articles including "Perfumery in ancient India", pp. 71-79 (issue no. 1); and G. Prasad, "Method of Science used in past India and its relevance to present day context", pp. 99-102 (issue no. 2).

22. N.K. Bose, "Theory of heredity in the Manu-Samhita", In *Bulletin of National Institute of Sciences of India*, 1962, 21, 226-27.

17

In Pursuit of Reality
Oriental Mysticism and Modern Science

N.C. Rana

The search for the nature of matter — *bhutah* — is a fundamental one to both scientists and non-scientists. A careful thought to this process leads to the fact that it ought to be some kind of a realisation in the form of human perception, awaiting an expression. Over the years, people from different disciplines of science and humanities have acquired some wisdom of how this perception can (or cannot) be expressed in terms of their own 'languages'. Even though all languages, be they mathematicians or any other mortals, are symbolic and are chosen as a matter of conventions, we have gathered here with the hope to understand each others' language, and see where exactly we all are in this game. I call it a search for reality, and shall try to express my own understanding of some of the viewpoints of the modern scientists and philosopher-cum-spiritualists of the oriental traditions in a language supposedly comprehensible to people of both the categories.

Is there anything common in the ways the two Categories of People practise their own Disciplines?

If we are to compare our views across the table in a serious manner, we better start with our modes of practising.

Practising science has, broadly speaking, three stages: (i) providing the logistics, for example, laboratory, computing facility, library, training facilities, institutionalised schools of people of common interest, and so on; (ii) performing the experiments and/or theoretical calculations and ending up with seminal presentation of results in a logical manner and in the most concise form; and (iii) reaching the results of pure research to the laypersons by way of popularisation or writing science fictions, and transforming the knowledge of pure science into technology for improving the standard of everybody's day-to-day life. More often than not, all these three stages representing actually three categories of activities are not practised by the same persons. Obviously, pessimists may find in the first category, a possible promotion of dogmatism in a big way, keeping the second one, of course, relatively free from such prejudices, if any, and in the third one, an average citizen is on the whole expected to be benefited tremendously but eventually might turn into hapless victims of the hazards of man-made pollutions, or dreadful star wars due to possible abuse of the pedagogical results of scientific inventions. Who would then set the guidelines for a sane approach to scientific research and technological transformations?

A parallel to the above scenario can be found in the ways of practice of the other side in what is known as *Prasthanatraya*, meaning three paths to perceiving the reality with a possibly better introspection: (i) through the door-way of *Sruti-prasthana*, or the head/revealed texts, such as the four *Vedas* (*Rk*, *Sama*, *Yajuh*, *Atharva*) and six *Vedangas* (*siksa*, *kalpa*, *vyakarana*, *chanda*, *jyotisa*), for which the priest's (or teacher's, as the case may be) instructions are the final; (ii) through the door-way of *Nyaya-prasthana*, such as the classical six *darsanas* (schools of philosophies), such as *Samkhya*, *Yoga*, *Nyaya*, *Vaisesika*, *Purva-mimamsa*, *Uttara-mimamsa*, and others, for which the superiority of either logic or some methodology of practice is accepted; (iii) through the door-way of *Smrti-prasthana*, or the remembered, i.e., secondary, texts based on the *Vedas*, such as, *Manu-smrti*, eighteen *Puranas*, *Ramayana*, *Mahabharata*, and *Srimadbhagavadgita*. Again, in the fold of mysticism and philosophies, religious dogmatism plays a key role in making virtually each one of the so-called religions as a fundamentalist's ritualistic sanctions on the methods of training of the would-be scholars. But the second door-way has by and large remained free of dogmas, unless the scholar really ends up in justifying the pre-existing form of the logical basis of the school of thoughts he/she belongs to. The third path does really aim to set some well-defined moral and social codes for their own communities in order to enable any ordinary individual not only to promote himself/herself to exercise the highest moral standards, but also to achieve the highest realisations under certain special circumstances.

How far can the Concepts of Reality in Religion and Science be Stretched to be Compared at par in Principle?

Let us consider *Vedanta*, one of the oldest disciplines of acquiring a knowledge of the Self as well as the external world, which claims that the question of the perception of reality in the external world is intimately related to that of the perception of the Self. One of the denominations of the Vedantic schools (*Advaita Vedanta*) claims even further that the world external to ourselves does not simply exist, or more precisely, does not have an ontological status at par with our own selves. Using inductive logic, they say, it is merely our ignorance that leads to an illusory perception of the whole world external to ourselves. They do not say that 'the world does not exist' is a false statement, but it appears otherwise so long as one remains ignorant of its falsehood. The most common allegory used in this regard is the following:

> A piece of string may appear to some people as a snake under circumstances. So long as one imagines the reality of a snake in it, the piece of string is indeed a snake to the best of one's perception, but the moment the person realises the piece of string to be a piece of string, the snake ceases to exist in the piece of string. So, they say, it is merely the different degree of our ignorance that drives us to ascribe some or other quality in a substance that we perceive. At any given instant, either we believe a thing, or we do not believe it. The moment we change our conclusion, we transcend from one substratum of perceiving the truth to another substratum of it, and in this manner we keep on updating our previous notions. Therefore, at no stage, are we in a position to say that we have known the real truth, else the real truth, by this logic, ought to be unchangeable. They also add that the real truth is 'unknowable,' too, to the limited scope of human mind and perception.

If we now begin to analyse how we proceed in our scientific mission of understanding the nature, we find that the process is qualitatively very similar to the one stated above. How can we convince ourselves of a thing beyond what we have already been able to convince ourselves up to that moment? Most scientists start with a set of *a priori* postulates, build up their ladder of arguments leading to certain conclusions which, under circumstances, though rare enough, do return to the falsifiability of the initial postulates, thus making at some stage or the other, the chain of the logic to be circular. This provision for any feedback mechanism to operate on it makes the system of logic to be self-regressive in nature. Without a feedback or *a posteriori* observation and experimentation, the methodology of scientific empiricism cannot work. Thus, every scientific assertion including its basic postulates is endlessly falsifiable, so long as the switch of its feedback mechanism is not turned off. The ultimate scientific truth, if it exists, can never be reached by any finite process of the scientific methodology, unless, of course, we hit by chance the real truth itself. At that point, the system of logic ought to become closed and remain absolutely self-consistent thenceafter. Thus, even in science, the real truth ought to be unchangeable, if at all it can be hit upon par chance.

Therefore, there is no inconsistency between science and certain schools of philosophies and religious denominations, even if the later category dares to claim that it has reached the Absolute Truth, but in that case, it would be their responsibility to provide answers to all possible questions. There are enough examples of such obsessive tendency that are prevalent in practically all of the religious denominations, a process which has perhaps made many philosopher-scientists turning a totally deaf ear to their sayings beyond what any sensible logic could permit to digest. This obsession has to be controlled, and a *Yogi* is supposed to have mastered in that art in the sixth stage of his/her eight-fold *Yogasiddhis*. In this respect, both scientists and philosophers (and Seers) are often found to be quite ordinary human beings only, not rationalists. Why Maharsi Krsnadvaipayana Vadarayana Vyasadeva, supposedly the composer of *Mahabharata*, *Brahmasutra* and *Puranas*, has put *Dhyanayoga* (the art of mastering over mind) above the *Karmayoga* (the art of mastering over one's activities without having an expectation of reward/curse of any kind), *Jnanayoga* (the art of proving anything, right or wrong, by the sheer power of the intellect and knowledge) in the *Gita*, supposedly the quintessence of all the *Vedas*, *Upanisads* and *Darsanas*, may provide you with some further foods for thought. I shall return to this point once again why he put *Samkhyayoga* in the second chapter, and attributes of matter (physical as well as psychic) in the fourteenth chapter of the *Gita*.

Is it possible to Eliminate the Subjective Elements from Science, Philosophy and Religion?

Let us now move on to have a closer look at the ways or the modes of expressing a fact in science or otherwise. The mode of delivery of this talk, for example, is verbal (and also visual). It is a process by which the desired content of information of my lecture is codified into a train of propagating, sound and electromagnetic, waves in the air, which are received by your appropriate sense-organs, and these are expected to be decodified in some standard way. I am emphasizing the phrases, expected and standard, because they are my *a priori* assumptions that are made use of in the act of conveying a particular set of messages from my head to your head. Let us analyse the process a bit more critically in the following way.

Surely, I want to convey some ideas of mine. To the best of our knowledge, the ideas, by themselves, are abstract. They are surely given an explicit form, by way of generating sound waves and all that. You are assumed to have been trained in the same standard way, I believe, I am trained to enable myself to encode as well as decode an idea. We know that the sounds or the trains of light pulses, thus produced are by no means the idea themselves, yet the ideas must have also been carried with these forms, else how can we reconcile with the fact that you would most probably get the same idea as I wanted to transmit? This time of very apparent contradictions exist at all levels of our day-to-day life. Let us give another example. While reading a book, we merely look at a page which contains, materialistically speaking, nothing other than some patterns of some chemicals, called inks, on a sheet of paper, supposedly made up of some other chemical substances. A mere pattern of the ink cannot be the idea itself, but at the same time it ought to carry the idea somehow. According to Karl Popper, the art of understanding the exhibits of fine arts, be they created by the humans or by the maiden nature, requires what is called the cultural training by a perceptible and imaginative mind. Here, as in other cases, a set of conventions are likely to act as the vehicles of an otherwise totally abstract idea. This process seems to be far from being understood by the biophysicists at present.

If reasoned in the above way, it becomes obvious to us that our understanding of the outside world is an involved process that goes on in our head only. The system is not closed, as it interacts meaningfully with the external world, but it is not necessarily open, as our brain can reconstruct any event in our head using what is called the power of imagination. This second possibility has far-reaching significance, and to emphasise that a *Vedantin* might argue in the following way. When I say that a table really exists in the external world before my eyes, all I mean is that my brain is perceiving an image through its assembly of the sense-organs, that compares reasonably well with its prototype that already exists in some cognisable form in our brain. Now, in order to perceive an image, a distribution of photons is required to be incident on the retina, or more correctly, the optical nerves must be stimulated in a particular way. We also know that in our dreams, we do simulate such images without receiving any stimuli from the external world. Further, in dreams, we do recognise the simulations as real as we perceive them when we are awake. Then, how can one be confident enough to distinguish between a dream and the so-called reality, particularly when, in a dream, it is difficult to realise that it is a dream. The converse is, however, not true because when we are awake, we are able to distinguish between a dream and reality. The inherent power of imagination in the humans to create fake images by simulation only has really put us in a state of confusion between reality and dream or hallucination. Whether in the sojourn of our human lives we are in a state of superdream or not cannot be answered without facing a circular argument.

At this point, we may have a brief look at what revolution the computer technology has brought into our understanding. A computer, when bought, does not have any softwares loaded, much like a newly born child, having its memory not stuffed with pride and prejudices. Through constant interaction with the outside world the child develops its own culture. Now, we have come to a stage where the network of computers are found to work in unison, much like a matured person interacting with other people in a society. However, whether computers or robots can acquire an artificial intelligence or not is a matter of further research, but abstraction without a form or pattern has not so far been achieved in the field of computer technology.

Much more than that, one can see that the process of creative thinking or finding a new solution to a problem cannot proceed without making explicit use of the potential faculty of telling a lie or imagining attributes to the face-value of the reality of any object of study. By this, basically I mean that a poet's vision (for example, imagining a 'woman' in a tree or cloud or river) is not much more unreal than a scientist's or philosopher's vision of the outside world (for example, a 'cloud' of electrons in an atom, or electric field as 'something' like a streamline flow of an invisible fluid). Now, how can we hope to succeed in the pursuit of truth by making the best use of basically the precious faculty of 'lying and imagination'? We simply cannot. The very basis of the notion of so-called 'objectivity' cannot in principle come out of the vicious circle of 'subjectivity'.

Even though I have spent more than a page to discuss about, this fact is nothing new to the scientists. Of course, time and again, fraudulent claims of some extra-ordinary phenomena, such as decay of protons, cold fusion and detection of magnetic monopoles, do come up, and one vital criterion for checking the scientific objectivity, namely, the ability to repeat the experimental results elsewhere (for theoretical claims, thorough re-checking of the calculations and the mathematical logic), has so far proved to be quite effective on deciding the issues. Nevertheless, even if 100 scientists firmly argue in support of a theory against even one individual who does not subscribe to it, there are enough number of historical evidences to suggest that the consensus alone was not the most reliable measure of scientific objectivity. In fact, the progress of science has suffered many set-backs in the past due to the prejudice of some of the 'great' scientists.

What does the Modern Science say about the Nature of Matter?

Since science is an evolving discipline of knowledge, we need not have to bother about what mistakes the previous scientists did in the past, where this notion of past may refer to even as late as yesterday.

As of today, scientists have indeed pursued the nature of matter in a very diverse way. For some, the quest is one, of acquiring the knowledge of the ultimate microscopic structure of matter; for others, it is to know what kind of symmetries in the form of laws of motion of matter obeys on different scales of length and time; yet for others, it may be a question of how matter is created, and so on. A few notable observations can be made in the following points:

(i) One of the profound discoveries of the previous century is that heat, electricity, mechanical work, etc. are merely some form of 'energy', which is indestructible but only mutually interchangeable in its form or the brand name. However, it was further realised that all natural processes have an inescapable tendency to transform all other forms of energy into heat, leading to Jeans' fatalistic prediction of the heat death of the whole universe. Heat was linked with the chaotic motion of the microscopic particles, and therefore, gradual increase in the heat content implied a gradual but sure change from any existing ordered structure or ordered motion into a totally disordered state, devoid of any structure.

Today's universe as it appears to us is highly structured and ordered, and so is the highly ordered state in the prevailing life forms on earth. But the most surprising and revealing fact is that our past was in a less ordered state than our present, be it in regards the form of life on earth or the overall state of the universe. Somehow the second law of thermodynamics seemed to have been violated in the working principle of life on one hand (virtually perpetual engines are running to produce work at a constant temperature) and the universe on the other (virtually homogeneous and isotropic universe turning into a structured and clumpy one)!

The physics behind the evolution of life forms is not yet clearly understood, but it is the negative specific heat of gravitating systems (namely, an evolved star continues to emit radiation causing its temperature rather to increase than to decrease with time) that is known to be responsible for violating the second law of thermodynamics in gravitating systems, such as the universe.

(ii) The concept of energy (E) is an integral part of the notion of inertia of matter (represented by its mass m) through the famous equation $E=mc^2$, where c is the speed of light in vacuum (=299,792,458 metre/second, exact by definition). The energy can be potent and can act like an inertial mundane object, but if it is fully released, it would still carry the same amount of inertia. Given a finite amount of energy, whether one would call it energy or inertia, makes absolutely no difference to a physicist. However, given a mundane object having a finite rest mass, its total transformation into an active form of energy is usually not possible, except for a small fraction and that, too, depends on the situation. Just by measuring the amount of energy released in a chemical or thermal or electrical or nuclear process, the amount of inertia corresponding to that amount of energy ($\Delta m = \Delta E/c^2$) is only converted, which is usually very small compared to m itself.

(iii) The greatest import of quantum mechanics is the concept of 'quantum', as opposed to the classical idea of continuity or infinite divisibility. Planck's constant (h) is its sole representative. It does not mean that everything is quantised. To start with, the energy of a light-carrying particle, called photons, were quantised with the Planck law of radiation which says that the energy content (E) of a photon is intimately related to one of its classical attributes, namely, the frequency v of the electro-magnetic radiation (representing now the photon), by the relation $E=hv$, where h (=6.626 x 10^{34} joules/sec) is a universal constant. A few years later, the angular momentum or the spin, and another subtle classical concept, 'action' were also quantised. The implications of these new inputs were tremendous as well as revealing. The Planck law paved the way to the development of the wave-mechanics, and wave-particle duality, a concept hardly could be reconciled in a totally classical manner. Similarly, the classical idea of spin can be perceived if and only if a particle has an inherent structure. It was very soon realised that classically an electron cannot be thought of an object smaller than a certain size (simply because, the amount of electric charge *e* it contains will lead to have a store of some finite electrostatic potential energy, which cannot be allowed to exceed its inertial rest-mass energy $E = m\hat{e}c^2$, '$m\hat{e}$' being its rest-mass; that is, potent energy cannot exceed its internal rest-mass energy). This required size (5.85×10^{-15} metre, for $m\hat{e} = 9.11 \times 10^{-31}$ kg and $e = 1.602 \times 10^{-19}$ coulomb) is so tiny that even if its equatorial parts are allowed to rotate with a speed as fast as that of light in vacuum, its maximum possible angular momentum will fall short of the Planck constant by a factor of several thousands. So it was hopeless to think of the elementary particles in a manner our classical concepts would allow for, and this fact alone demonstrates that the concept of spin is non-classical.

Losing the battle on such fundamental issues, it was no more considered to be painful to picture the elementary particles as structureless. The wave-particle duality of photons and the elementary particles became the part of our life. Till the advent of quantum mechanics, physicists were quite content with the idea that the complex numbers were only mathematical tools for simplifying certain mathematical problems and all solutions having a root in the form of complex quantities were rejected as unreal solutions. But in the hands of Schroedinger, the differential equation of motion itself could not get rid of the use of i (= h — 1), thus raising the status of complex numbers to describe the reality of the quantum world. Even though Max Born was bold enough (and correctly so) to re-establish the prime role of the real numbers to describe all measurable physical quantities, the role of complex numbers in the context of the Hilbert space, in resolving the mystery of wave-particle duality in the Argand plane of complex numbers, in the use of unitary matrices and unitary groups to describe the unification of forces of nature, in the idea of Minkowskian space-time continuum retaining the Euclidean character, got its profound recognition.

Another major import of quantum mechanics, namely, how to define the process of measurement and what the genuine observables are, has raised a lot of controversies, leading to Schroedinger's cat problem, Einstein-Podolski-Rosen (EPR) paradox, Bohm-Aharonov effect, etc. There is at present a mixed feeling about the role of an observer in the process of observation, a process leading to spontaneous collapse of wave function, which basically amounts to collapse of the observer's ignorance about the eigenstate of the quantum system to which the measurement process out to 'collapse' and hence 'reveal' it to the observer. In Schroedinger's cat problem, the system with the measuring device is such that the probability of collapsing to one of the two possible eigenstates is exactly 0.5, and therefore, the revelation is the only option left to the observer to know the real state. In the EPR paradox, the two measuring devices are placed wide apart, the probability of collapsing to one of the two possible eigenstates is 0.5 for either of the two measuring devices, but the EPR case is formulated in such a manner that revelation of the result in one device will 'spontaneously' determine what the revelation would be at other device, without allocating any time to inform each other's observational results. To some, these instances are bothersome and they see a role of the conscious decision of the observer, to others there is nothing mysterious. Scientists of both the categories have learnt to live with such instances. In the Bohm-Aharonov effect, one attempts to devise a case in which a supposedly non-observable quantity becomes measurable, and this chosen non-observable quantity is such a fundamental one that its reality as well as non-observability is responsible for what is called the principle of gauge invariance of elecromagnetic theory. All such propositions are based on a hypothesis of some hidden variables to defy the claims of the standard formulation of the quantum mechanics, and to that effect, Bell's inequality, a very cleverly designed test for distinguishing between the two schemes, has lost by a wide margin on real experimentation over the past 15 years. The Copenhagen interpretation of the standard quantum mechanics is still found to be valid, and the Einsteinian concept of physical reality seems to have remained illusive in the wizard world of the microcosmos.

(iv) Originally, the space and time were considered to be as merely concepts, which did not have any ontological status. But in Einstein's hand, the general theory of relativity, has unified the space, time and matter to such a level that space-time is no longer assumed to be concepts only, thus allowing the possibility of gravitational waves (fluctuations in the space-time continuum, not of matter) to be given the same ontological status as electro-magnetic waves are endowed with. Similarly, nobody believed before Maxwell that mere electric and magnetic fields in free space could sometimes behave like physical entities as tangible as the 'light' itself.

(v) The uncertainty principle due to Heisenberg has shaken the firm classical belief that the principle of causality is a sacred one, namely, all effects are precisely predictable if their cause (the law) is stated clearly. This principle was blatantly violated by the world of the atoms and electrons. The culprit was finally found to be no other than the vacuum itself. Even Maxwell had suspected that vacuum was not simply void; as he thought, how vacuum could produce electric currents, called displacement currents! Vacuum is known to have finite electric polarizability, magnetic permeability, and can witness processes such as annihilation and creation of particles and anti-particles, and transmutation of particles. Today's vacuum is a dynamic world full of virtual particles, unrealisable potentialities, and eagerly awaiting a proper chance to manifest itself as cognisable entities. In science, a theory however nice and beautiful it be, its ultimate test is to get some or other observable or experimentally measurable effect. If we merely say that vacuum is full of virtual pairs, it will not become a fully acceptable theory. In fact, Lamb shift and Casimir effects are the two pillars for us to witness the reality of the above theory of vacuum. The sound of music of vacuum can really be compared to that of an orchestra having an infinite number of strings of all the possible lengths of chords. Similarly, the above-mentioned Bohm-Aharonov effect ought to manifest in some or other way if the basis of the electro-magnetic gauge invariance ought to get the actual scientific recognition.

(vi) The elementary particles, more precisely, the fields representing them, such as electrons or neutrons or quarks, are assumed not to have a structure at all. No one would be in a position to give any idea of how exactly two such field entities do encounter in space and time, even though the results of interactions are predictable by the appropriate laws of the quantum world. Physicists are very much concerned about revealing the aesthetic beauty in the form of unifying principles of symmetry in the diverse behaviour of the whole world. For this, they had to pay a very heavy price. The behaviour of the known elementary particles suggests that many of them have finite rest mass, and therefore, obey laws of lesser symmetry. Everytime one moves from the plane of higher symmetry to a lower one, some of the field entities are to be endowed with some finite rest mass from an original state of their zero rest mass. This mass-giving ceremony is christened as Higg's mechanism (also recall Mach's headache regarding the origin of inertia of matter), supposedly an outcome of the spontaneous (causeless) symmetry breaking principle but so far not been directly witnessed in any of the laboratory experiments. Of course, long before Higgs, Einstein talked of the spontaneous emission of photons. If one has to be so fussy about the concept of spontaneity, Newton can hardly be spared of introducing it in his celebrated third law of motion, in which any creation of momentum in any internal or external process needed to be complemented by the simultaneous creation of exactly equal momentum but opposite in direction. In order to save the principle of Newtonian causality, spontaneity had to be allowed to get its way into the realm of physics at the hands of the very person who founded the subject itself.

(vii) Let us now have a look at the cosmos. Although the modern foundation of cosmology was laid by Einstein in 1917, the subject of cosmogony began with Gamow's idea of the hot big-bang in 1946, soon to be followed by Bondi, Gold and Hoyle's idea of a steady state universe in 1948 (the title 'big-bang' was for the first time used in a BBC radio talk delivered by Hoyle in 1950). One of the key differences between these two models is that the creation of matter in the universe takes place at a finite and continuous rate in the steady stat model, when in the hot big-bang model the entire creation took place some finite time ago. The popular mandate is to let the process of creation of matter, space and time an altogether, a painful process no doubt, be it for once and once only at the very beginning for the big-bang models, or on a continuous basis (begging the vacuum to do it) for all the time for the steady state model. However, the pandora box of the ultra-high energy particle physics has been equally kind to both the possible options. Once the sanctity of vacuum is gone, it is gone forever; now it is no crime to ask vacuum to provide a continuous creation or creation in bangs, mini or macro. Of course, the idea of the hot big-bang has unified the origin of a macroscopic world with that of the microscopic particles. So in the Beginning, if there was any, the whole learnt to respect for its tiniest parts, and these tiniest parts assumed the wholeness, for reasons still quite mysterious to both particle physicists and cosmologists.

(viii) The general theory of relativity and the quantum mechanics have in one sense ruined the possibility of deriving infinite energy out of the collapse of a finite system into a structureless point. Quantum mechanics has given stability to atoms and nuclei by putting them on to some kind of ground states, even though classical mechanics and classical electromagnetism allowed them to derive infinite amount of energy out of it by the process of spiralling into a point. The same is true with the collapse of a star into a blackhole which would be in a position to convert only a fraction of its total mass-energy content, but classically gravity allowed the possibility of deriving an infinite amount of energy from the gravitational collapse. However, general relativity could not give stability to matter, it led to an unavoidable singularity in case all other forces of nature surrendered to gravity. When quantum mechanics and general relativity were combined at the hands of Steven Hawking, it was found that a blackhole ought to die out and would make almost 100 per cent conversion of matter into energy possible in the long run, with the tiniest bit of the remnant left, which is a particle of Planck mass (~ 10^{-8} kg). Similarly, the very nascent phase of the hot big-bang model also cannot get rid of this effect of quantum-gravity, and therefore, it ought to begin with finite density and radius, both having the tiniest Planckian dimensions. Philosophers must note the implication of this interesting consequence, namely, even though the potentiality of a finite system appeared to be infinite about 80 years ago, today's physics has been able to put a limit to the extent to which the actual manifestation is possible, which is nearly 100 per cent, though under some extraordinary circumstances only.

(ix) There has been another interesting development over the past few years. When matter changes its state through what is called phase transition, the clustering or reassembling of the constituents may not evolve as a three or two-dimensional object does, obeying the Euclidean type of geometry, even though they are all supposed to be embedded in the Euclidean type of space only. Their hierarchical growth is found to follow a non-integral dimension, that is, growth with an effectively fractal dimension of space.

(x) The quantum world has proven not to be in a position to dismiss the uncertainty principle, and the price one pays in the form of lising the most fundamental and classically aesthetic principle of causality. Then what is the link between chaotic behaviour and the exact mathematical prescriptions that lead to definite and quantitative predictions, even though it had to be statistical in nature? Can we really say that the mathematical laws governing the quantum world is precisely acting the role of a task master to obey certain set of equations as absolute laws, namely the overall conservation of measurable energy, of linear and angular momenta, of lepton and baryon numbers under the most general conditions? There is indeed a kind of continuity maintained, but that might be absolutely in the form of some covariant mathematical equations or some sacred quantities that are to be conserved in most cases. Without allowing at least one of these expected properties to serve duly the purpose of maintaining a continuity in the form of some or other conservation law(s), physics cannot in principle work at all.

(xi) Having said so much about the physicists' profound ignorance and revelations, let me switch over to biology. In the age of genetic surgery, it might not be an act of sin, if we talk about what makes a body assume life. If it is merely the result of assemblage of the biochemical molecules in some particular order, then it would be possible to revive a dead animal either by the process of resurrection or by superfast transplantation of a live head in place of the dead head. The question remains, if parts of the brain could be set right by surgery, why not the whole.

Again, if we carefully look at the history of evolution of life on earth during the past 3,600 million years, we find that the record begins from the unicellular proto-viral form to the most complex form in the human beings. It is a long journey, nevertheless, at every stage, the process of natural procreation has ensured to develop a miniature form of the adult in the foetus starting from a single cell, a most cleverly codified result of experimentation in the nature that took several billion years of time, in usually less than a year's time. If we compare the complexity of the primeval cells with those of human's, it is no more than a factor of 100 or so. Molecular biologists have not so far been able to synthesize a complete cell in the laboratory. So it would be a tall claim if they begin authentically to state that life has originated on the surface of the earth (that is, emphasising on absolutely no need for any seed of life to have come from extra-terrestrial sources). So far as mind and consciousness are concerned, both physical and biological sciences are too premature to address such issues at the present.

The pace at which the cultural evolution is taking place in the *Homo Sapiens*, the modern humans do not need to wait for solving their problems (ecological or otherwise) by the extremely slow process of biological adaptation cum evolution. Humans are indeed meeting all their needs by way of inventing new ideas and techniques in the name of discovery or inventions, a process that takes place at the neuronal level in the cerebral cortex in the form of creative thinking or restructuring of a tiny portion of the neuronal network. Therefore, the need for biological evolution for solving survival problems has ended in the cultured humans, and the nature has been able to produce such a highly intelligent and exalted form of life as it would have surely been required to perceive its own manifestation with awe and wonder. (Of course, it sounds like claiming a fundamental basis for the anthropomorphic principle). But the fact remains that being and becoming are the two sides of the same coin for witnessing the fun of nature by no other than the nature itself!

Whether this coin subscribes to an eternally existing entity (namely, whether 'soul' or 'consciousness' is perishable with the decay of the body or not) cannot be answered at this stage: speculations as diverse as arguing in favour (such as, when the brain stops functioning biochemically it dies along with its harbours, namely mind and all that), or arguing against (by giving an analogy, for example, except for some portions of the cerebral cortex, the whole body is known to have been continuously replaced with its replica cells on a time scale of a few weeks to years without losing the sense of the identity of one's self at all; there is then no guarantee that mind and soul will not continue to exist even when the cerebral cortex is totally discarded) can hardly be distinguished on a firm scientific basis. Only if the future research turns out to support the latter possibility, then and only then, one would be in a position to talk about the eternity of souls and all that in a scientific manner.

(xii) No science can be practised without mathematics. Before Godel (1930) most people thought that mathematics is something that ought to exist irrespective of whether there is any human being to comprehend it. Godel's famous incompleteness theorem demonstrated that mathematics is an invention of the human brain only. Numbers, symbols and algebra are no sacred entities by themselves, they are basically some adopted conventions, and the logic of connecting them are also conventions. Matter or entities serve merely as vehicles for adopting these conventions, but a conscious brain, if of course required to formulate these conventions. Then, there is a whole machinery of the complex numbers and their beautiful applications in solving physical problems. If the real numbers are obliged to describe the physical world in a quantitative fashion, the complex numbers should also do the same under some special circumstances. Its reality in physics has now been proved in the way the mathematical formulation of quantum mechanics depends upon it. Another most crucial test will definitely be provided if the Bohm-Aharonov effect becomes 'visible'. Even though mathematics is considered to be figs of 'imagination', the reality of all abstract mathematics must in some or other way ought to have an application in the experimental science, today or tomorrow. This has indeed been happening so far.

(xiii) Subjects like psychology and sociology are regarded as separate disciplines of science, but in both the cases, statistics brings in some meaningful quantifications, otherwise psychic and social attributes are by and large still awaiting to be quantified.

A Brief Account of the Oriental Conclusions from the Religious and Philosophical Traditions

As a scientist, my primary job has been to present my views on the scientific developments, but at the same time, I also wish to present my perceptions of the teachings of various traditions of oriental philosophies and religions in a scientifically acceptable perspective. I am not much worried about the distinguished philosophers in this respect, because they have by now got the messages in the previous sections as to what scientific results are relevant to their respective schools of thoughts.

(1) Unlike science, religious and philosophical traditions are dogmatic in the sense that they try to preserve the quintessence of their logic and teachings of their own schools established by some spiritual leaders or highly placed philosophers in the past. However, just as two textbooks on any subject in science are never identical, yet they ought to teach the same subject-matter, the schools of religious and philosophical traditions have written textbooks on their specific themes and they are traditionally regarded as commentaries on their respective original texts. The commentators have by and large tried to follow the progress in the knowledge of relevant topics in other disciplines and updated the viewpoints, if such a need was felt, but the originality of the commentators are also respectfully acknowledged by the peer scholars belonging to their schools.

Since the race of the modern humans is believed to have originated in Africa, Egyptians and Hebrews were perhaps the first ones to develop an agro-pastoral culture. On the other side, the Mongoloids were not far too behind, as the recession of the recentmost Ice Age made more northern latitude zones more habitable for the humans later in the history, but the early Caucasoids (having darker skins) who survived through the Ice Ages in South India basically continued their hunting cultures (there was hardly any need for developing an agro-pastoral culture for them). By about 6000 BC, the natural forces and the heavenly bodies became their first subjects of worship. The Sumerians, Babylonians, Aryans, Mongolians and the tribals habitating in Asia founded the earliest religions, and developed languages for expressions verbal as well as literal. Even with the two distinct approaches to constructing alphabets and vocal sounds by Caucasoids and Mongoloids, the early civilizations had indeed interchanged their cultural, social, religious views more freely than what we practised in the more recent past.

(2) The original texts in all religions are claimed to be The Revelations from some

mythical Supreme Lord, be He referred to as Lord Brahma for the Aryans, Siva for the Dravidians, Ra or the Sun God for the Egyptians, Anu for the Babylonians, Gaea for the Greeks, Jeovah or God or the Moon God Sin for the Hebrews (Jews and Christians), Allah for Moslems, Ahura Mazda or the Fire God for the Zoroastrians, no God for the Buddhists and Jains, Hu for the early Chinese, Tao (Yin and Yam) for Taoists, and myriads of Gods for Shintos in Japan, for example.

The earliest propounders and their oldest Canons in the form of verbal instructions or written scriptures or inscriptions may be given tentatively as follows: Pyramid texts of the Egyptians were written in hieroglyphs by the priests of Heliopolis (*ca.* 2400 BC), their Coffin texts (2190 BC-1786 BC), the Book of the Dead (1590 BC), monotheistic faith during the reign of the king Amenhotep (1350 BC), 12 large clay tablets by a Babylonian king, *Gilgamesh Epic* (*ca.* 2000 BC), the Greek epics, *Iliad* and *Odyssey*, of Homer advancing polytheism (*ca.* 750 BC), the Call of Abraham in the land of Cannan (somewhere between Mesopotamia and Egypt, *ca.* 1700 BC) followed by the Call of Moses with his Ten Commandments (the oral version of the Old Testament) on behalf of 12 tribes of Israel (1200 BC), emergence of Seers and Ecstatic Prophets, such as Samuel, Saul with a well defined concept of God (1025 BC), the written version of the first five books of the Old Testament (900-850 BC) and Deuteronomic Reforms banning the use of sacred prostitutes and child sacrifices during the reign of Josiah (621 BC). The poetical books, such as the song of Solomon appeared during 400-200 BC, the Synoptic Gospels of the Christian faith emerged sometime between 60 and 100 AD, the New Testament of the Holy *Bible* emerged about 150 years after its propounder, Jesus Christ was crucified and got its establishment under the patronage of the Roman emperors since then. The Christianity arrived in India before the fourth century A.D Out of the Christianity, Islam has branched out under the leadership of the Prophet Muhammad, and his revelations (obtained from Gabriel) were recorded in the Holy Book of *Qur'an* (or, *Koran*) in 610 A.D. Muhammad's sayings and his life were recorded *ca.* 810 AD in the book *Hadith*. The predicaments of the Old Testament were to be continued religiously followed by the Israelis (the so-called Jews) till today.

The following revelations in the *Qur'an* are relevant to this topic: The Book of Revelations is in Arabic for men of understanding (41: 1), Allah is the Almighty and the One, and is the Creator of Heaven and Earth (35: 1). The unbelievers shall be sternly punished, but those that accept the true faith and do good works shall be forgiven and richly rewarded (35: 7). Allah created you from dust, then from a little germ. Into two sexes he divided you. No female conceives or delivers without His knowledge. No man grows old or has his life cut short but in accordance with His decree (35: 8). For every soul there is a guardian watching over it. Let man reflect from what he is created. He is created from an ejected fluid that issues from between the loins and the ribs (86:1).

However, the Islam got soon divided into Shia and Sunni doctrines following the blood-shedding paths of history, and paved the way to evolving Sufism, a peaceful and popular version of the orthodox Islam. This is much like presently existing various Christian denominations based on some new interpretations of the New Testament. Islam has by and large remained bound by too much of its imposing rituals, very rigid moral codes, and social obligations. Judaism, Christianity and Islam have seen so much of political warfare that fundamentalism had to become the way of their lives.

(3) The branch of civilization that undergoes in the name of the Indus Valley civilization, archaeologically dates back to about 3000-1700 BC. (the Mohenjo-daro and Harappan cultures) with at least seven times being flooded (extinct) and rebuilt along the river Indus and in its fertile valley. The threat for survival compelled them to migrate all over the Indo-Gangetic plane, and the agro-pastoral culture they developed goes by the name of the Aryan culture.

They are the founders of the four *Vedas*, the oldest being the *Rk* and the latest being the *Atharva*. The astronomical information contained in the 8th (containing 5 *slokas*) and 9th (containing 14 *slokas*) stanzas (*sukta*) of the 1st chapter (*anubak*) of the 19th volume (*kanda*) of the *Atharva Veda* suggests that these were not composed later than the fifteenth century B.C. We really do not know when the *Rk Veda* was formulated (it can be anytime between 1700 BC and perhaps 5000 BC.).

The *Rk Veda* was composed (by scholars of the clans beginning with Sakala, Vaskala, Bharadvaja, Vasistha, Kanva, Angira, and many others) in the praise of all the natural forces and the celestial objects. The *Sama Veda* (composed by about 50 scholars) is basically the songs in the praise of the gods. The *Yajurveda* (composed mainly by Yajnavalkya and his contemporaries) prescribes the actual ritualistic procedures to be adopted in order to please these gods. The *Atharva Veda* is concerned about medicines, social norms and customs, magic, anatomy, how to acquire wealth, processes of love-making and sex, descriptions of various diseases, how to live long, and so on.

Each *Veda* has basically two parts: one is the collection of hymns (*Mantras*), called the *Samhitas*; and the other is the discussion of pedagogical (philosophical and moral) issues in the *Brahmanas* in the form of prose and poetry.

The examples of the *Samhitas* of various *Vedas* are as follows: *Sakala Samhita*, *Vaskala Samhita*, etc. of the *Rgveda*; *Samaveda Samhita* of *Samaveda*; *Vajasaneya Samhita* of *Sukla Yajurveda* (the story behind this goes like this: the teacher of Yajnavalkya was displeased with him, so Yajnavalkya prayed to the Sun God, who revealed the True Knowledge to him and the other disciples of his previous teacher had to learn it from Yajnavalkya assuming the form of falcons, *Baja paksis*, but before he began to pray to the Sun God, he attempted to acquire his own teacher's knowledge by sheer meditation, and this knowledge was also shared by the other disciples of his same teacher assuming the form of sandpipers, the *Tittir paksis*, hence the term *Taittiriya*); *Katha Samhita*, *Maitrayanni Samhita*, *Svetasvatara Saṃhita*, *Taittiriya Samhita*, etc. of the *Krsna Yajurveda*; and *Paippalad Samhita*, *Saunaka Samhita*, etc. of the *Atharvaveda*. In order to give you an idea of the size of the *Vedas*, the number of hymns *Mantras* in the *Samhita* parts alone, of all the four *Vedas* turns out to be 10,552 + 1,875 + 1, 975 + 5,977 = 20,379 (I have personally counted from my own collections).

While performing a sacrificial rite, a *Rtvik* will perform the rite for the welfare of a *Yajman*, duly assisted by a set of people singing/chanting with musical voice and another set of people telling the *Rtvik* what to do and when. In that respect, most parts of *Samaveda Samhita* are taken word by word from the *Rgveda* except for only 75 hymns, but the difference is that each hymn belonging to the *Samaveda Samhita* has a prescribed note, rhythm and the name of its composer.

The *Brahmana* parts were mainly written by the people of the so-called *Brahmana* class, and these have again two parts: the *Aranyakas* (composed in the secluded places such as deep inside the forests) and the *Upanisads* (the philosophical and pedagogical aspects regarding the origin of life, origin of the universe, the nature of matter and life, etc.) The kings and learned people from the warrior class, later to be known as *Ksatriyas* when the system of castes emerged, also took part in these discussions. The examples of the *Brahmanas* are *Vahvrca Brahmana*, and *Samkhyana Brahmana* of the *Rgveda*, *Tandyamaha Brahmana*, *Tandya-ssa Brahmana*, *Devatadhyaya Brahmana*, *Arseya Brahmana*, *Samhitopanisad Brahmana* and *Chandogya Upanisad Brahmana* of the *Samaveda*; *Kanva* and *Madhyandin* branches of the *Satapatha Brahmana* of the *Sukla Yajurveda*; *Taittiriya Brahmana*, *Maitrayani Brahmana*, *Ballabhi Brahmana*, *Satyayani Brahmana*, etc., of the *Krsna Yajurveda*, and the *Gopath Brahmana* of the *Atharvaveda*.

There are 12 main *Upanisads*, namely *Aitareya*, *Kausitaki*, *Chandogya*, *Brhadaranyaka*, *Taittiriya*, *Kena*, *Katha*, *Svetasvatara*, *Isa*, *Mundaka*, *Mandukya* and *Prasna*, of which the first six are the oldest ones and they formed the cream part of the *Vedanta Darsana*. The contents of the latter six are so similar in constituents and arguments to those of *Samkhya* (due to Kapila) and *Yoga Sutra* (due to Patanjali) that these six *Upanisads* were perhaps their precursors, or might even be contemporaneous. However, so far as the number of *Upanisads* are concerned, 50 *Upanisads* were translated into many different languages other than Sanskrit, and to date, the total number is about 120. That there is The One Ultimate Reality behind the phenomenal world (which may be real or unreal) was the sum and substance of all these *Upanisads*.

Even though the ascetic way of life was considered to be the fourth stage (quarter) of life in those days by tradition, it was nowhere spelt out that it was a must for perceiving the above Truth.

So far as the non-Aryans (Anaryas) were concerned, they also had deified the natural forces of calamities. As regards their perceptions about the origin of the world, their theory was very naive and simple. As they could see, a baby is born due to sexual union of male and female, and so they worshipped the Lord Siva in the form of Sivalingam, which, according to *Siva-purana*, is an explicit representation of the *Anadi lingam* placed inside the *Gauri pata*, the *yoni* of Gauri. Later on, *Samkhya* combined this idea of Siva as the *Purusa* or the inert, but potent, male principle, and *Prakrti* as the active and manifestive, female principle. The most modern form of it is found to be in the concept of the Siva-Kali form, where Siva is actually made to lie inert with his potent of creation, while the naked and outrageously vibrant form of Sakti, the Kali, standing on the body of Lord Shiva laid in His supine posture below the walking feet of Kali, to be worshipped in a crematorium.

(4) Between 850 and 400 BC, there were many other interesting developments that took place in India, Persia and China. Jainism, though claiming to be almost eternally existing, had their 23rd saint or *Tirthankara* (the other 22 are mythical), Parsvanath (born in 850 BC) took an ascetic way of life and gathered around him a community of naked monks (*Nigranthas*) who aspired for nothing other than salvation. It was the 24th saint, Mahavira (599-527 BC), who laid down the rules and the philosophy (the scriptures, namely, 11 *Angas* and 12 *Upangas*, were written between 300 - 550 AD) for the Jain community with 12 commandments for the lay followers (they must not kill, and are not to lie, not to steal, not to be greedy, be faithful in marriage, avoid unnecessary walking to avoid killing ants, etc., practice regular meditation, give alms to poor, must become a monk/nun for some period, and so on). There are basically two sects of Jains: the *Digambaras* (= naked monks), and the *Svetambaras* (= white-clad monks with brooms). Like the Hindus, they never embarked upon missionaries or made converts, but their philosophy is one of negation, non-violence and self-humiliation.

Taoism was founded in China by Lao-tzu, a legendary figure born in 604 BC, with his writings *Tao-Te-Ching*. According to this philosophy, the Tao or the 'Way' came to be represented as the living principle pervading the universe, and in the popular form of Taoism, Tao is worshipped as a deity. Its existence is assumed to precede anything in nature, and though described as inactive, inert, invisible, intangible and impersonal, it was the source of all being as a result of the union of the female principle Yin and the male principle Yang. The Taoist canon of literature *Tao Tsang* began to emerge in written form since fourth century BC, and developed into 1100 volumes over the next 1500 years. Confucianism in China began with the teachings of

Confucius (actual name K'ung Fu'tzu, 551-479 BC), the only mystique without claiming for having obtained a divine revelation. He concentrated on setting more of moral than of religious codes for lay people with the declared five cardinal virtues: benevolence, righteousness, wisdom, trustworthiness and propriety. Later, both Taoism and Confucianism were immensely influenced by the arrival of Buddhism in China.

In Persia, Zarathustra (628-551 BC) received divine revelations in 598 BC from an arcangel, Vahu Manah, who was sent from the True God, Ahura Mazda. He preached monotheism, One God, the Creator of the Universe. He could make his contemporary Iranian king a convert. Zoroastrianism survived in Iran until the aggressive arrival of Islam in 652 AD, leading to exodus of a handful number of them to India, to be known as Parsis today. The personified aspects of Ahura Mazda, The Holy Immortal, are the good mind, right order, divine power, devotion, perfection, and immortality.

(5) Back in India, there came Siddhartha Gautama Buddha (563-483 BC) who attained the state of Buddhattva while meditating under a *pipal* (Bo) tree on the bank of the Niranjana river in Bodh Gaya sometime in 521 BC and was since then referred to as one of the many incarnations of the *Tathagata* (or Bodhisattva). Buddha's teachings were based primarily on the Vedic traditions, perhaps as much as the Islam did on the Judaism and the Christianity. He preached his first sermons to five ascetics in Varanasi in the language of the common people, called Pali, instead of Sanskrit, the 'official' language of the Hindu scholars (even today there are about 40 families in South India who use Sanskrit as their true mother tongue). He was also the first 'Revealed Personality' to let the door open to the common people for attaining the highest state of knowledge (called *Nirvana*) irrespective of the cast and creed of the aspirant (Note that in *Chandogya Upanisad*, Uddalak Aruni accepted Jabal Satyakama, an illegitimate son of Jabala, with the presumption of his unknown father being a *brahmana*, because such a shameful truth could have been acknowledged by none other than a *brahmana*, supposedly the truthful one by heart and deed). Buddha was also the first to initiate the 'missionary' activities as a travelling teacher of *Dhamma*, and built monastries, called the *Sanghas*, for both monks and nuns. All Buddhists must abide by Five Precepts (not to take life, not to steal, not to be sexually impure, not to lie and not to take drugs or consume alcohol), better ones including the monks and nuns would further abide by another Five Precepts (not to eat after midday, not to listen to music or watch dancing, not to use any cosmetics, not to sleep on any comfortable bed, and not to accept silver or gold).

There are in fact a total of 227 rules stated in the book *Vinaya* for the Buddhist ascetics, who should live only on alms. Those who adhered strictly to all these rules laid down by Buddha belong to the *Hinayana* school, and by about 350 BC, another moderately stringent adherent school of Buddhists, called the *Mahayana*, who soon outnumbered the former school, developed a philosophy later to be known as the *Madhyamika* philosophy.

The precepts of the former school, the (*Theravada*), acknowledging Buddha as merely a great preacher (there is no place for God or soul in the actual Buddhism), travelled wide across to Sri Lanka, Burma (now Myanmar), Thailand, Cambodia, Laos, Indonesia, and Greece under the royal patronage of the King Ashoka and before him by some army staff of Alexander, during the third and fourth centuries BC. The actual scriptures in the three volumes of the *Tripitaka* were however written down in the first century BC.

The latter school, namely the *Mahayana* school, projected Buddha as The Saviour, a divine principle and an object of worship in the form of an idol, translated the Pali Canon of *Theravada* into Sanskrit, Chinese and Tibetan, wrote the *Sutras*, *Sastras* and *Tantras* sometime between the first and fifth centuries AD, and paved the way to form various sects of *Mahayana* Buddhists, such as the Pure Land and Ch'an Schools in China, Nichiren and Zen Schools in Japan, and Lama School in Tibet.

(6) It was only then the so-called Brahmanism received the greatest possible jolt, and discovered that Buddhism has taken all the good elements of Brahmanism, and has very cleverly given a transformation to its legends, allegories, philosophical constituents in evolving a fully self-consistent scheme of thoughts, namely, the *Madhyamika* philosophy. Not that between 400 BC and 600 AD, Brahmanism remained idle, but unfortunately, it also developed two major systems of philosophies in the same lines of thought.

The *Samkhya* (the accepted number of elementary attributes, psychic as well as corporeal, being 25) and *Yoga* (the accepted number of both the category of elementary attributes being 13) putting a lot of emphasis on the reality of the physical world only, and a well-defined methodology of sheer practice to attain this highest state of realisation. The concept of the Almighty Creator was virtually eliminated in these philosophies. The *Nyaya* (the accepted number of elementary attributes being 16) and *Vaisesika* (the accepted number of elementary attributes being 7) systems laying emphasis on the superiority of the pedagogical arguments leading to revelations of the same truth, namely, the reality of the physical world only. In addition, the ritualistic part of all the *Vedas* was summarised by Jaimini (*ca.* 200 BC) in his voluminous work *Purva-Mimamsa Darsanam*, and the pedagogical part by Badarayana (almost contemporary of Jaimini, as the two texts refer to each other at some points) in four volumes of his *Uttara-Mimamsa Darsanam* (*Brahmasutra*). The two *Mimamsas* differed both in their objectives and methods, the former accepted the plurality of Selves or Souls, the Reality of the Universe, and righteous actions are the means to self-realisation, whereas the latter only identified the Self with the Omnipresent and

Eternally Conscious, the *Brahman*, which was claimed not to be realisable by the finite mind and finite intellect, let alone the righteous actions.

All these philosophies did however accept that the *Vedas* are eternal and are revealed only to certain *Rsis*, the Seers. As such the authority of the *Veda* was regarded unquestionable. The *Mimamsas* go a little further and claim that even words are eternal (*Sabda* = *Brahman*) and their meanings are therefore fixed, whereas the *Nyaya* and *Vaisesika* claimed that the meanings of words were subject to change, and hence in principle, the structures of the logic. Between the *Nyaya* and *Vaisesika*, the former school argued that matter is infinitely divisible, the sense of finiteness arises from the way we perceive them, and the forms are mere representatives of finiteness, and therefore, cannot be the true nature of matter. But the latter school believed that matter is not infinitely divisible, at some stage the discreteness is bound to manifest, and the gross matter would form as composites of these elementary and discrete entities, called *Anus*. At such face values, the *Samkhya* supported the *Purva-Mimamsa* and did not accept the *Purusa* as the Almighty Creator but only as the Potential Cause for all the Actions, the *Prakrti*. The *Yoga Darsana* laid down the procedures and practices for the absolute control on one's body and mind, in the form of the *Astangik Yoga Marga*, namely, *Yama*, *Niyama*, *Asana*, *Pranayama*, *Pratyahara*, *Ekagrata*, *Dhyana* and *Samadhi*, required for attaining the highest state of the Realisation (the first seven were essential for performance of miracles, the so-called *Hathayoga*, and all the eight were required for the *Rajayoga*).

By the turn of the eighth century AD, the *Madhyamika* and *Yogacara* schools of Buddhism took a full control over the Brahmanism. In short, the *Madhyamika* philosophy as propounded by Nagarjuna, Aryadeva and others, is known as the *Sunyavada*. It claims that the Ultimate Reality is *Paramarthic*, that is, transcendental to human intellect. It is neither subject to the processes of creation, persistence and annihilation, nor eternal or divisible. The Phenomenal Reality is *Samvrttik*, that is, intelligible but either illusive (= *tattvasamvrtti*, for instance, a sensual perception cannot be the substance itself) or non-existent (= *mithyasamvrtti*, for instance, an optically virtual image produced by a mirror). There are three categories of Phenomenal Realities: (i) all disappointments and unhappiness in life (*duhkha samudaya*), (ii) the cause of all such disappointments and unhappiness (*duhkha karana*), and (iii) the cessation of all disappointments and unhappiness (*duhkha nivrtti*). But (iv) the Way to Transcend all these three kinds of phenomenal realities (*duhkha nivrtti marga*) leads to the Realisation of the Ultimate Reality, known as the *Nirvana* or the *Tathagata Dharma*. It has ten stages with the last one being the attainment of the state of the *Bodhisattvabhumi*, the state of attributeless, which is equated to the *Sunyatva* or nihilism. This is the gist of the so-called *Bauddha Madhyamika Sunyavada* or Buddhistic Theory of Nihilism. On the other hand, the

Bauddha *Yogacara* school, as propounded by Maitreyanath and Acarya Asanga, claims that the Phenomenal Reality is the virtual image of the Ultimate Reality. The state of *Buddhattva* cannot be attained till the knowledge of the Self as a perceiver persists somewhere in the mind, thus the state of *Nirvana* is the cessation of all attributes, merging one's own self with the eternal *Sunyatva* or Nihilation. There are two other schools of Buddhist philosophy, namely *Vaibhasika* and *Ksanavadi* schools, who differ from the above schools in some minor details.

So, both the Buddhist camp and the majority of the contemporary Hindu camp (except for the hard core Vedantins) developed their philosophies in almost the identical lines before 800 AD.

(7) The stage was then set for the arrival of Acarya Sankara (788-820 AD). Originally, he was a defender of the *Samkhya*, then he wrote the *Sariraka Bhasyam*, a commentary on the *Vedanta Darsanam*, and this had made him realise the true achievements of the philosophy of *Vedanta*. He then went on a long pilgrimage, and confronted with all the best scholars of Buddhism, Jainism, *Samkhya*, *Yoga*, *Nyaya* and *Vaisesika*, and *Mimamsakas* of his time and defeated each and everyone by unparallel arguments in favour of what is known as the *Visuddha Advaita Vedanta*, the Pure Monism. All he had to do was to replace the atheist's *Nirvana* or total dissolution of the self at the point of realisation into an undescribable nothingness, by the *Akhanda Saccidananda Param Brahman*, or in other words, the state of nihilation was replaced by the state of all-pervading and eternally present consciousness, The One and The Very Same Reality in Every Object and Subject of the Universe. What was the Phenomenal Reality for all the atheists as the Only Reality, was interpreted by Acarya Sankara as *Mayik pratibhasa*, an illusive projection of the Self-evident *Brahman* created in the mind of an individual perceiver, arising due to the mere ignorance of the perceiver about its own Reality of the Self, the (*Atmajnanam*). He showed that the reality of the phenomenal world cannot be established by any acceptable arguments or by any experiments, simply because it all ought to occur in the head of a perceiver. No words can express it, no mind can fathom it (*Abangmanasagocaram*). Nobody could argue against the fact that the sense of 'I' does exist, but at the same time 'It' could not be expressed, because how a thing can be expressed solely by itself to itself. The modern science also says the same thing, yet differences in opinion arise (or may arise) when Acarya Sankara claims further that this so-called 'I', the Soul, is eternally existing even after the clinical death of the corporeal body. Legends say that he had in fact demonstrated it in his own life, for a different reason though: he left his body, occupied the clinically dead body of a king, his disciples safely guarded their teacher's body for a month, and he returned to resume his body again. Legends also say that Jesus Christ left his body and appeared before some of His disciples assuming the same corporeal body. Yet, there are sound philosophical reasons behind why Hindus

prefer to cremate a dead body than preserve it for the day of Resurrection. Hindus believe that the Soul is immortal and that it will take up another body for rebirth, whereas many others think that the same body is going to be resurrected on the Day of Judgement. For Hindus, such judgements depend on their cumulative actions, the *karmas*; and their sufferings and pleasures are derived exclusively by making bad or good use of their so-called Free Will, a faculty enjoyed equally by each and every Soul.

After establishing the *Advaita Vedanta* for once and all, he literally revived the glorious past of the Hinduism, drove away Buddhism from India (later on Hindus of course have given the place for the Ninth Incarnation, the *Avatara*, of the God to the Lord Buddha), literally converted all the giant atheistic personalities of *Samkhya*, *Yoga*, *Nyaya*, *Vaisesika*, and *Purva-Mimamsa* into theistic ones by showing where and how they had deviated from the authenticity of the *Vedas*, and established the Hindu monastery systems of the *Dasanama Sampradaya* at the four corners of the country (*Tirtha* and *Ananda sampradayas* at the Sarada Math in Dwaraka in the west, *Vana* and *Aranya sampradaya* at the Govardhan Math in Puri in the east, *Giri*, *Parvata* and *Sagara sampradaya* at the Jyotirmath in Jyotirdham in the north, and *Sarasvati*, *Bharati* and *Puri sampradaya* at the Srngeri Math, in Rameshwardham in the south). Even today these *Mathas* are having their *Acaryas* in the 67th generation or so of the respective *Mathadhisas*.

(8) After Sankaracarya, the commentaries of *Samkhya* and other Hindu philosophies were written with due recognition to preserve the integrity of the Vedic conclusions, but not just the conclusions of the *Vedanta*, as interpreted by Sankaracarya. In fact, today no scholar of the Hindu *Darsanas* would claim to be atheists or *Nirisvara-vadis*. Buddhists did not change their standpoint, and therefore, they had to quit India, and those who stayed back home reduced to a minority as the Jains or Parshis are today. Of course, we should not give the full credit to Sankaracarya, because before him Vyasadeva composed the Epic of *Mahabharata* (nobody knows who transcribed it later into written form and when), and there he had expressed fully the theistic viewpoints of *Samkhya*, *Yoga*, *Jnana*, *Vijnana*, *Bhakti*, *Guna*, *Moksa*, etc. in the *Gita* portion, and declared the *Gita* to be the quintessence of all the *Upanisads*. It is a kind of the Biblical Canon readily digestible even by an ordinary individual. In fact, it contains precisely 730 *slokas* which can be read and contemplated once through a year if the reader proceeds with chanting and contemplating on one *sloka* in the morning and one in the evening of everyday of the year. The point I want to make is that what Vyasadeva did accomplish with great ease, took Sankaracarya to adopt a path of highly pedantic and aggressively warring battle. Nevertheless, it initiated another phase of highly pedagogical activities in India, much like the European Renaissance, in the field of religion and philosophy, in spite of the fact that the Pathans and the Mughals were to soon flood the country bringing in a totally different culture

and religion with also the privilege of using their political power.

In the following centuries, after Sankaracarya, Madhvacarya propounded the theory of Dualism *Dvaitavada* (in which entity is of two kinds: The Eternally Free and Determinant, The *Isvara* = Srihari = Siva = Purusa = Brahma; and Everything Else being subject to Causality and to the God, The *Prakrti* = *Jagat* and *Jiva* (representing the inert as well as conscious constituents as perceived through the sense-organs). All other theories of reality can be classified under the title of some or other kind of Pseudo-Monism, in which the individual selves and the material world were regarded as constitutionally one and the same as the Universal Consciousness, the God or the *Paramatma*. The metaphor they use is that wood and table are constitutionally one and the same, the former being merely a generic name, which can assume any form or shape to manifest itself as the latter, a chair or table or any other wooden furniture. Just to name a few such theories, we may refer to *Bhedavedavada* due to Acarya Bhaskara, *Acintyavedavedavada* due to Acarya Valadeva Vidyabhusana, *Dvaitadvaitavada* due to Acarya Nimbarka, *Suddhadvaitavada* due to Acarya Ballava, *Visistadvaitavada* due to Acarya Ramanuja, *Sivavisistadvaitavada* due to Acarya Srikantha, and *Visesadvaitavada* due to Acarya Sripati. In order to maintain a balance between the *Samkhya-Patanjal* and the *Nyaya-Vaisesika* theories, Acarya Vijnanabhiksu wrote a commentary on the *Vedantadarsana*, which is known as *Samanjasyavada*. Later on some commentaries on *Vedantadarsana* appeared from the *Sakta* cults which can be categorised under the Pseudo-Monism, for example, *Saktavisistadvaitavada* due to Bhattacarya Pancanana and *Saktadvaitavada* due to Maharsi Haritayana.

However, history had to wait till the arrival of Swami Vivekananda (1863-1902), who in 1898 interpreted all these isms to be nothing but the last few steps for the latter leading to the ultimate realisation of the undescribable state of the Principle of pure Monism. His explanation for the illusory nature of *Maya* is very simple: if we become desperate to see ourselves, we can at best place a mirror before us, and we ought to be satisfied with viewing some artificial and illusory projections of ourselves only, else we close our eyes and believe that 'I exist'. There is no other choice. Once again, he only reiterated the glorious past of Hinduism, and gave a proper interpretation of idolatry before the world.

(9) Interestingly enough, a combination of *Saiva*, *Sakta* and *Vaisnavas* is found to have taken place in the development of the cults, such as *Tantrikas* and *Mantrikas*, both aiming at making some curious combinations of geometrical symbols (*Yantras*) and extra-physical skills (*Tantras*) directed towards achieving any particular miracle following anyone or more of the ten *Mahavidyas*. The ultimate success (*Siddhi*) of the practitioner, usually rests upon his/her absolute control on the sexual impulses in all kinds of *Vamacar Sadhanas*. At present there are about 400 known *Siddha Tantrikas*

and *Mantrikas* in the country, but as a scientist, I have been impressed by at least one account of the *Tara Sadhana* by one Mr. Vasudev Sharma under the guidance of Dr. Narayandutta Srimali (Jodhpur), which can be scientifically verifiable, as the methods are prescribed in most precise terms in the Proceedings of a convention of the *Tantrikas* held at Kamakhya in 1988. It is a matter of only 15 night's *sadhana.* (I do not dare to attempt to practise it by myself as I have paid a heavy price for practising *Rajayoga* in 1972 without a Guru's instruction leading to severe heart conditions. Moreover, the fact remains is that most *Siddhas* are so short-tempered and rude that hardly any scientist would accept such personalities as their teachers and practise these *sadhanas* with patience, even though a modern graduate student would not turn into a rebellion if he/she fails to write a paper after putting two or more years of hard work. We all prefer to go by the customs and conventions of the day.)

Another off-shoot of combination of Sufism and Hinduism has led to Sikhism, formulated by its Ten Preachers. Political and Brahmanic oppressions have made them choose the path of war, but the monistic preachings in *Granthsaheb* by Guru Nanak (1469-1533 AD) assured every Sikh of an absolute self-defence with their identifying makers of five *k*'s (*kesa* = uncut hairs, *kaccha* = short trousers, *kada* = an iron bangle, *krpan* = a short dagger, and *kangha* = comb), and the Sikhs fought bravely against Moslem rulers. Today, Sikhs are the best farmers and the best sentinnels in the Army, but also vulnerable to taking aggressive measures at the slightest provocation on religio-political issues. For political reasons, many Hindus were also forced to take Islam, and this was considerably checked by Sri Caitanyadeva (1485-1533 AD) by making the Vaisnava *dharma* extremely popular.

(10) Over the past two centuries, the eastern philosophies have seen a lot of influences by the Western philosophies, and *vice versa.* The Christian missionaries along with their colonism in the Asian countries have brought about revolutions in the fields of science and technology, sociology, economics, and religious traditions. Idolatry has become a taboo for many intellectuals, and Marxism has played its role too, even if Marx ought to have been worshipped like an idol. It seems that there is no substitute for idols, as one's mind cannot work unless something tangible is placed before one's eyes, and keep aside the abstract mathematicians.

During the British colonial period, it was Raja Rammohun Roy, who was the first to remove the idolatry from Hinduism and tried, historically once again, to revive the symbolic Monism from the *Upanisads.* His ardent followers soon established the Brahma Samaj, a breakaway sect from the then existing orthodox Hindu society, and accepted the principle of Brahman as merely a symbol, *Om,* without assigning any attribute of any kind to it. Similarly, there emerged the Arya Samaj, the Theosophical Society, and so on in the same line. They had of course declared themselves as non-Hindus, but not the so-called Indian Marxists, however. Side by side, Hindus also gathered together under the leadership of various religious personalities, and paved the way to formation of Ramakrishna Mission, Bharat Sevashram Sangha, Satsang, Satya Sai Baba Society, Hare-Krishna Society, and many others, including the religio-political ones, such as Shiva-Sena Dal, Ananda Margis and Vishwa Hindu Parishad. All claim to be Hindus, and their preaching texts mostly root back to the authenticity of the *Vedas* or the *Upanisads*.

Relevance of *Vedanta* in the Present-day Society

It is beyond doubt that *Vedanta* contains something so vital that has made it viable time and again against all possible rough times in its history of rise and fall over the past three millennia. It was Swami Vivekananda, who demonstrated the relevance of *Vedanta* in our social life. He used to quote one of his Guru Sri Ramakrsna Paramahamsadeva's instructions, namely, *Siva jnane Jiva seva*, which means, 'Serve your fellow person (in need) assuming him/her as an incarnation of the Lord Shiva'. In my opinion, concurring fully with Vivekananda's, this would be the most practical applications of *Vedanta* in the present-day civil life, if one can indeed practise and live up to this standard. He said that there is no need for worshipping a God (whatever be its form, as inert as an institution, or as alive as a film star, for example) spending colossal amount of money on performing *Yajnas* (whatever be its modern form), if the neighbour has to die of hunger. Swami Vivekananda said that to serve the destitutes and truly needy people are the highest object of worship for today, and that individual's Salvation can be achieved by executing merely its own duties towards the society (*Atmanomoksartha jagaddhitaya ca*), because it is after all the society that has given us all the privileges we consider to be so essential for leading a 'decent' life.

All differences of opinion between two individuals arise because they fail to place themselves in the heart of each other's. Obviously, nobody expects that any two individuals would have the identical views or approach to life. Some we call stupids, some we call demoralised, some we just pity upon, and some we do adore and respect. A person develops certain moral and social principles depending on his/her background of education and the society he/she lives in. When we were born, we hardly had any softwares loaded in our brains, the circumstances have led us to become what we are today. If, and only if, we can see ourselves in the heart of everybody else (*Sarvabhute Atmadarsanam*), there cannot arise a situation for quarrel. No philosophy other than *Vedanta* has ever proclaimed that every individual is indeed Him and Him only, the Almighty, and not merely one of His subordinates. We are all potentially divine, and 'education' is merely the process of unfolding this infinite potentiality into useful actions. By the clause of the 'Free Will' in the decree of the Divine Lord (= Self for a *Jnani*, much like the possibility of any worthy citizen of a democratic nation to become its First Citizen), we are totally free to choose our own paths and courses of action. If we ponder on it a bit carefully, we should be able to see that we do really possess the free will, the greatest possible virtue that anyone could have. Vivekananda thus proclaimed, 'Truth, purity and unselfishness – wherever these are present, there is no power below or above the sun to crush the possessor thereof. Equipped with these, one individual is able to face the whole universe in opposition.' Let us not forget that Hinduism is the only religion which allows even the atheists or the non-believers to be a part of it. Let us all practise it in this very right spirit.

List of Contributors

Hakeem Altaf Ahmad Azmi	Jamia Hamdard New Delhi - 110 062
Pushpa M. Bhargava	Centre for Cellular and Molecular Biology Hyderabad - 570 007
Chandana Chakrabarti	Centre for Cellular and Molecular Biology Hyderabad - 570 007
A. K. Chakravarty	Midnapur (W. Bengal)
Arshad Hussain	Department of History of Medicine and Science Jamia Hamdard New Delhi - 110 062
P. G. Lalye	Bhandarkar Oriental Research Institute Pune - 411 004
S. C. Malik	Centre for Contemporary Studies Nehru Memorial Museum, and Library New Delhi - 110 011
P. K. Mukhopadhyay	FAMTSIT Jadavpur University Calcutta (W. Bengal)

N. Mukunda
Centre for Theoretical Studies: and Deptt. of Physics
Indian Institute of Sciences
Banglore - 560 012

S. R. N. Murthy
307-C/10, 18th Main
Vijayanagara
Bangalore - 560 040

Jayant V. Narlikar
Inter-University Centre for Astronomy and Astrophysics
Ganeshkhind
Pune - 411 007 (Maharasthra)

Raja Ramanna
National Institute of Advanced Studies
Banglore (Karnataka)

N. C. Rana
Inter-University Centre for Astronomy and Astrophysics
Ganeshkhind
Pune - 411 007

M. P. Rege
Prajna Pathashala Mandal
Wai

Baidyanath Saraswati
Indira Gandhi National Centre for the Arts
New Delhi - 110 001

B.V. Subarayappa
Centre for History and Philosophy of Science
Indian Institute of World Culture
Bangalore - 560 004

E. C. G. Sudarshan
Physics Deptt. and Centre for Particle Physics
University of Texas
Austin, Texas - 78712

Kapila Vatsyayan — Indira Gandhi National Centre for the Arts
New Delhi - 110 001

C. V. Vishveshwara — Raman Research Institute
Bangalore (Karnataka)

Index